JUDY HALL

Crystal Companion

An Hachette UK Company
www.hachette.co.uk

First published in Great Britain in 2018 by Godsfield, a division of Octopus Publishing
Group Ltd, Carmelite House, 50 Victoria Embankment, London EC4Y 0DZ
www.octopusbooks.co.uk

ISBN 978-1-84181-471-1

A CIP catalogue record for this book is available from the British Library.

Printed and bound in China

1 3 5 7 9 10 8 6 4 2

Disclaimer
No medical claims are made for crystals in this book and information given is not
intended to act as a substitute for medical treatment. Healing means bringing mind,
body and spirit back into balance, it does not imply a cure.

Publisher's Note
Always buy your crystals from a reputable supplier.

Commissioning Editor: Leanne Bryan
Art Director: Yasia Williams-Leedham
Copy Editor: Sian Parkhouse
Designer: Isabel de Cordova
Editorial Assistant: Nell Warner
Photographer: Michael Illas
Model: Josie Roberts
Hair & Make-up: Angelika Samocka
Picture Research Manager: Giulia Hetherington
Picture Library Manager: Jennifer Veall
Production Controller: Dasha Miller

JUDY HALL'S

Crystal Companion

ENHANCE YOUR LIFE WITH CRYSTALS

GODSFIELD

Contents

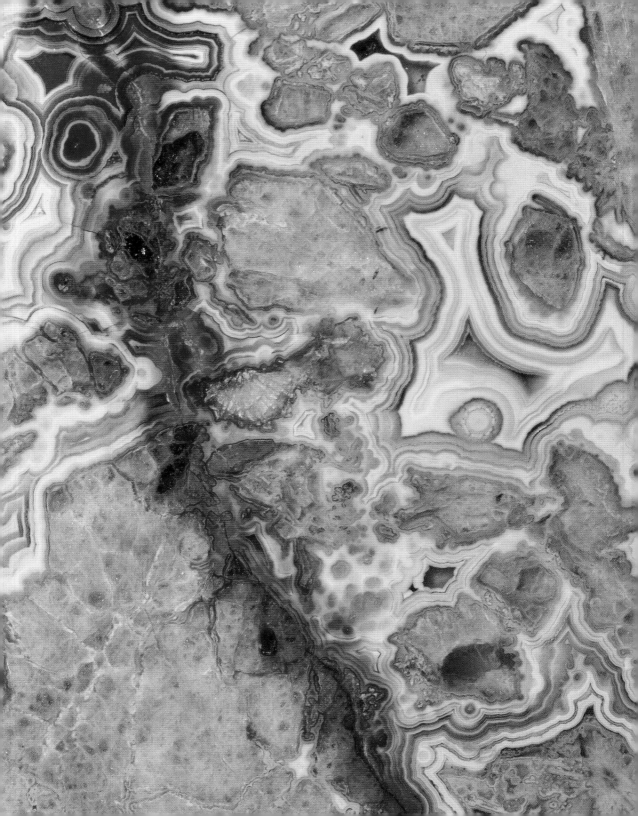

Welcome to my crystal world

The culmination of a lifetime's intuitive exploration of crystals, this book is immensely practical. It shares with you how I personally work with these potent entities. These are techniques that I, my clients and workshop participants have found to be particularly fruitful. You'll find familiar, tried-and-tested crystals and more recently available stones. In addition to bringing the body back into balance, I delight in exploring what crystals offer above and beyond their traditional therapeutic properties. How they heal not only the present but past and future. How they expand consciousness and connect to my soul. How far out into the cosmos we journey together. How deep into Earth a crystal takes me. How they enhance my environment and that of the planet. And experiencing how crystals facilitate enlightenment ('en-lighten-ment'). I invite you to join me.

How this book works

Potent working tools, crystals are not just beautiful objects. An essential foundation, this book introduces techniques for working to best effect. It has been designed as a practical workbook. Please don't skip the preparatory section or you'll be disappointed with the results. If you don't know how to cleanse and dedicate crystals, you won't feel their maximum impact and they become toxic. If you don't ask your crystals to cooperate, they won't know what they are supposed to do, or work at full capacity. Knowledge of energy centres and crystal grids makes a huge difference to the effectiveness of your interaction with crystal power.

The book is divided into sections, such as healing for body, mind, ancestors or spirit. It clears your space – or your karma. If you have a specific healing requirement, or want to expand awareness, go to the relevant section. Each section is prefaced by information on how to use crystals productively. By understanding different applications of crystal power, you'll build a toolkit that can be implemented across a variety of applications. Each section is completed by 'portraits' of appropriate crystals. Two main crystals are highlighted first, with other choices in the pages that follow to ensure you find exactly the right crystal for you.

Before that, there are introductions to major crystal families. These give you the generic properties of major groups of healing and consciousness-expanding crystals and their variants. You'll meet their offspring in the crystal portraits that follow (*see* pages 68–307).

A glossary at the end of the book helps you to understand unfamiliar terms.

Do bear in mind that there is no one particular right way to work with crystals. There is only the way that works for you.

Caution

Some crystals have toxic trace minerals bound up within their structure. This includes gemstones that have been worn and crystals that have been used in healing for thousands of years without harm. Indeed, these are some of the most potent healing crystals. Make essences from these crystals using the indirect method (*see* page 30). Wash your hands after handling these stones and use them in a tumbled version where possible. Do not inhale their dust. Caution indications (●) are given throughout this book.

Hints and tips

- Choose stones appropriate for your personal energy field.
- Crystals do not have to be perfect. Chipped, raw or oddly shaped crystals work equally well.
- Cleanse and reactivate your crystals regularly (*see* pages 27–8).
- Take your time. Switch off your phone.
- Explore crystals without preconceptions or expectations.
- Remember that changes may occur over time rather than immediately.
- Be prepared for a healing challenge, dizziness or nausea to occur. If so, remove crystal(s) and sit with a grounding crystal such as Smoky Quartz or Flint at your feet or on your belly. Breathe deeply and slowly, making the out-breath longer than the in-breath. Push the energies down through your feet until equilibrium returns.
- Drink plenty of pure spring water after a crystal session.
- Rest and relax after a session to allow the energies to integrate.

You know the world is a magical place when Mother Earth grows her own jewellery.

www.wildwomansisterhood

The building blocks of life

Earth is a product of alchemy and transformation. Over aeons of time, whirling clouds of dusty star matter and gases containing minerals constituting all life on this planet were drawn together. They contracted into a white hot, molten ball spinning in space. As this fiery sphere began to cool, crystals and rocks came into being. There is a constant process of creation, destruction and re-creation. Psychogeology, the influence of geology on the mind, suggests that the rock beneath our feet has a fundamental effect on how we experience life. Crystals, too, exert influence, profoundly affecting mood and wellbeing.

Born of fire

Crystals in igneous rocks are some of the oldest on the planet, and also some of the youngest, as formation processes continue. They are primary creations, constructed out of star material and magma. Born when minerals in the gaseous dust cloud condensed, or when molten lava bubbled through Earth's crust, igneous crystals reflect internal tensions in the planet. Many potent healing crystals are created by igneous processes. Aventurine or Peridot form at high temperatures from liquid magma. When lava is expelled through faults in Earth's crust and cools rapidly, Obsidian, Basalt and Jasper result. Where liquid magma rises up into the crust and cools slowly in a pool, it produces Rose Quartz and Peridot. Gaseous magma under high pressure permeates hollow rocks to bring Amethyst, Tourmaline and Smoky Quartz into being. Aragonite, a potent earth-healer, cools slowly in hidden vents. Igneous crystals restore stability after change and ground energies. But first, igneous crystals impel change to take place, stimulating growth processes and healing the past.

Rebirthed by pressure

Metamorphic crystals such as Garnet, Serpentine and Jade are created when existing minerals melt under intense pressure and enormous heat. Laid down in recrystallized plates, which in turn are crushed, folded and bent, these are some of the most potent transformation crystals. Metamorphic crystals facilitate change and transmutation, and processes of soul scouring and reconfiguring that precede soul growth. As reborn crystals, metamorphic rocks are also associated with processes of building, rebuilding and shapeshifting.

BORN OF FIRE Black Tourmaline
REBIRTHED BY PRESSURE Garnet

Reborn of water

Crystals in sedimentary rocks drip into being. Some of these transmutative crystals were created from sediments that settled at the bottom of a body of water and were compressed over millions of years. Calcite and other sedimentary crystals form from erosion. Surface rocks break down and mineralized water drips through rock, or a river lays down weathered material, which becomes cemented together. Selenite came into being when recycled mineral-laden water dripped into fissures. These calming crystals assist with survival issues and riding out long cycles of time. Teaching the value of going with the flow, they patiently facilitate understanding the impact of the environment on health and wellbeing, assisting letting go of rigid belief patterns and ingrained thoughts, opening the way for change.

Born of air

A handful of crystals come from the stars, literally flying through the air, or are a fusion of star matter with the ground on which they impact at huge velocity. Moldavite, Tektite and Libyan Gold Tektite have all travelled to the planet bringing knowledge from outer space. Moqui Marbles have a sandstone kernel, surrounded by Hematite from fragmented iron meteorites that hit Earth, raining small particles that fused with sand.

Crystals born of air open the mind. They usher in new ideals, fresh possibilities, rebuilding ancient concepts into deeper knowing. Visionary air is the element of liberation and freedom. It offers room to breathe – and opens the soul to transmutation.

Air works internally too. When minerals oxidize, they produce a potent crystal. 'Oxidize' literally means taking on oxygen. Iron oxidizing onto the surface of Quartz produces beautiful iridescent coatings on Rainbow Mayanite and other Quartzes. Stunning pink Rhodochrosite is created through oxidization of manganese. The brightness and lightness are joyful and lift the spirit.

Born of nature

Certain 'crystals' form from transformed organic material. Amber is a tree resin, Shungite a natural organic carbon compound compressed into 'bucky ball' form. It retains traces of the earliest forms of life. Stones such as Turritella Agate exhibit remnants of sea creatures, shells and fossils. Natural materials mineralize – dinosaur bone and petrified wood being examples. Stunning crystals are created when creatures such as Ammonites fossilize and infill with Aragonite, Opal, Calcite, Pyrite and trace elements. All contribute to the rainbow flash (an iridescent coating or an internal colouring) and gentle healing effect. These crystals teach the value of going with the flow, opening to transformation without struggle or pressure. Simply allowing.

REBORN OF WATER Moldavite Calcite
BORN OF AIR Moldavite
BORN OF NATURE Amber

Crystal vibrations

According to the laws of physics, everything in the universe vibrates and has its own resonant frequency. Although a term often applied to acoustics, resonant frequency relates to objects, too, as they have a mechanical or electromagnetic resonance – that is, they give off waves of energy. Where there are energetic waves, there is resonance. This resonance can be tested by specialist equipment but, for crystal workers, it is something felt rather than measured. Crystals have vibrational frequencies that range from deep and earthy ('lower') to exceedingly fine and cosmic ('higher'). These are not judgemental terms; no one vibration is better than another. Each has its part to play. Some crystals combine both ends of the spectrum, assimilating and grounding higher vibrations into the physical plane. That is to say, they step down high, refined 'cosmic' vibrations so that they can be utilized in the denser vibrations of Earth. It is through these varied vibrations that crystals interact with physical and subtle bodies to bring about healing.

Earthy (lower) vibration

Earthy is the lowest and densest frequency of vibrational resonances. Earthy crystals function well in the physical world, grounding and anchoring energies. They are protective, cleansing and transmutational, soaking up negative energies and transmitting beneficial vibes. This is the resonance of pragmatic concerns, body and physical wellbeing, home, prosperity and material possessions. It brings things into manifestation. A seed vibration of inspiration, fertilization and creativity, it kickstarts new projects. Earthy crystals carry an abundant supply of Qi, or lifeforce. They resonate with the earth star chakra (*see* page 20) holding you in incarnation (your physical form on Earth), and with base and sacral chakras (*see* pages 20 and 21) to bring projects to fruition. Earthy crystals channel energy from Earth throughout the whole chakra system to energize and activate all levels of life.

Earthy crystals: Smoky Quartz, Flint, Hematite

Cosmic (high) vibration

High-vibration crystals operate at exceedingly refined resonances beyond the physicality of Earth. These cosmic crystals work at the level of spirit and soul and their effects filter 'down' into the physical. Cosmic vibrations assist spiritual wellbeing, channelling higher consciousness to Earth, taking you into unity consciousness and universal love, accessing your soul's plan. They facilitate the ability to be in several dimensions at once. High-vibration crystals open the highest crown chakras to reach way up into multidimensions. They activate the causal vortex, soul star and stellar gateway portals, and the alta major chakra within the skull (*see* pages 23–4).

Cosmic crystals: Anandalite, Trigonic, Petalite

Healing vibration

The healing vibration covers a wide spectrum of energetic resonances. Healing means integrating mind, body and spirit, returning them to a harmonious whole. Crystals combining high vibrations with earthy resonances are effective on the physical plane, promoting wellbeing. Wellbeing is a state of mind rather than a physical condition. These crystals facilitate understanding of the effect of the mind's and soul's needs on the physical body. They dissolve underlying causes of dis-ease: spiritual, environmental, karmic, psychological, ancestral, emotional or mental imbalances accrued over many lifetimes. Healing-vibration crystals facilitate handling change and adjusting to new circumstances, pointing the way forward. Healing crystals contain large quantities of Qi and bioscalar healing waves, a unique form of energy that can be harnessed and directed into solid objects or bodies placed in its field. They cleanse, energize, align and activate the chakras and facilitate assimilation of higher vibrations into physical and subtle-energy bodies.

Healing crystals: Bloodstone, Que Sera, Quantum Quattro

Combination (lower and higher) vibrations

Combination-vibration crystals are dynamic, energetic tools for transformation and wellbeing. Crystals with combined earthy and high vibrations bridge frequencies of the earth-plane with cosmic dimensions to integrate dualities, infuse higher consciousness into the everyday and ensure wellbeing on every level. They harmonize physical and subtle-energy bodies, integrating them with the environment and multidimensions that surround us. These crystals elevate denser vibrations and re-form subtle matter. As they have a near-perfect vibration, they entrain energy – that is, return a state of disorder to order. Combination crystals purify and detoxify at an energetic level, drawing in earthy or cosmic energies as appropriate, and assimilate new frequencies into a purified, receptive physical body. They unify higher chakras above the crown with the earth star and Gaia gateway, integrating refined frequencies throughout the whole chakra system.

Combined crystals: Elestial Smoky Quartz, Brandberg Amethyst, Auralite 23, Shiva Lingam

EARTHY Flint

COSMIC Pink Petalite

HEALING Bloodstone

COMBINATION Brandberg Amethyst

Colour vibrations

Each colour has its own unique vibration. This means that different colours of a basic crystal may exhibit significant disparities in their healing effect.

Chalky white, grey, silver, brown or black: Useful protectors, these crystals anchor grids. (Grids are patterns laid using empowered crystals for the purpose of manifesting a desired outcome, or for cleansing and safeguarding a space. *See* pages 32–3.) They ground the physical body and detoxify negative energies.

Bi-colour: Excellent integrators, bi-coloured crystals harmonize and unify.

Red: Best used for short periods, red crystals stimulate and strengthen. Activating creativity and revitalizing potency, red crystals may over-excite volatile emotions or over-energize the body, creating hyper-conditions.

Pink: Ideal for long-term use, gentle pink crystals offer unconditional love, nurture and comfort, and are excellent for heart healing. They release grief, calm emotions and facilitate acceptance.

Orange: Less volatile than red and appropriate for longer periods of use, orange crystals activate and release. Building up supportive energetic structures, orange attracts abundance and stimulates creativity.

BLACK **Black Kyanite**   BI-COLOUR **Ruby in Fuchsite**   RED **Zircon**   PINK **Pink Muscovite**   ORANGE **Orange Sphalerite**

Yellow: Active at mental and feeling levels, yellow and golden crystals awaken and organize the mind and energize situations. They rebalance and calm emotions and overcome seasonal disorders, such as Seasonal Affective Disorder (SAD), hayfever, sensitivity to pressure changes, coughs and colds.

Green: Perfect for environmental healing and the heart, green crystals calm and rebalance. They sedate energy and pacify emotions.

Blue: Calming and clarifying, blue crystals facilitate communication and self-expression. They ground spiritual energy, and assist intuition and channelling.

Purple, indigo and lilac: Integrating and aligning higher energies, these crystals have powerful spiritual awakening qualities, stimulating service to others. These colours cool over-heated energies.

White and clear: Clarifying situations and opening intuition to gain insight, white or clear crystals purify and focus energy. They link to the highest realms of being and expanded spiritual consciousness.

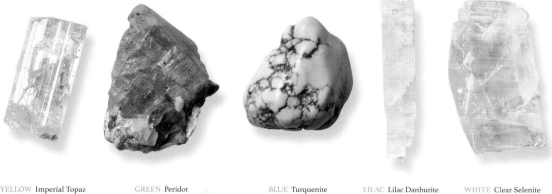

YELLOW Imperial Topaz   GREEN Peridot   BLUE Turquenite   LILAC Lilac Danburite   WHITE Clear Selenite

What is crystal healing?

Crystal healing is an integrated, therapeutic, energetic process. It is holistic, working with the whole person rather than what is most probably a symptom of deeper dis-ease. It acts on body, psyche, soul and environment. The definition of healing that I find most useful is:

'Illness is a dis-ease, the final manifestation of spiritual, environmental, psychological, karmic, emotional or mental imbalance or distress. Healing means bringing mind, body and spirit back into balance and facilitating evolution for the soul, it does not imply a cure.' (*Crystal Bible*, Judy Hall)

To facilitate that 'coming back into balance', I use crystals. Why so many? Well, each crystal offers unique properties. There may be a need to cleanse, unblock, sedate or activate energies. For that, different colours and disparate crystals are required, according to the vibrational state of the person or environment. There is no 'one size fits all' in crystal work. Each person has their own specific frequency, which differs from anyone else's, due to past experiences, ancestral inheritance, environment, nutrition, beliefs and so on. Finding the crystal that resonates with you and brings you back into balance is key to maintaining wellbeing and evolving spiritually.

Crystal affinities

Across aeons of time, the perceived properties of crystals have remained remarkably consistent. Hematite has an affinity with blood, exactly as it did in Mesopotamia and Egypt thousands of years ago. Selenite is still regarded as crystallized divine light. A vast body of knowledge has built up regarding affinities between crystals and organs of the body and chakras, mapping physiological interaction. Crystals energetically regulate the hormonal and other systems in addition to bringing mind, body and spirit into harmony. Light and colour have a profound effect on the functioning of pineal, pituitary and other glands in the body, supporting traditional use.

Crystals for healing

The most direct method of using a crystal for healing is to place it over the site of dis-ease or pain and leave it in place for 5–15 minutes once or twice a day. You could, of course, wear a crystal for long periods of time, but remember to cleanse it regularly (*see* page 27). The other main methods are through chakras (*see* pages 18–24) or grids (*see* pages 32–3). The crystal activates, cleanses and re-energizes the energy centre and organs connected with it, realigning and harmonizing chakras where appropriate, or purifies and protects the whole body or space. This book includes crystal techniques for environmental and multidimensional healing.

A healing challenge

If you find yourself having a strong reaction or feeling particularly averse to a specific colour or crystal, it may have an incompatible vibration. Or it could indicate something you are hiding from yourself. This may be a feeling or an attitude repressed because you, unconsciously, deem it 'unacceptable' or too painful. Such repression leads to psychosomatic dis-ease (caused by internal conflict or stress). The suppressed feeling manifests itself physically within the body, or as a subtle sense of all not being well. This feeling is sometimes projected into the outside world. It could be that the crystal is having a cathartic or detoxifying effect, or triggering internal conflicts and conflicting agendas in your unconscious mind. Putting the crystal aside and gently exploring the cause of your reaction with a cleansing and grounding crystal such as Smoky Quartz at your feet assists. Once you have drawn off the initial source of distress, and dispersed it into the grounding crystal, you may need the support of a crystal that instils a complementary healing resonance. So, if the crystal has triggered jealousy and resentment, for instance, holding Rose Quartz would dispel this.

ABOVE A Prairie Tanzanite layout around the head to calm the mind and release a tension headache.

Chakras and subtle-energy bodies

The chakras and subtle-energy bodies are an integrated system that maintains health and wellbeing at all the levels covered within this book. Blockages and imbalances may result in dis-ease.

The chakras

Whirling vortexes of energy, chakras act as linkage and assimilation points between subtle-energy bodies and the physical body. Perception, emotions and self-expression are powerfully affected by how active these energy centres are, and whether they are stressed or functioning optimally. When blocked or stagnant, they permit subconscious fears and feelings to rule unchallenged. Centres that are wide open and whirling out of control allow the outside world to influence all too strongly. Operating at optimum, chakras test and challenge ingrained perceptions. They download and assimilate higher vibrational energy that lifts the soul beyond what has been known before.

As ancient chakra diagrams indicate, there are many more chakras than the seven traditional 'personal chakras' shown on conventional modern chakra diagrams. (A multitude of chakras were pared down and formalized by occultists into the Theosophical coloured-chakra system at the beginning of the 20th century.) Higher-vibration chakras are once again being activated as consciousness expands and dormant energetic linkage points are opening up to connect the physical body and the Earth with cosmic energies. 'Secondary chakras' also connect into the ancestral and past-life realms. (*See* pages 20–4 for descriptions of these chakras.)

Types of chakra

The chakras can be divided as follows:
- **Personal chakras** These 'traditional' chakras include the base, sacral, solar plexus, heart, throat, third eye and crown.
- **Transpersonal chakras** These 'higher-vibration' chakras include the earth star, gaia gateway, heart seed, higher heart, soma, causal vortex, soul star and alta major.
- **Secondary chakras** These include the palms, knees, past life, dantien and spleen.

OPPOSITE The major chakras run from below the feet, up the spine, to above the head. Others are positioned on one or both sides of the body.

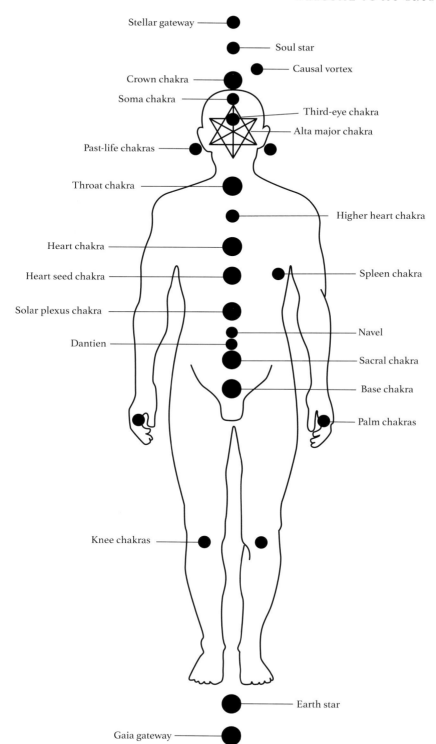

Stellar gateway

Soul star

Causal vortex

Crown chakra

Soma chakra

Third-eye chakra

Alta major chakra

Past-life chakras

Throat chakra

Higher heart chakra

Heart chakra

Heart seed chakra

Spleen chakra

Solar plexus chakra

Navel

Dantien

Sacral chakra

Base chakra

Palm chakras

Knee chakras

Earth star

Gaia gateway

Earthy (subpersonal) chakras

Earthy energy centres function below everyday awareness, keeping you anchored in incarnation. When you interact with the ground beneath your feet and the energetic forces that run through the body of the planet, they anchor you in the central core of your being, physical and spiritual. When they do not function optimally, you feel rootless, alien and isolated, literally 'from a different planet'. When they are functioning optimally, you feel as though you belong on Earth.

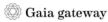 **Gaia gateway**
PLANETARY SOUL CONNECTION
Location: Deep beneath feet
Function: Connecting your soul to the soul and spirit of Earth, Gaia and Mother Earth, the Gaia gateway assimilates and anchors high vibrations into the physical body and that of Earth, adjusting your electromagnetic field (EMF) frequency to remain in harmonic resonance with that of the planet.
Functioning optimally: You are aware of being a part of a sacred whole. (The Gaia gateway is energetically linked to the stellar gateway.)

Earth star
ANCHORING AND GROUNDING
Location: Beneath feet
Function: The earth star is a place of safety and regeneration, keeping you grounded. Connecting to Earth's electromagnetic fields and energy meridians, it goes deep into the core. Actualizing plans and dreams, it anchors new frequencies and downloads of cosmic information, creating a stable and strong centre.
Functioning optimally: It creates a natural electrical circuit and a powerful source of vital energy. (The earth star is energetically linked to the soul star.)

 Knees
FLEXIBILITY, BALANCE AND WILLPOWER
Location: Knees
Function: All major energy meridians pass through the knees, as does the sciatic nerve, the longest in the body. Knee chakras facilitate nurturing and supporting yourself, manifesting what you need from day to day.
Functioning optimally: You are flexible, able to adapt to changing circumstances, going with the flow, yet having perseverance when needed. Well-balanced knee chakras support in stepping into a new way of being.

Personal chakras

Personal energy centres function within everyday reality. Mediating between inner and outer worlds – physical body, environment and energies of Earth – these chakras assimilate energies at the lower end of the vibrational scale. They control how Qi is utilized. Personal chakras govern how you react – or respond – to the world around you, which may be a knee-jerk reaction to emotions or ingrained habits. These chakras bring body and psyche back into balance.

 Base (root)
BASIC SURVIVAL INSTINCTS AND SECURITY ISSUES
Location: Base of spine
Function: Relating to your roots, willpower and ability to make things happen, this is where you connect with your tribe and where you feel safe. You discover yourself as an individual and take responsibility for your Self. The base chakra represents home and career, and how secure you feel in each. Imbalances lead to sexual disturbances and stuckness, anger, impotence and frustration – and inability to let go. Linking core connection to Earth, the 'sacred bone' is where kundalini (a subtle but extremely dynamic psycho-spiritual energy) rests before it is awakened.
Functioning optimally: You trust the universe.

Sacral

CREATIVITY, PASSION AND FERTILITY

Location: Below navel

Function: An important part of the core energy system, the sacral chakra stimulates production of feel-good hormones, having a powerful effect on moment-to-moment mood. It holds boundaries steady. This is where you handle the immediate environment and matters such as money, career and authority figures. It affects how easily you express your sexuality and how you feel about relationships, holding parenting issues and connection to family, in addition to hooks from previous relationships.

Functioning optimally: You have the ability to bring things into manifestation.

Dantien

POWER

Location: Below navel, above sacral

Function: An energy storage vault, when the dantien is full, you have inner resources on which to draw. You are literally power-full. An adjunct to the sacral chakra and point of balance for the physical body, the dantien stores Qi, and earths the body.

Functioning optimally: A place of inner strength, stability and balance, when connected to the dantien, you have more physical energy and are unaffected by life's ups and downs, emotionally stable and can resist stress.

Navel ('belly button')

NURTURE

Location: Centre line, below waist

Function: A potent ancestral-line connection point, the navel links to the mother and matriarchal line and is strongest pre-birth. The navel is vulnerable, known as the belly 'button' for good, largely unconscious reasons as it is the trigger for ancestral memories, especially fear and trauma. Transgenerational messages, DNA, cellular disorders and matriarchal imperatives lodge here, plus ancestral strengths and feminine wisdom.

Functioning optimally: You are able to access and utilize the wisdom of past generations and nurture yourself.

Palms

ENERGY MANIFESTATION, TRANSMUTATION AND UTILIZATION

Location: Palms, fingers, lower arms

Function: Interacting with the world on an energetic level, the palms are powerful sensors, where you experience expanded awareness, collecting and radiating energy and impressions.

Functioning optimally: Palm chakras receive energy from the universe – or crystals – and channel this into another energy field. Palms increase creativity in the physical and subtle-energy worlds.

Solar plexus

EMOTIONS

Location: Above navel

Function: Emotions stored in the solar plexus have a deeply psychosomatic effect. The point of digestion on all levels, this is where you assimilate nourishment and absorb energy and emotions from outside yourself. Emotional hooks from other people locate here. Having a powerful effect on the ability to assert your will, this chakra governs self-confidence and self-esteem in addition to emotional stability.

Functioning optimally: Linked to intuition, it is the seat of 'gut instincts' and bodily knowledge.

Spleen

SELF-PROTECTION AND EMPOWERMENT

Location: Below left armpit

Function: A seat of power, the spleen is where energy vampires hook in to get their fix, leaving you depleted at immune and vitality levels.

Functioning optimally: Energy easily flows around the physical and subtle bodies, and you are protected.

Heart seed

SOUL REMEMBRANCE

Location: Tip of breastbone

Function: A soul linkage point, the heart seed recalls the reason for incarnation, showing how to return to the original soulplan if you have deviated.

Functioning optimally: Assisting in renegotiating outdated soul purpose, it activates karmic tools to actualize your soul potential. It brings a profound connection to the lightbody and multidimensional consciousness. (The lightbody is a subtle-energetic envelope that forms part of the aura but extends beyond it into higher dimensions. *See* page 25.)

Heart

UNCONDITIONAL LOVE AND NURTURING

Location: Towards base of breastbone

Function: The heart chakra facilitates unselfish self-love and self-worth, rising above egotism. With the higher heart and heart seed, it forms the three-chambered heart chakra. Integrating the whole chakric line, the heart chakra is the core of your being, where the physical body and soul meet. The site of bonds made with other people, it governs relationships and interaction with wider worlds.

Functioning optimally: You 'live from the heart', safe, compassionate and non-judgemental.

Higher heart (thymus)

IMMUNITY AND WELLBEING

Location: Between heart and throat

Function: Governing physical and psychic immune systems, this centre controls how well you protect yourself, and has a profound effect on wellbeing. The first gland to develop, it is a core component of the body *in utero*, governing which genetic potential is switched on, and how much natural immunity you have. Blockages in the chakra connect to and reflect ancestral DNA and past-life patterning, which in turn results in a compromised immune system and consequent dis-ease.

Functioning optimally: You have natural physical and psychic immunity.

Throat

COMMUNICATION

Location: Centre of throat

Function: This chakra has a surprising amount to do with willpower and choices that arise in life. Mediating contact with the external world, the throat is where you express yourself, including feelings and emotions coming from the heart or solar plexus as well as thoughts. If closed, there is no outlet for these feelings and thoughts, leading to psychosomatic dis-ease.

Functioning optimally: Opinions and feelings are clearly communicated.

Third eye (brow)

INTUITION AND MENTAL CONNECTION

Location: Above and between eyebrows

Function: Where inner sight meets outer vision and bonds into intuitive insight, the third eye sees beyond everyday reality into what really is: sensing unseen worlds and higher dimensions. Imbalances result in being bombarded by other people's thoughts, or overwhelmed by irrational intuitions with no basis in truth. Controlling or coercing mental hooks from outside influences lock in here.

Functioning optimally: Intuition can be relied upon.

Soma

SOULBODY CONNECTION

Location: Mid-hairline above third eye

Function: Where soul and etheric bodies attach to the physical, the soma anchors the 'silver cord' holding subtle-energy bodies in contact with the physical. It links to angelic realms and spirit guides. Out of balance, it is easy for the soul to disconnect, or for discarnate spirits to attach, and involuntary out-of-body experiences to occur that may literally blow your mind.

Functioning optimally: It gives the clarity necessary to achieve enlightenment. Cosmic light anchors the soulbody to the physical and the greater whole.

Past life
MEMORY AND HEREDITARY ISSUES

Location: Behind ears

Function: Where memories of previous incarnations are stored together with deeply ingrained soul programmes and emotional baggage, past-life chakras hold soul contracts, intentions, traumas, dramas, gifts and lessons from many lifetimes. It links to the karmic etheric body that stores soul wounds, physical or emotional, re-creating psychosomatic dis-ease or physical disease through subtle DNA memory traces. Activating these chakras brings up memories for release. Soul contracts can resemble curses or hexing moving down a family or karmic line.

Functioning optimally: Facilitates moving forward with no baggage, freed from karmic deficits, drawing on karmic credits.

Crown
SPIRITUAL COMMUNICATION AND AWARENESS

Location: Top of head

Function: A place of spiritual, intellectual and intuitive knowing, the crown chakra connects to multidimensions and multiverses. When blocked, excessive environmental sensitivity, delusions or dementia result.

Functioning optimally: Soul purpose is actualized, leading to self-understanding. Certain of your pathway, you are attuned to the cycles of life, recognizing lessons programmed in before birth and soul gifts you seek.

Transpersonal (spiritual) chakras

Transpersonal energy centres vibrate at a higher resonance and are located within the human energy field, or at its outermost edges where that field merges with the greater energy field. Transpersonal chakras include the Gaia gateway (*see* page 20), as it is energetically linked to the stellar gateway.

Alta major (ascension)
EXPANDING AWARENESS

Location: Inside and around skull

Function: Anchoring the multidimensional lightbody, the alta major shows the bigger picture. Holding the ancestral past and ingrained patterns that govern human life, in conjunction with the causal vortex and past-life chakras, it accesses past-life karma and contractual agreements plus the soul's plan.

Functioning optimally: The subtle endocrine system harmonizes auric bodies with the physical. There is a strong sense of direction.

Soul star
ULTIMATE SOUL AWARENESS

Location: Above head

Function: An interface between spirit and matter, when out of balance this chakra creates spiritual arrogance, soul fragmentation or messiah-complex, or is the site of spirit attachment, extraterrestrial invasion or being overwhelmed by ancestral spirits. The soul star links to the earth star.

Functioning optimally: This energy centre recalibrates extremely high spiritual frequencies to be assimilated and integrated into matter. (The soul star is energetically linked to the earth star.)

✹ Stellar gateway

COSMIC DOORWAY TO OTHER WORLDS

Location: Above soul star

Function: A dimensional portal, the stellar gateway connects to the divine and to multiverses. When this chakra is imbalanced, the soul is a 'space cadet', fragmented, disintegrated, unable to function in the everyday world.

Functioning optimally: Two-way communication with higher dimensional beings is facilitated and spiritual illumination results. (The stellar gateway is energetically linked to the Gaia gateway.)

✹ Causal vortex

SOUL JOURNEY

Location: Above and to side of head

Function: A universal and cosmic worldwide web, the causal vortex accesses the Akashic Record to reveal how far you've travelled on your spiritual journey. (The Akashic Record is a cosmic memory bank of all that is, has been or ever could be – *see* page 216.) A repository for ancestral and karmic dis-eases, the causal vortex brings subtle and physical bodies into alignment, activating DNA potential.

Functioning optimally: Wisdom and guidance, illuminating lessons planned and highlighting karmic skills and abilities, are received and integrated.

The aura and subtle bodies

Biomagnetic fields, subtle-energy bodies, radiating out from the physical body in interpenetrating waves, connect via the chakras. These auric fields link to multidimensional frequencies and are blueprints holding information, bio-memories and engrams (bundles of energy holding deeply traumatic or joyful memory pictures), from which the physical body is constructed. Crystals entrain subtle bodies back into equilibrium, healing energetic 'holes': energy depletion, distortion or imprinted patterns that no longer serve and which, ultimately, create physical dis-ease.

✹ Physical-etheric body

Function: A biomagnetic programme holding imprints of past-life dis-ease, injuries and beliefs, the physical-etheric body contains subtle DNA activated or switched off by behaviour, emotions and beliefs. This in turn affects DNA in the physical body.

Chakra connection: Seven traditional, lower-frequency chakras and soma, past life, alta major and causal vortex chakras.

✹ Emotional body

Function: Imprinted with emotions and feelings, attitudes, heartbreaks, traumas and dramas from present and previous lives, the emotional body contains engrams. Dis-ease in this body is reflected in knees and feet, which act out insecurities and fears, or heart and abdomen.

Chakra connection: Knees, solar plexus, base and sacral, throat, heart.

✹ Mental body

Function: Created from thoughts, memories, credos and ingrained limiting beliefs from past and present lives, the mental body holds imprints of authority figures from the past, along with inculcated ideologies, attitudes and points of view.

Chakra connection: Throat and head chakras and lower body.

Karmic body

Function: Holding imprints of all previous lives and the purpose for the present life, the karmic body contains mental programmes, physical imprints, emotional impressions and beliefs that may be contradictory and create internal conflict. When balanced, evolutionary intent is actualized.

Chakra connection: Past life, alta major and causal vortex chakras; may affect soma, knee and earth star.

Ancestral body

Function: Everything that is inherited down both sides of ancestral lineage at the physical, or more subtle, levels is held in the ancestral body, including family sagas, belief systems, attitudes, culture, loss, expectations, traumas and dramas. Healing sent down the ancestral line to the core experience rebounds forward to heal the future. Ancestral imperatives must be released before soul evolution occurs.

Chakra connection: Soul star, past life, alta major, causal vortex, higher heart, earth star and Gaia gateway chakras.

Planetary body

Function: Linking into the physical planet and Earth's etheric body and meridians, the planetary body connects to the wider cosmos, luminaries, planets and stellar bodies. Cosmic or soul dis-ease is corrected through the planetary subtle body.

Chakra connection: Past life, alta major, causal vortex, soma, stellar and Gaia gateway chakras.

Spiritual or lightbody

Function: An integrated, luminous, vibrating energy field, the lightbody connects the physical body, subtle-energy bodies, with spirit or soul and the wider cosmos.

Chakra connection: All, especially soma, soul star, stellar gateway, Gaia gateway, alta major and causal vortex.

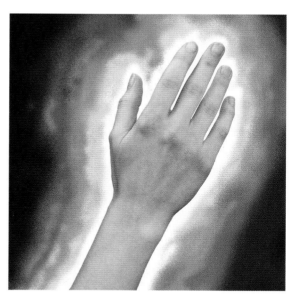

ABOVE The biomagnetic field around the physical body is visible to the psychic eye as a subtle field of light.

Crystal selection, care and programming

The easiest way to select your crystal is to use your intuition. Glance through relevant crystal portraits in this book (*see* pages 68–307). When a particular crystal catches your eye, focus on it. The same applies when you purchase a crystal. Choose one that catches your attention. Or, if you are unused to trusting your intuition, dowse for the right crystal (*see* below). Finger-dowsing provides an easy way to select stones.

To ensure that a crystal works to its highest potential, attune it to your personal vibration, asking it to work for your highest good.

To finger-dowse

Loop the thumb and finger of your non-dominant hand together. Slip your other thumb and finger through the loop and close together. Ask your question. Pull steadily. If the loop breaks, the answer is 'no'. If the loop holds, the answer is 'yes'.

To pendulum-dowse

Hold your pendulum between thumb and forefinger of your most receptive hand with about a hand's length of chain hanging down. Wrap the remaining chain around your fingers. Hold the pendulum over the crystal or its photograph in this book.

To ascertain a 'yes' and 'no' response: Hold the pendulum over your knee and ask: 'Is my name [state correct name]?' The direction that the pendulum swings indicates 'yes'. Ask: 'Is my name [incorrect name]?' to establish 'no'.

The pendulum may swing in one direction for 'yes' and at right angles to that axis for 'no', or a backward and forward swing for 'no' and a circular motion for 'yes'. A wobble indicates 'maybe', that it is not appropriate at that time or the wrong question is being asked. If so, check you are framing the question correctly. If the pendulum stops, it is inappropriate to ask at that time.

BELOW Finger-dowsing quickly and easily establishes the right crystal for you.

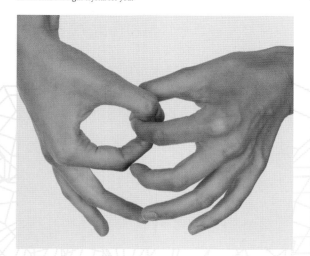

BELOW Pendulum-dowsing utilizes your body's intuitive knowing.

Crystal cleansing methods

Crystals soak up vibrations – negative and positive – by absorbing energy from the environment. Unless cleansed, a crystal carries energy from everyone who has handled it or places where it spent time. Crystals require frequent cleansing and re-energizing. Crystal descriptions throughout the book list appropriate and inappropriate cleansing methods.

Water Robust, non-soluble crystals are cleansed by running under water for a few moments and placing in sun or moonlight to recharge.

Brown rice Place crystal in brown rice overnight and recharge afterwards in sunlight. Do not reuse the rice – compost or dispose of it.

Sound A singing bowl, tuning fork or tingshas (small cymbals) transmute negative vibrations. Sound over the crystal, or place the crystal in the bowl and strike the bowl. Recharge the crystal in sunlight.

BELOW Tap water can be used to cleanse crystals but spring water is better.

Return to earth Robust crystals may be buried. Mark the spot. After retrieving the crystal, leave it in sunlight to recharge.

Smudge Smoke from a smudge stick or incense cleanses a crystal before recharging in sunlight.

Crystal A large Quartz, Citrine, Chlorite Quartz or Carnelian cleanses and recharges a smaller crystal but needs cleansing afterwards. (Although Citrine and Kyanite are self-cleansing, they still benefit from regular cleansing.) Placing a small crystal on a larger version of itself recharges a crystal, restoring its energetic frequency.

Light Passing a crystal through light from a candle or visualizing it surrounded by light purifies it. Placing the crystal in sun or moonlight recharges it.

Purpose-made essence Purpose-made crystal cleansing and recharging essences are available (*see* Resources and Further Reading, page 311). Make your own cleansing essence by selecting a few crystals from the clearing and recharging list (*see* page 31).

Salt

Salt, unless in a salt ring or as Halite, is best avoided, as it damages delicate crystals.

Activating your crystal

A crystal needs to be activated and programmed to begin working. Rub your hands briskly together to activate your palm chakras. Hold the crystal in your hands and wait a few moments to attune to it. Check out how you feel. A crystal in harmony with your energy field feels peaceful and calm, or buzzing and busy. If a crystal feels unpleasant, it may have triggered a release or may not be appropriate (*see* page 17).

Picture light surrounding the crystal and formulate your intention. Be specific because focused intention is part of the process, but don't limit your intention. If using the crystal for healing, say precisely for which condition and the result you seek. But leave room for underlying factors to materialize. Always add the statement: 'This or something more for the highest good.' This opens the way for things to happen that you may not have envisaged.

When you are totally in tune, say out loud: 'I programme [ask] this crystal for/to [state your purpose]. This or something greater for the highest good of all who come in contact with it.'

If using your crystal for protection, be less specific: a generalized 'protect me from anything negative that may harm me' suffices.

Wear the crystal, place it on your body, position it where you see it frequently or keep it in your pocket.

OPPOSITE Wearing a crystal is the perfect way to benefit from its healing energies.

Maintaining your crystals

Treat your crystals gently. Keep coloured crystals out of sunlight as they may fade. Layered or clustered stones such as Halite are water-soluble, eroding in a damp atmosphere. Polished surfaces are easily scratched, but tumbled stones are more robust. When not in use, wrap your crystals in a silk or velvet scarf. This protects the crystal against absorbing negative emanations. It avoids a mishmash of crystal energies permeating your home or environment and allows space for those that are working to function optimally.

Manmade crystals

Some natural crystals are shaped into new forms, such as wands or balls, that direct but do not amend the crystal energy. Increasingly, however, crystals are being grown in laboratories (and may be passed off as 'natural' by unscrupulous vendors). Crystals may also be altered either by heating (for example, Citrine and Tanzanite), coating (for example, Aura Quartz) or colour infusing (for example, Turquenite). Swarovski crystal is manmade from lead and, in my view, has no healing properties, although it has aesthetic value. Some manmade stones have strong healing properties: Bismuth is lab-grown and Goldstone is an alchemical combination of glass and metal flakes. The type of metal or mineral used determines the colour: copper creates red, cobalt blue, chromium oxide green and manganese purple.

Crystal essences and Shungite water

Essences encapsulate the healing power of crystals. Crystals can be combined to make an essence, provided you check compatibility by dowsing (*see* page 26). Crystal essences transfer subtle vibrational energies and minute concentrations of the minerals of crystals into water. Water stores the vibrations and transfers them to chakras, physical or subtle bodies and the environment.

ABOVE Crystal essences should be made in a glass bowl.

Exercise

Making a crystal essence

You will need: An appropriate crystal, one or two clean glass bowls, spring water and a suitable bottle in which to keep the essence (coloured glass is preferable to clear or plastic). Use spring water rather than tap water that may have toxic chlorine, fluoride and aluminium added. Always ensure that the crystals are thoroughly cleansed and activated (*see* page 28) before use.

Direct method

1 Place sufficient spring water in a glass bowl to cover the crystal(s).
2 Stand the bowl in sunlight for several hours. (If the bowl is left outside, cover with a glass lid or clingfilm.) If possible, leave the bowl overnight in moonlight.
3 Bottle as directed below.

Indirect method

Use this method if a crystal is potentially toxic or fragile.

1 Place the crystal in a small glass bowl and stand the bowl within a larger bowl with sufficient spring water to raise the level above the dry crystal in the inner bowl.
2 Stand in sunlight for several hours. (If the bowl is left outside, cover with a glass lid or clingfilm.) If possible, leave the bowl overnight in moonlight.

Bottling and preserving

1 Remove the crystals.
2 Pour the essence into a glass bottle. If the essence is not to be used immediately, top up one-third essence with two-thirds brandy, vodka, white rum or cider vinegar (otherwise it may become musty).
3 Label with the date and contents and store in a cool place. This is the 'mother essence', which is to be diluted for use.
4 To make a dosage bottle, add seven drops of mother essence to a small bottle containing two-thirds water and one-third brandy.

5 If you are making a spray, add seven drops of mother essence to pure water. For prolonged use, add vodka or white rum.

Using a crystal essence

For short-term use, sip every few minutes, rub on an appropriate chakra (remembering that these extend several feet out from the physical body), place on a crystal or grid, spray around the aura or space, or drip onto a crystal on an ancestral or other photograph. Apply to skin, either at the wrist or over the site of a problem, or add to bath water. Hold in your mouth for a few moments if taking orally. For longer-term application, use three times a day.

Exercise
Crystal cleansing and recharging essence

Chose one or two crystals from each of the following lists.
Clearing crystals: Black Tourmaline, Blue or Black Kyanite, Halite, Hematite, Shungite, Smoky Quartz.
Recharging: Anandalite™, Carnelian, Golden Healer, Citrine, Orange Kyanite, Quartz, Red Jasper, Selenite, Quartz.

To make the essence
1 Hold the crystals in your hands and ask them to cleanse your crystals or space. Follow the instructions for making a direct essence above. (Note: Although Selenite and Halite are soluble, place them directly in water for this particular essence.)
2 Remove the crystals and pour the essence into a glass bottle.
3 Add a few drops of essential oil such as frankincense, sage or lavender, and top up with vodka or white rum. This is the mother essence.
4 Label bottle with date and contents. Keep in a cool place.
5 Fill a spray bottle with spring water. Add seven drops of mother essence.
6 Lightly mist crystals or space.

Shungite water

To become biologically active, for example to be able to kill off bacteria or viruses, water needs to have Shungite immersed in it for 48 hours. If you prefer, make water by the indirect method for crystal essence (*see* opposite), placing Elite (Noble) Shungite in a container within the water and standing it in sunlight for 48 hours. Shungite water is cleansing and preventative. It isn't further diluted, but is used as it is.

Exercise
Making the water

You will need: 2 litre (4 pint) filter jug, 5cm (2in) fine mesh bag, 10–100g (⅓–3½oz) raw Shungite

1 Place the mesh bag of Shungite in the base of a filter jug (or place Noble or Elite Shungite in the base of a closed glass container).
2 Fill the jug with water (if using tap water, pass it through a commercial water filter first).
3 Stand for 48 hours.

Cleanse Shungite frequently under running water and re-energize in sunlight or fresh air. Small pieces of Elite Shungite will keep small bottles of pre-activated water potent and ready for use.

Once the first batch is made, refill the filter jug after each use. Raw Shungite is more effective than tumbled or Elite but, no matter how often non-vitreous Shungite is washed and the use of a mesh bag, it leaves a suspension of fine black particles. This is part of the process.

Crystal grids and layouts

Crystal grids are energy transmitters laid out according to the principles of sacred geometry. Ranging from the simplest of shapes to the most complex forms, they harness fundamental forces of the universe, synergizing them with crystal vibrations into a vast energetic net. These work at personal and environmental levels.

Layouts are particularly useful for protecting your space and transmuting detrimental energies (*see* pages 284–307). They fill the space with beneficial energy.

Cleanse crystals before laying in a grid. A few basic grids are all you need and you'll find layouts throughout the book. For additional crystal ideas, see the crystal portraits on pages 68–307.

Triangle

A triangular grid cleanses and protects a space. Triangulation neutralizes negative energy and electromotive forces (EMFs), and draws in positive vibes. This layout is particularly helpful placed around your bed.

Suitable crystals: Flint, Shungite, Black Tourmaline, Herkimer Diamond

1 Place one crystal midway along a wall or above the head.
2 Place a crystal in each opposite corner or below either side of the feet.
3 Join points with a crystal wand or the power of your mind.

Five-pointed star

The five-pointed star is a useful protection layout or caller-in of cosmic energies and healing. (*See* page 293 for an example grid.)

Suitable crystals: Shungite, Aragonite, Kambaba Jasper

1 Place one crystal at the top point.
2 Follow the line down to the bottom right of the star.
3 Follow the line up to the top left.
4 Follow the line straight across.
5 Follow the line down to the bottom left.
6 Join up the star with a wand, returning to the first crystal to complete the circuit.
7 You can place a keystone in the centre.

Star of David

The Star of David is a traditional protection layout that creates a perfect manifestation space. (*See* page 61 for an example grid.)

Suitable crystals: Bronzite and Black Tourmaline, Black Tourmaline and Selenite, Garnet, Rose Quartz

1 Lay the first triangle and join up the points. (Lay it facing downwards to contain energy and facing up to draw it in.)

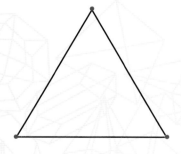

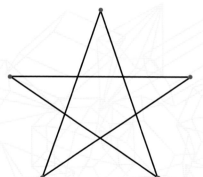

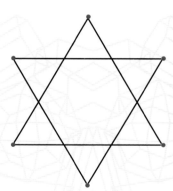

2 Lay a second triangle over the top but facing in the opposite direction.

3 Join up the points.

4 A keystone can be placed in the centre or an anchor stone below the grid.

Zig-zag

The zig-zag heals sick-building syndrome and counteracts environmental pollution. Lay in a zig-zag pattern so that the crystals touch the walls on either side.

Suitable crystals: Smoky Quartz, Black Tourmaline, Shungite or Flint alternated with Selenite or Quartz

1 Place appropriate crystals as shown in the diagram, starting on the left-hand side.

2 Finish on the right-hand side.

3 Both or all sides of a room can be gridded to give even stronger protection.

4 Cleanse regularly.

Spiral

Spirals are abundance creators and re-energizing layouts. A spiral draws energy into the centre or radiates it out as required. (*See* pages 288–91 for example grids.)

Suitable crystals: Citrine, Goldstone, Herkimer Diamond, Smoky Quartz

1 If drawing energy into the centre, start at the outer edge. If radiating energy out, start at the inner point.

2 A keystone can be placed at the centre.

3 Lay crystals in a spiral. (If using crystals with points, position point towards the centre to bring energy in and point outwards to radiate it into the environment.)

Square (or rectangle)

Squares cleanse and protect a space. Lay a crystal at each corner of a room or around a building, your bed or in the environment to neutralize an EMF source or geopathic stress line.

Suitable crystals: Flint, Tourmaline, Shungite and Herkimer Diamond

1 Place one crystal at each point.

2 Join points with a crystal wand or the power of your mind.

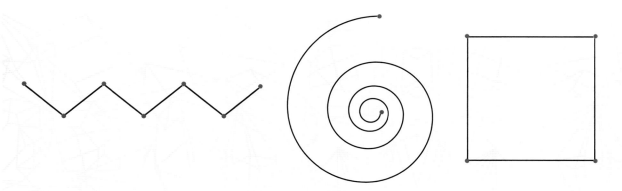

The Flower of Life grid

The Flower of Life is an incredibly versatile grid that represents the eternal cycle of life. It contains within it the Seed of Life, Fruit of Life, Vesica Piscis, Tree of Life, Merkaba and Metatron's Cube, all suitable grids for the crystals in this book (*see* pages 61, 126, 157, 191, 213, 242, 289 and 293 for examples of Flower of Life layouts).

Suitable crystals: All, according to the purpose of the grid – see the crystal portraits on pages 68–307.

ABOVE The Flower of Life

BELOW A chakra-balancing layout laid on a Flower of Life grid.

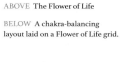

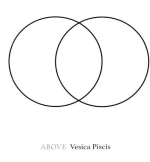

ABOVE Vesica Piscis

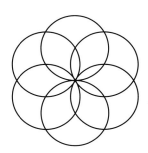

ABOVE The Seed of Life

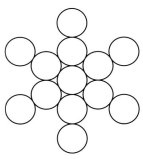

ABOVE The Fruit of Life

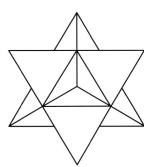

ABOVE Merkaba

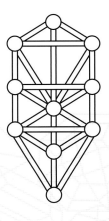

ABOVE The Tree of Life

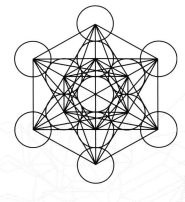

ABOVE Metatron's Cube

Crystal families

In this section you'll find the characteristics and generic
properties of major healing crystal groups. Examples
of their offspring are found throughout the book.

Quartz

Master healer and paterfamilias of the largest crystal family on the planet

Source: Worldwide

Vibration: Earthy to exceptionally high, according to type

Formation process: Present in igneous, metamorphic and sedimentary rocks

Subsets: Agate, Jasper, Chert, Flint, Onyx

Chakra: All

Physiology: Quartz maintains all organs and systems in the body

Cleansing: All

Quartz generates, stores and radiates vibrant energy.

MAIN Generator Quartz pillar
FAR LEFT Orange River Quartz
LEFT Lemurian Tangerine Quartz

Characteristics

Quartz's simple atomic makeup creates a stable and reliable vibrational core. It takes on myriad external shapes, varieties, vibrations and colours, however. The structure varies from a dense, microcrystalline form with a fine-grained uniform texture, visible under magnification, to individual crystals visible to the naked eye. The basic properties remain constant, but are enhanced and expanded by form, colour and vibration. Quartz generates, stores and radiates vibrant energy. Colour is created by incorporation of additional minerals and trace elements, or, as in Aura Quartzes, by electrostatic enhancement with precious metals. Other colour-saturation processes may be utilized, as with Crackle Quartzes. Crackle Quartz undergoes thermal shock to create the fracture-pattern.

Generic properties

Quartz purifies and amplifies energy, working in harmony with each individual using it. It doubles the biomagnetic field around the body and takes energy back to the most perfect state possible. It is a master healer, so you can use it for any condition, although different colours and forms work better for specific tasks, according to their vibration. The crystal stimulates the immune system and returns the body to balance, harmonizing the chakras and aligning the subtle bodies with the physical. Quartz, particularly types with extremely high vibrations, works at a soul and multidimensional level. It holds some of the highest known vibrations and many types act as a spiritual library for cosmic knowledge. A crystal computer, Quartz is ideal for programming for distance healing, communication or manifestation, as its stable energy holds the programme for long periods and radiates the energy appropriately. Excellent for transmuting negative energies and grounding higher energy into the physical world, at a psychic level Quartz dissolves outgrown mental programmes and karmic seeds, 'trace elements' carried over from another lifetime that can be activated by actions or meeting someone from the past at any time during the present life. Opening the third eye and attuning to soul purpose, it filters out distractions, enhancing meditation and visioning.

ABOVE Spirit Quartz
BELOW Clear Quartz cluster

Specific properties

Each type of Quartz has specific properties in addition to the generic:

Smoky Quartz (*see* page 78)
Orange River Quartz (*see* page 80)
Green Ridge Quartz (*see* page 83)
Kundalini Quartz (*see* page 83)
Chrysocolla in Quartz (*see* page 85)
Tanzine Aura Quartz (*see* page 88)
Rose Quartz (*see* page 102)
Tanzurine (Emerald and Cherry Quartz) (*see* page 115)
Lithium Quartz (*see* page 140)
Indicolite and Blue Quartz (*see* page 144)
Anandalite™ (Aurora Quartz) (*see* page 160)
Angel Aura Quartz (*see* page 170)
Ajoite and Ajo Quartz (*see* page 173)
Smoky Amethyst Elestial Quartz (*see* page 177)
Amphibole Quartz (*see* page 178)
Rutilated Quartz (Angel Hair) (*see* page 179)
Faden Quartz (*see* page 179)
Himalayan Quartz (*see* page 181)
Nirvana Quartz (*see* page 182)
Trigonic Quartz (*see* page 185)
Tourmalinated Quartz (*see* page 198)
Tangerine Aura Quartz (*see* page 204)
Snow Quartz (*see* page 208)
Crackle Quartz (*see* page 209)
Ice Quartz (*see* page 233)
Lodalite (Shaman Quartz) (*see* page 234)
Phantom Quartz (*see* page 234)
Celestial Quartz (*see* page 235)
Celtic Golden Healer (*see* page 254)
Celtic Chevron Quartz (*see* page 256)
Ancestral Timeline (*see* page 257)
Cathedral Quartz (*see* page 257)
Elestial Smoky Quartz (*see* page 301)
Chlorite Quartz (*see* page 304)
Candle Quartz (*see* page 306)
Manifestation Quartz (*see* page 307)
Spirit Quartz (*see* page 307)

ABOVE LEFT Lithium Quartz
ABOVE RIGHT Ajoite
CENTRE Chrysocolla in Quartz
'Ajoite Quartz'
BELOW Fire and Ice Quartz

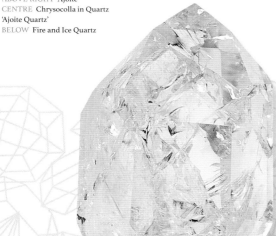

Aura Quartzes: born of alchemy

The alchemists of old sought to turn lead into gold – if you believe the pragmatic version of alchemy. Metaphysically, it is said that the alchemists were seeking to transmute the soul. Whichever version you choose to believe, alchemical crystals are the legacy of those ancient alchemists and they assist with deep transmutation. Goldstone was an offshoot of alchemical experimentation. Copper and ground Quartz were fused together. The resulting effect was pleasing to the eye, and so was continued. Nowadays it attracts prosperity and abundance.

Modern-day alchemists electrostatically bond precious metals onto crystals such as Quartz to heighten the effect of the underlying crystal. These Aura Quartzes have a profound effect on the soul, taking it to a higher frequency. Dyed or coated crystals, which mimic the effect, have no additional properties, however, and may be detrimental rather than beneficial. (Always buy Aura Quartz from a reputable source.) Crystals such as Crackle Quartz are colour-infused. The colour may have an effect on the energy field, but basically the effect relies on the energetic resonances of the underlying Quartz, which can vary widely.

BELOW LEFT Aqua Aura Quartz
BELOW CENTRE Angel Aura Quartz
BELOW RIGHT Tanzine Aura Quartz

Quartz facets and shapes

Quartz points have different facet shapes on the termination, or pointed end, each with their own unique properties, and specific shapes of Quartz have unique properties.

Single points

- **Point:** Quartz points naturally form a hexagonal, six-sided, faceted top, culminating in a point. A point with a faceted termination at one end and a flat base channels energy in the direction in which the termination points.

- **Long point:** A long point acts as a natural wand, channelling energy in a specific direction, or joining the points of a grid.

- **Tabular/Tabby:** A long, flat crystal point allows energy to flow freely in one direction, and links heart and mind.

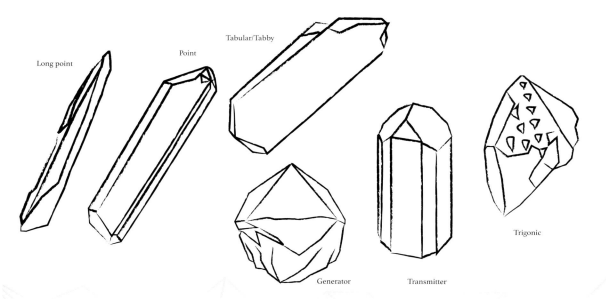

Long point

Point

Tabular/Tabby

Generator

Transmitter

Trigonic

Facets

- **Generator:** Six equal-sided triangular faces meeting at a point generate energy and attract abundance.

- **Transmitter:** Two seven-sided faces with perfect triangular facets between them facilitate absent healing or energy transmission.

- **Trigonic:** Inverted triangles running down a crystal face connect to the soul and to cosmic beings.

Formations

- **Double termination:** Pointed terminations at each end bridge two energy points, breaking outdated patterns.

- **Cluster:** Radiates energy in all directions.

- **Self-healed:** Point that has broken from its base and begun growing again, or has many small structures on one end or internally partway along its length. As the crystal has been wounded and healed again, it is an excellent tool for cellular, spiritual and emotional levels.

- **Phantom:** Smaller, usually triangular, ghost-like crystal within a larger one.

- **Barnacle:** Large crystal covered with smaller crystals on some part. The larger crystal is an 'old soul' that has attracted 'younger souls' for the purpose of learning. Barnacles assist families and those whose work involves service.

- **Bridge/penetrator:** Part of one crystal partially penetrates another, forming a bridge between the physical and spiritual worlds. This bridge facilitates inner-child work.

- **Cross:** One crystal crosses another, usually larger, at right angles. It unites or repels energy.

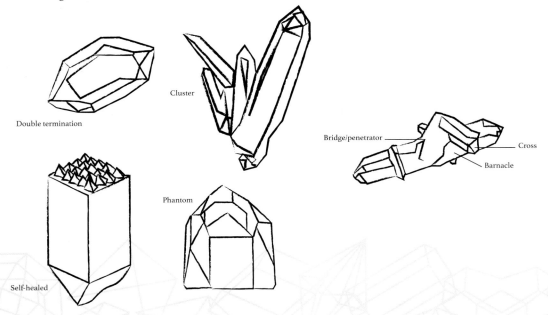

Double termination

Cluster

Self-healed

Phantom

Bridge/penetrator

Cross

Barnacle

- **Elestial:** Numerous terminations and facets folded over an inner structure create an elestial. Often double-terminated, Elestials regulate energy flow within the human body or that of the planet. When smoky, they draw off negative energy.

- **Etched:** Markings engraved into a crystal contact star beings and read ancient languages or encoded information.

- **Mother and child:** Large crystal 'holding' a smaller one assists inner-child work and heals young children. Dolphin formation, where one crystal carries another smaller one on its back, is similar.

- **Mentor:** Large crystal surrounded by upright small ones is a teacher.

- **Manifestation:** Small crystal fully enclosed within a larger one attracts abundance.

- **Twinflame/soulmate:** Two equal crystals side by side from the same base attract a soulmate or twinflame.

- **Timelink:** Backward-pointing rectangle below a crystal facet assists looking back into the past. A forward-pointing rectangle goes to the future.

- **Sceptre:** Rod with a thicker crystal around one end is a conveyer of power.

- **Record keeper:** Etched or raised triangles contain the record of the soul's journey and the universe's past.

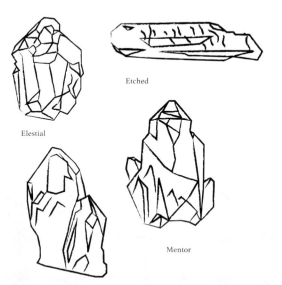

Etched

Elestial

Mentor

Mother and child

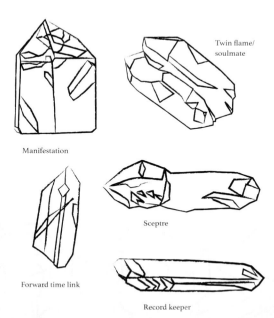

Twin flame/ soulmate

Manifestation

Sceptre

Forward time link

Record keeper

Agate
Stabilizing

Source: Worldwide

Vibration: Earthy to high, according to type

Formation process: Metamorphic

Chakra: Earth star, base, sacral, plus others according to type

Physiology: Digestive organs, blood vessels, eyes, uterus, skin, lymphatic system, pancreas

Cleansing: All

Perfect for grounding energy.

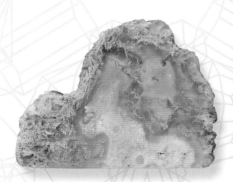

MAIN Crazy Lace Agate
FAR LEFT Dendritic Agate
CENTRE Ziaimara Agate
BELOW Raw Moss Agate

Characteristics

There is enormous variety in the colour and appearance of the Agate family, and its applications. Garishly coloured Agate slices are usually dyed, adding no supplementary properties. But beautiful, naturally subtle-coloured examples exist, such as those from the Arizona and Gobi Deserts, or beautiful Blue Lace Agate from South Africa. There are some vibrant, strikingly coloured examples, such as flame-bright Condor Agate from a remote location in Argentina and others that are, at first glance, dull and yet exhibit subtle colouring that becomes more fascinating the longer you look into it. The distinctive bands of colour were formed as the chemistry of the fluids moving through the host rock changed according to the temperature and rate of crystallization.

Generic properties

Agate is perfect for grounding energy. It acts slowly but surely. This centring stone provides an unshakeable sense of safety and security. Soothing and calming, it brings balance at the physical, emotional and intellectual levels, harmonizing yin and yang, positive and negative. Meditating with Agate brings hidden information to the surface, including the subtle causes of dis-ease. Agate has a powerful cleansing effect, physically and emotionally. Gently dissolving anger and resentment, it heals emotional trauma that underlies an inability to accept love. The stone encourages starting again. Agate purifies and stabilizes the aura. Supporting all matters of the heart, it rebuilds self-confidence and assists self-acceptance. Mentally, it facilitates analysis, concentration and perception. Whatever form it takes, Agate supports truth and integrity. This beautiful stone assimilates life's experiences and seeks the gift in them, no matter how traumatic. Its layers take you into a deeper connection with the oneness of life.

Specific properties

Each type of Agate has specific properties in addition to the generic:

Botswana Agate (*see* page 76)
Blue Lace Agate (*see* page 87)
Plume Agate (*see* page 138)
White Agate (*see* page 151)
Shiva Agate Eye (*see* page 201)
Crazy Lace Agate (*see* page 201)
Pink Agate (*see* page 203)
Wind Fossil Agate (*see* page 226)
Snakeskin Agate (*see* page 248)
Montana Agate (*see* page 253)
Turritella Agate (*see* page 270)
Banded Agate (*see* page 271)
Fire Agate (*see* page 277)
Sage Amethyst Agate (*see* page 283)
Tree (Dendritic) Agate (*see* page 298)
Gobi Desert Agate (*see* page 300)

ABOVE Fire Agate
RIGHT Moss Agate
CENTRE Botswana Agate
FAR RIGHT Blue Lace Agate

Jasper

Supreme nurturer

Source: Worldwide

Vibration: Earthy to high, according to type

Formation process: Metamorphic

Chakra: All according to type

Physiology: Circulatory, digestive and sexual organs

Cleansing: All

Stable and protective, Jasper grounds all areas of life.

MAIN Heart-shaped Mookaite Jasper
LEFT Kambaba Jasper
OPPOSITE LEFT Ocean Jasper
OPPOSITE CENTRE Red Jasper
OPPOSITE RIGHT Porcelain Jasper

Characteristics

Jasper is extremely stable and protective, grounding all areas of life. A reliable support during prolonged illness or traumatic events, it prevents burn-out. Jasper facilitates ending situations that are no longer for your highest good with gentleness and grace, and protects your energies during tie-cutting. Each variety of Jasper is unique, and new varieties are discovered and named almost every day. The stone is found in virtually every colour in the spectrum and many combinations. It may be striped, speckled or multicoloured and differs from Agate in that Agate is translucent whereas Jasper is granular and opaque. Jasper is quicker-acting and more immediately transformative in effect. It aligns the chakras and the various colours create chakra-balancing layouts. Each colour is appropriate to a specific chakra, and the brown and deep-red varieties make excellent grounding stones as they are strongly connected to Mother Earth.

Generic properties

Jasper sustains and supports during periods of stress and unifies all aspects of life. This nurturing stone facilitates shamanic journeys, dowsing and dream recall, providing protection. Jasper absorbs negative energy, balances yin and yang, and aligns the physical, emotional and mental bodies with the etheric realm. It protects against electromotive force (EMF) or geopathic stress (created by earth disturbance) and environmental pollution. Bringing the courage to face problems assertively, and encouraging honesty with yourself, Jasper imparts determination to all pursuits and support during necessary conflict. It assists quick thinking, promotes organizational abilities and seeing projects through. It stimulates the imagination, transforming ideas into action.

Specific properties

Each type of Jasper has specific properties in addition to the generic:

Poppy Jasper (*see* page 78)
Yellow Jasper (*see* page 81)
Mookaite Jasper (*see* page 81)
Bumble Bee Jasper (*see* page 82)
Porcelain Jasper (Exotic Jasper) (*see* page 140)
Spiderweb Jasper (*see* page 196)
Dragon's Blood Jasper (*see* page 200)
Ocean Jasper (*see* page 224)
Picture Jasper (*see* page 224)
Kambaba Jasper (*see* page 255)
Polychrome Jasper (*see* page 269)
Rainforest Jasper (*see* page 304)
Kiwi Jasper (Sesame Jasper) (*see* page 305)

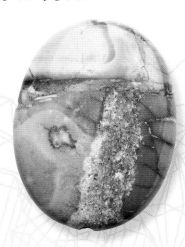

Calcite

Purifying

Source: Worldwide

Vibration: Earthy to extremely high

Formation process: Sedimentary

Chakra: All, according to type

Physiology: Skeleton, teeth, skin, kidneys, pancreas, spleen, blood

Cleansing: All

Calcite speeds up development and growth.

MAIN Blue Calcite
LEFT White Calcite

Characteristics

Although working slowly and gently, Calcite speeds up development and growth. This serene stone varies in form from the earthy solidity of marble to the highly refined vibrations of Merkabite or Stellar Beam Calcite, with their inter- and multidimensional connections. Calcite is available in virtually every colour, and purifies and harmonizes the chakras accordingly. It ensures safety when journeying into expanded consciousness and the inner self. Calcites such as Optical Calcite focus in on the smallest matter or expand your view as widely as possible. No matter the vibration, the energetic effect is powerful and supremely cleansing and centring. Calcite is an energy purifier and amplifier, great for distance healing.

Generic qualities

Calcite removes stagnant energies, revitalizing the body and the environment. It encourages calcium uptake in bones, but dissolves calcifications, strengthening the skeleton and joints. The crystal promotes inner peace and spiritual connection. It supports learning at every level, clarifying the mind and facilitating soul intention. This crystal promotes emotional intelligence, opening the heart to restore hope and inner serenity. It increases trust in yourself and others.

Specific properties

Each type of Calcite has specific properties in addition to the generic:

White Calcite (*see* page 91)
Cobalto-calcite (Roselite) (*see* page 109)
Mangano Calcite (*see* page 110)
Green Calcite (*see* page 142)
Blue Calcite (*see* page 148)

RIGHT Yellow Calcite
FAR RIGHT Moldavite Calcite

Garnet

Revitalizer

Source: Worldwide

Vibration: Earthy to high, according to type

Formation process: Metamorphic

Chakra: Base, sacral, heart

Physiology: Blood, liver, heart, lungs, spleen, metabolic system, pituitary gland, DNA

Cleansing: All

Garnet is an energizing crystal of regeneration and rejuvenation.

Characteristics

The major types of Garnet are Almandine, Pyrope, Spessartite, Grossular, Andradite and Uvarovite, but there are countless minor, yet still powerful Garnets such as Rhodolite. Available in a wide spectrum of colours, members of the Garnet family have similar properties and internal structure, but vary in chemical composition, hence the colour range. Garnet is an energizing crystal of regeneration and rejuvenation. It boosts the energy of an entire system and stabilizes it. Garnet has a long history of inspiring love, devotion and commitment. Ameliorating extremes, it balances the sex drive and alleviates emotional disharmony. Useful in a crisis, this stone instils courage into seemingly hopeless situations, especially when life has fragmented or is traumatic. The crystal also fosters mutual assistance.

Generic properties

Garnet sharpens perceptions, dissolves ingrained, outdated behaviour patterns and bestows self-confidence. As a guardian stone, it links with the angelic realm and creates a protective talisman steeped in magical power. Laid on the past-life chakras, it stimulates expanded awareness and past-life recall. Garnet has anti-inflammatory powers, restoring vitality to the blood. It was traditionally an antidote to poisons and calmed fevers. In industrial applications, Garnets are prized for their abrasive, cutting and filtration properties. The same properties emerge in healing, as they clear away all that is not energetically healthy and restore the system to balance. ●

Specific properties

Each type of Garnet has specific properties in addition to the generic:

Hessonite Garnet (*see* page 106)
Rhodolite and Raspberry Garnet (*see* page 106)

MAIN Grossular Garnet
BELOW LEFT Red Garnet
BELOW CENTRE Orange Garnet
BELOW RIGHT Uvarovite Garnet

Opal
Iridescent fire

Source: Australia, Mexico, USA, South America, UK, Canada, Brazil, Czech Republic, Slovakia, Ethiopia

Vibration: High

Formation process: Infill in sedimentary or igneous rocks

Chakra: All, according to type

Physiology: Female reproductive system, pancreas, blood, kidneys and adrenals, eyes, fluid balance, abdomen, lower back, intestines, liver

Cleansing: Avoid water or earth

Attracts love and passion, desire and eroticism.

MAIN Blue Opal
ABOVE Black Opal

Characteristics

Protective Opal reaches out to cosmic consciousness and induces metaphysical and mystical visions. Its non-crystalline structure is created from tiny spheres of silica gel. Energy passes rapidly through an amorphous crystal – there's nothing to slow down its passage as there are no internal lattice walls, as there is with an internal crystalline structure. Opals are strong-acting and virtually instant in their effect. There are two types: the 'precious' form, which shows scintillating iridescent flashes of colour, and the opaque 'common' Opal that displays little or no iridescence. The latter are more robust and less likely to fracture. Seductive Opal has always been associated with love and passion, desire and eroticism. It encourages positive emotions and exploring your deepest feelings, but you need to be centred before using Opal. Have other stones standing by to assist with release and integration of transformed emotions, if necessary.

Generic properties

A karmic stone, Opal teaches that what you put out comes back. It amplifies deeply ingrained traits, whether those traits are deemed 'good' or 'bad', and draws characteristics to the surface for transformation and to discover the gifts hidden within. Absorbent and reflective, Opal picks up thoughts and feelings, amplifies them and returns them to the source for examination. Exploring karmic dis-ease, this stone shows what your emotional state has been previously, especially in other lives, and teaches how to take responsibility for how you feel now. Opal heals Earth's energy field, repairing depletions and re-energizing and stabilizing the meridian grid, a system of subtle-energy channels that run close to the surface of the globe.

Specific properties

Each type of Opal has specific properties in addition to the generic:

Boulder Opal (*see* page 105)
Pink Opal (*see* page 112)
Mount Shasta Opal (*see* page 174)
Yowah Nut (*see* page 200)

BELOW Pink Opal
CENTRE LEFT & RIGHT Ethiopian Opal
FAR RIGHT Owyhee Opal

Tourmaline

Psychic shield

Source: Brazil, USA, Sri Lanka, Tanzania, Nigeria, Kenya, Madagascar, Mozambique, Namibia, Afghanistan, Pakistan, Sri Lanka, Malawi

Vibration: Earthy to extremely high

Formation process: Igneous and metamorphic

Chakra: All, according to type

Physiology: Spine, throat, brain hemispheres, detoxification

Cleansing: All

Tourmaline forms a protective shield around the body.

Characteristics

Highly energetic, Tourmaline is piezoelectric and pyroelectric, creating electricity under heat and pressure. It emits far-infrared rays and negative ions. The far-infrared spectrum boosts the immune system and promotes detoxification. Ions profoundly affect mood and wellbeing. Positive ions impair brain function and suppress the immune system, causing symptoms such as anxiety, breathing difficulties, chronic fatigue, headaches, irritability, lack of energy and more. Negative ions tranquillize, stimulate and detoxify the body and psyche, as appropriate. They promote oxygenation in the brain and regeneration of blood. Tourmaline grounds spiritual energy, clears and balances the chakras, forming a protective shield around the body. The striations along the side of Tourmaline enhance energy flow, making it excellent for healing, energy enhancement and removal of blockages. Each of the colours has its own specific healing ability. This is a deeply grounding stone.

Generic properties

Tourmaline cleanses, purifies and transforms toxic energy into a lighter vibration. It is ideal for counteracting EMF emanations and for protecting against ill-wishing. The stone rebalances the energy meridians, cleansing and realigning the chakras and subtle-energy bodies. Tourmaline facilitates understanding yourself and others. It takes you deep into your Self, promoting self-confidence, diminishing fear and banishing victim mentality. The stone promotes inspiration, compassion, tolerance and prosperity. Tourmaline is a potent mental healer, balancing right–left hemispheres of the brain and transmuting negative thought patterns into positive ones. It overcomes dyslexia as it improves hand-to-eye coordination, and the assimilation and translation of coded information. ❶

Specific properties

Each type of Tourmaline has specific properties in addition to the generic:

Rubellite (Pink/Red Tourmaline) (*see* page 80)
Watermelon Tourmaline (*see* page 115)
Green Tourmaline (Verdelite) (*see* page 205)
Paraiba Tourmaline (*see* page 232)
Black Tourmaline (*see* page 272)

MAIN Blue and Black Tourmaline
OPPOSITE Dark Green Tourmaline
FAR LEFT Rubellite Tourmaline
CENTRE Paraiba Tourmaline
RIGHT Black Tourmaline

Crystals for the body

Crystals in this section have been specially chosen for their healing effect on the physical and subtle-energy bodies. As we have noted, illness is a dis-ease, the final manifestation of spiritual, environmental, psychological, karmic, emotional or mental imbalance or distress. Healing through the chakras is an important part of crystal healing, as each chakra is traditionally linked to organs and physiological processes within the body. Crystal layouts over a chakra or along the whole system return the body to balance. However, crystals can be laid over an organ or gridded around the body to support wellbeing (*see* pages 32–3).

Common causes of dis-ease

Crystals are an holistic healing system that treats causes rather than relieving symptoms. Dis-ease is a state of imbalance. It eventually results in physical or psychosomatic ailments. Psychosomatic does not mean imaginary. Internal conflict or stress, toxic emotions and destructive thought patterns directly affect the body's ability to function optimally. Except in cases of direct physical injury, dis-ease establishes itself at an energetic level first. It is located in chakras and subtle-energy bodies (see pages 18–25). If not restored to equilibrium, dis-ease moves into the physical body to create deeper maladies.

Intervention with crystals restores energetic balance before dis-ease establishes a permanent hold. Even in cases of physical injury, crystals such as Magnetite and Bloodstone have a long history of assisting in the relief of inflammation, bruising, broken bones and muscular aches and pains. The minerals in crystals are still part of medicine today. Lithium-rich crystals such as Kunzite form the base of anti-anxiety medication, and Klinopotilolith creates a powerful chemotherapy drug.

Common causes of physical dis-ease

- Malfunctioning immune system
- Viral, bacterial, environmental or chemical pathogens, including the side effects of previous medication or treatment
- Physical injury
- Stress and tension or inadequate rest
- Toxic emotions or negative thoughts
- Emotional exhaustion and energy drain
- Shock or trauma
- Anxiety or fear
- EMF pollution and geopathic stress, sick building syndrome and the like (see page 260)
- Karmic or transgenerational transfer (see pages 212–15 and 238–9) and Ancestral Healing (see page 242)
- Soulplan, which maps out the soul's intention for the present lifetime (see page 154)

Exercise
Supporting the immune system

Keeping the immune system energetically supported ensures wellbeing. If the immune system is running too slowly, invigorating healing crystals, such as Bloodstone or Cherry Quartz taped over the higher heart chakra (mid upper chest) or gently tapped either side of the breastbone stimulates it. If it is running too fast, soothing crystals such as Que Sera, Emerald Quartz or Quantum Quattro calm it.

1 Lie down and place the immune crystal in the centre of the upper chest midway along the breastbone.
2 Relax and breathe gently.
3 Leave in place for 15–20 minutes before removing.
4 Cleanse crystal after use.

Exercise
All-purpose revitalizer layout

Suitable crystals: Red Jasper, Hematite Quartz, Flint keystone. *See also* the crystal portraits on pages 68–307.

1 Lie down and place a crystal either side of the base of your armpits.
2 Place a crystal on your pubic bone.
3 Join up the triangle with the power of your mind.
4 Lay two crystals either side of your waist.
5 Lay a crystal in the centre of your breastbone.
6 Join up the second triangle with the power of your mind.
7 Place a keystone on the navel.
8 Keep in place for 15–20 minutes.
9 Remove stones in the reverse order – that is, keystone first.
10 Cleanse crystals after use.

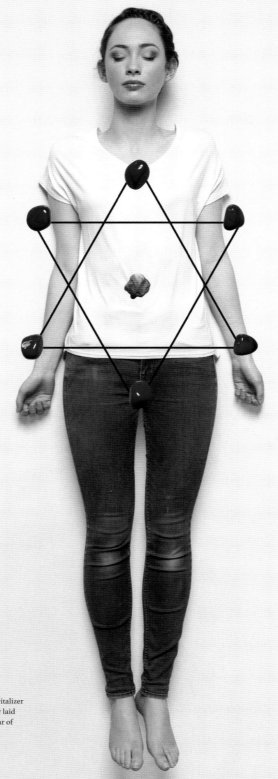

RIGHT The all-purpose revitalizer layout consists of Red Jasper laid around Orange Flint in a Star of David arrangement.

Chakras, physiology and dis-ease

Laying crystals on the chakras or auric field corrects imbalances and systems of the body. The chakras and how well they are operating play a vital role in regulating dis-ease (*see* pages 18–25). Chakras may be over-active and need calming, or under-active and blocked, in which case they need stimulating, which is why traditional chakra colour correspondences may not be appropriate. Many crystals relate to specific chakras but are not the 'traditional' colour, because this colour system was only formulated just over 100 years ago, whereas the chakra-related crystals have been in use for issues connected to those chakras for hundreds, if not thousands, of years. A crystal from the other side of the colour wheel may be more suitable.

Chakras and physiology

Gaia gateway
Physiology: Subtle-energy bodies, linking into Earth's subtle bodies and meridian system.
Typical dis-eases: Supra-physical. Inability to ground kundalini and higher frequencies leads to subtle dis-ease.

Earth star
Physiology: Physical body, electrical and meridian systems, sciatic nerve, sensory organs.
Typical dis-eases: Lethargic or invasive. Myalgic encephalomyelitis (ME), arthritis, cancer, muscular disorders, depression, psychiatric disturbances, auto-immune diseases, persistent tiredness.

Knees
Physiology: Brain, kidneys, lumbar spine, heart, bladder and kidney meridians, sciatic nerve.
Typical dis-eases: Disabling. Knee problems, arthritis, cartilage and joint problems, bladder infections, cold feet, Reynaud's disease, Osgood-Schlatter disease, bursitis, osteoarthritis, poor leg circulation, sacroiliac pain, eating disorders, malabsorption of nutrients, kidney diseases.

ABOVE The colour wheel. Colours opposite to the 'traditional' chakra colours may be more appropriate for chakra healing.

Base

Physiology: 'Fight or flight' response, adrenals, bladder, elimination and immune systems, gonads, kidneys, lower back, lower extremities, sciatic nerve, lymph system, prostate gland, rectum, teeth and bones, veins.

Typical dis-eases: Constant, low-level or flare-up. Adrenal response is permanently activated. Stiffness or tingling in joints, poor circulation in lower limbs, sciatica, chronic lower back pain, renal, reproductive or rectal disorders, fluid retention, constipation or diarrhoea, prostate problems, haemorrhoids, varicose veins or hernias, bi-polar disorder, addictions, glandular disturbances, personality and anxiety disorders, skeletal/bone/teeth problems, auto-immune diseases, insomnia and disturbed sleep, waking unrefreshed.

 Sacral

Physiology: Bladder and gall bladder, immune and elimination systems, kidneys, large and small intestine, lumbar and pelvic region, sacrum, spleen, ovaries, testes, uterus.

Typical dis-eases: Pernicious and psychosomatic. Premenstrual syndrome (PMS), muscle cramps, sciatica, reproductive blockages or diseases, prostate problems, impotence, infertility, fibroids, endometriosis, allergies, addictions, eating disorders, diabetes, liver or intestinal dysfunction, irritable bowel syndrome, chronic back pain, urinary infections.

 Dantien

Physiology: Autonomic nervous and energy-conduction systems, regulation of internal organs and involuntary processes such as breathing and heartbeat. Sensory impulses to the brain.

Typical dis-eases: Physical dysfunction. Nervous system disturbance, auto-immune diseases, cardiac problems, high blood pressure, orthostatic hypotension, palpitations, adrenal overload, chronic fatigue, ME, Reynaud's disease, Parkinson's disease, digestive problems, diabetes, lightheadedness, powerlessness, ill at ease in incarnation.

 Navel

Physiology: DNA, ribonucleic acid (RNA) and 'junk DNA' (DNA that does not seem to serve any useful purpose – *see* page 238), epigenetics, blood and lymphatic system, uterus and reproductive area, autonomic nervous system, filtration systems.

Typical dis-eases: Inherited through the matriarchal line. Difficulty in giving birth. Deeply ingrained fears trigger auto-immune diseases and endocrine malfunctions. If the mother's womb was noxious, breathing difficulties result.

Palms

Physiology: Nerves, tendons, ganglions, skin, hands, fingers, nails.

Typical dis-eases: Incapacitating. Arthritis, brittle nails, carpal tunnel, Dupuytren's contracture, eczema, plantar fasciitis, psoriasis, rashes, allergies, shin splints, gut-disturbances, repetitive strain injury.

Solar plexus

Physiology: Adrenals, digestive system, liver, lymphatic system, metabolism, muscles, pancreas, skin, small intestine, stomach, eyesight.

Typical dis-eases: Emotional and demanding. Stomach ulcers, ME, adrenaline imbalances, SAD, insomnia and chronic anxiety, digestive problems, malabsorption of nutrients, gallstones, pancreatic failure, liver problems, eczema and skin conditions, eating disorders, phobias, multiple sclerosis.

Spleen

Physiology: Spleen, pancreas, lymphatic system and liver.

Typical dis-eases: Depletion and lack. Lethargy, anaemia, low blood sugar, diabetes, pancreatitis, liver problems, auto-immune diseases.

Heart seed

Physiology: Integrated physical and subtle-energy systems.

Typical dis-eases: Depletion and disillusionment at a spiritual level.

Heart

Physiology: Chest, circulation, heart, lungs, shoulders, thymus, respiratory system.

Typical dis-eases: Psychosomatic and reactive. Heart attacks, angina, chest infections, asthma, frozen shoulder, ulcers, persistent cough, wheeziness, pneumonia, high cholesterol, mastitis, breast cysts, pancreatic problems.

Higher heart (thymus)

Physiology: Psychic and physical immune systems, thymus gland, lymphatic system, elimination and purification organs.

Typical dis-eases: Disordered immune system. Auto-immune diseases, repeated viral and bacterial infections, coughs, colds, glandular fever, ME, multiple sclerosis (MS), HIV/Aids, arteriosclerosis, flushing of chest and neck, tinnitus, epilepsy, vitiligo, psoriasis, alopecia, thyroid problems.

Throat

Physiology: Ears, nose, respiratory and nervous system, sinuses, skin, throat, thyroid, parathyroid, tongue, tonsils, speech and body language, metabolism.

Typical dis-eases: Block communication. Sore throat/quinsy, lump in throat, difficulty in swallowing, inflammation of trachea, sinus, constant colds and viral infections, tinnitus, ear infections, jaw pain, gum disease, tooth problems, thyroid imbalances, high blood pressure, attention deficit hyperactivity disorder (ADHD), autism, speech impediment, irritable bowel, psychosomatic and metabolic dis-eases.

Third eye (brow)

Physiology: Brain, ears, eyes, neurological and endocrine systems, pineal and pituitary glands, hypothalamus, production of serotonin and melatonin, temperature control, scalp, sinuses.

Typical dis-eases: Metaphysical. Migraine, mental overwhelm, schizophrenia, cataracts, iritis, epilepsy, autism, spinal and neurological disorders, sinus and ear infections, high blood pressure, learning disabilities, memory loss, eye problems. Nervous or hormonal disorders, hot or cold flushes, excessive perspiration, skin conditions such as psoriasis, eczema, impetigo, hives; allergies, sinus problems, adenoid and ear disorders, lack of energy and/or sex drive.

Soma

Physiology: Whole body including etheric bodies, subtle-energy systems and meridians, pineal and pituitary glands.

Typical dis-eases: Autistic, disconnected. Dyspraxia, autism, ADHD, chronic fatigue, delusional states, sinus or eye problems, migraine headaches, stress headaches, digestive difficulties.

Past life

Physiology: Karmic blueprint and etheric bodies. Wounds, attitudes and dysfunction in subtle bodies imprint onto the physical at a psychosomatic or genetic level. Psychological dis-eases impact on mind and body.

Typical dis-eases: Chronic. Immune or endocrine deficiencies, genetic or physical malfunctions, heart, liver or kidney problems, auto-immune diseases.

⬡ Crown

Physiology: Brain, central nervous system, hair, hypothalamus, pituitary gland, spine, subtle-energy bodies, cerebellum, nervous and motor control, posture and balance.

Typical dis-eases: Disconnection and isolation. Metabolic syndrome, hypertension, vague 'unwellness', lethargy, nervous system disturbances, electromagnetic and environmental sensitivity, depression, dementia, ME, Parkinson's disease, insomnia or excessive sleepiness, 'biological clock' disturbances, SAD, impaired coordination, headaches, migraine, anxiety, insomnia, depression, multiple personality disorder, mental breakdown.

⬡ Alta major

Physiology: Subtle and physical endocrine systems, hippocampus, hypothalamus, pineal and pituitary glands, brain function, cerebellum, voluntary muscle movements, medulla oblongata, breathing, heart rate and blood pressure, hormonal balance, occipital area and optic nerves, throat, spine, sleeping patterns.

Typical dis-eases: Inherited and karmic. Disorientation, metabolic dysfunction, eye problems, floaters, cataracts, migraine, headaches, memory loss, Alzheimer's or dementia, confusion, physical depression, dizziness or disconnection, loss of purpose, spiritual depression, fear, terror, adrenaline rush.

OPPOSITE Dumorterite
RIGHT Kyanite

⬡ Soul star

Physiology: Subtle bodies and the psyche.
Typical dis-eases: Psychological and psychiatric. Schizophrenia, paranoia, bi-polar disorder.

⬡ Stellar gateway

Physiology: Beyond physical.
Typical dis-eases: Spiritual and soul disconnection.

⬡ Causal vortex

Physiology: Etheric and karmic blueprint, inherited and karmic diseases, DNA and RNA.
Typical dis-eases: Ancestral and karmic.

Bloodstone (Heliotrope)

Immune stimulator

Source: Australia, Brazil, China, Czech Republic, Russia, India, Africa

Vibration: Earthy

Chakra: Higher heart. Aligns all

Physiology: Immune system, blood, blood-rich organs, liver, intestines, kidneys, spleen and bladder

Cleansing: All

Bloodstone is the traditional remedy for any kind of physical ailment.

Characteristics

Bloodstone is an excellent grounding shield, offering protection against pathogens as well as deflecting bullying or threatening situations. It imparts courage and teaches how to avoid dangerous situations through strategic withdrawal. Bloodstone encourages unselfishness and idealism, recognizing that chaos precedes transformation. It facilitates mindfulness and acting in the present moment. Calming the mind, it dispels confusion and clarifies the decision-making process. It revitalizes the mind as well as reversing the effect on the body of mental exhaustion. Facilitating adjustment to unaccustomed circumstances, it supports during chronic illness and brings spirituality into everyday life.

Generic properties

Bloodstone is the go-to stone of choice for physical ailments, especially when placed over the higher heart (thymus) chakra. An excellent blood cleanser, it regulates blood-flow and assists circulation. Use at onset of acute infections. Bloodstone stimulates the flow of lymph and metabolic processes, revitalizes and re-energizes the body and detoxifies liver, intestines, kidneys, spleen and bladder. It reduces irritability, aggressiveness and impatience.

Chinese Bloodstone

Greyish Chinese Bloodstone is transparent rather than deeply opaque. The vividness of its red inclusions makes it excellent for imparting energy and enhancing blood.

Seftonite (Vulcan Jasper)

Seftonite is an African Bloodstone with a softer colour than the dark-green variety. Although generic properties are much the same, it is calming rather than energizing for the immune system. Seftonite facilitates gaining admittance to the realm of the ancestors and is beneficial in ancestral healing. It grounds spirituality into everyday life, opening you to inner guidance, assisting clairvoyance and dreaming.

MAIN Bloodstone
BELOW LEFT Chinese Bloodstone
BELOW RIGHT Seftonite

Golden Healer

Pure golden light

Source: Worldwide, according to type

Vibration: High to exceedingly high

Chakra: Base, sacral, solar plexus, heart and higher chakras. Aligns all

Physiology: Autonomic processes, adrenals, lungs, sinuses, heart and muscular systems

Cleansing: All (except Rainbow Mayanite, Green Ridge or Arkansas as a cluster)

A potent healing crystal on all levels of being.

Characteristics

Golden Healer Quartz raises your vibrations to an exceedingly high level. A catalyst for profound spiritual activation, higher-vibration crystals such as Golden Healer resonate with the journey of the soul and the process of enlightenment. Crystals with ever higher frequencies are becoming available. This potent crystal contains a high ratio of Qi and bioscalar healing waves that create multidimensional healing. It penetrates between cells of the physical body to reprogramme DNA and switch on beneficial potential. The crystal purifies and re-energizes the chakras, rapidly releasing pernicious mental or emotional conditioning. It ameliorates depression, dissolves negative emotions and promotes compassion and empathy. Holding it calms anger and irritation, releasing the underlying cause, bringing things back into conscious control. Golden Healer overcomes malignant and toxic conditions. A powerful absorber of noxious energies from EMF smog and geopathic stress, it guards against psychic vampirism of heart energy.

Arkansas Golden Healer

Arkansas Golden Healer is incredibly active; iron oxide in the stone amps up the power exponentially and creates a multidimensional energy grid around the planet. Accessing interstellar healing power and bringing to Earth Christ Consciousness, a state in which all life forms of the universe are linked in universal love and awareness, it potentizes healing on all levels. The crystal prepares the lightbody for an influx of cosmic energy that expands awareness, so that your whole being helps the planet to ascend. It purifies, aligns and re-energizes chakras and rapidly releases ancient emotional conditioning from the solar plexus. The crystal harnesses the personal will held in that chakra with divine will in chakras above the crown, so that the Higher Self becomes the guiding light rather than ego. This stone facilitates making profound changes in life with minimum effort.

MAIN Golden Healer Phantom Pillar
BELOW LEFT Arkansas Golden Healer
BELOW CENTRE Phantom Golden Healer point
BELOW RIGHT Golden Healer tumble stone

Rainbow Mayanite

An exceptionally high-vibration light-bringer. *See* page 168.

Green Ridge Quartz

Green Ridge Quartz is a Golden Healer with intensely high vibrations. The more we align our own vibrations, expand awareness and interact with higher dimensions, the more information encoded within such crystals manifests. A Green Ridge Light-Golden plate, a flat plate with individual crystals encrusted on it, acts as a life-support system while healing work is undertaken. It takes over running physiological and autonomics systems for the physical body. This enables delicate healing to be undertaken that anchors into the physical body. Orange Green Ridge is highly energizing and creative, giving the sacral chakra an effective cleanse from previous relationship hooks and leaving it ready to start anew. It activates the soul star chakra, linking it into the chakric system at both higher and lower vibrational levels. *See* page 83.

Celtic (Welsh) Golden Healer

An exceptionally high vibration ancestral and karmic healer. *See* page 254.

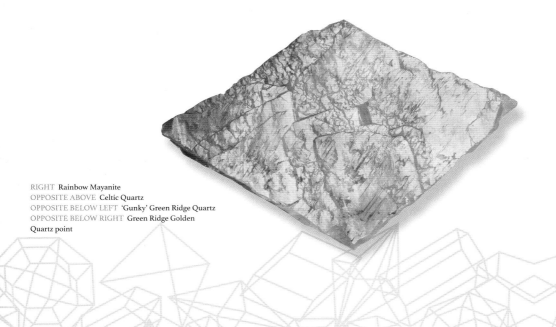

RIGHT Rainbow Mayanite
OPPOSITE ABOVE Celtic Quartz
OPPOSITE BELOW LEFT 'Gunky' Green Ridge Quartz
OPPOSITE BELOW RIGHT Green Ridge Golden
Quartz point

Golden Healer purifies and re-energizes the chakras.

Klinoptilolith

Detoxifier

Klinoptilolith is a powerful detoxifier, absorbing negative energy. It counteracts electromagnetic and heavy-metal pollutants, radioactivity and suchlike that disrupt cell function. This calming stone rebalances the body and enhances the immune system, facilitating production of T-cells. The stone removes energetic toxin-releasing implants, tracking devices, entities, hooks and negative constructs so that the body energetically regenerates itself to a more appropriate level of functioning, restoring the core energy field. Klinoptilolith supports assimilation of essential minerals required for optimum physiological functioning. ❶

Menalite

Feminine wisdom

Menalite reconnects the natural cycle of birth, death and rebirth, and facilitates passages through womanhood. Menalite comes to terms with death, removing fear. It assists men to relate to their feminine side and restores potency. This shamanic stone enhances divination and connects to power animals. It takes you journeying to other realms and into the womb of Mother Earth to remember your soul. Physically, Menalite maintains hormonal balance during puberty, menopause or childbirth. Keep a Menalite under your pillow during menopause and hold one during hot flushes or night sweats. Place one under the mattress to conceive.

Source: Turkey, New Zealand, Australia, Russia, Mexico, USA

Vibration: Earthy

Chakra: Cleanses and aligns all

Physiology: Connective tissue, cells and cell function, liver, kidneys

Cleansing: Avoid water

Source: Morocco, USA, Africa, Australia

Vibration: Earthy

Chakra: Base, sacral, earth star, Gaia gateway

Physiology: Female and male reproductive organs, breasts, hormonal system, skeletal system

Cleansing: All

Magnesite

Flexibility

A powerful antispasmodic, Magnesite induces deep relaxation. It releases the psoas muscle, source of much bodily tension. Opening the heart chakra, it stimulates heart-felt love for everyone, including yourself. Magnesite surfaces any form of self-deceit. It takes you into the past to recognize unconscious thoughts, feelings and multiple agendas that affect wellbeing. Brain-like Magnesite has a powerful effect on the mind, harmonizing hemispheres and stimulating ideas. It deals with emotional stress and overcomes irritability and intolerance. This stone supports nervous people. With high levels of magnesium, it detoxifies the body and lessens fevers and chills.

Magnetite

Lodestone

Magnetite has a strong polarity that makes it ideal for working with the body's own biomagnetic field. It energizes or sedates meridians and organs. Magnetite provides the energy necessary for recovery for bones and tendons. Grounding, Magnetite sustains life force and vitality in the physical body, connecting it to the planet. Antispasmodic, it relieves aches and pains. The stone attracts love, commitment and loyalty. It alleviates negative emotions, such as fear or anger, and instils tenacity. Use Magnetite to remove yourself from detrimental situations and point the way forward. This stone balances intellect with emotion, bringing inner stability. ⓘ

Source: Austria, Italy, Poland, South Africa, USA, Brazil

Vibration: Earthy

Chakra: Heart, third eye, crown, earth star

Physiology: Muscles, bones, teeth, intestines, gall bladder, kidneys

Cleansing: All

Source: USA, Canada, India, Mexico, Romania, Italy, Finland, Austria

Vibration: Earthy

Chakra: Earth star. Aligns all

Physiology: Lungs, muscles, blood and circulatory system, skin, hair

Cleansing: Avoid water

Pakulite™

Expansiveness

An extremely stable stone, born at the foot of a volcano, Pakulite™ has an intimate connection with Gaia and the fiery vibrations of inner earth. Anchoring those whose impetuous nature only has a toehold in incarnation and are always ahead of themselves, it facilitates living in harmony with Earth and attuning to its natural rhythms. Pakulite combines freedom with groundedness, holding the body in balance. The optimistic stone is packed with lifeforce and assists willpower to manifest constructively. It encourages vision, expansiveness, adventure and constructive use of freedom. With Pakulite's assistance, you look to the future with different eyes.

Botswana Agate

Smoker's antidote

Botswana Agate shields you and your family, encouraging protective love that is objective and non-smothering. Alleviating repression, it cuts ties that bind people together, removing judgemental 'oughts and shoulds' and leaving unconditional love, mutual respect and acceptance in their place. The stone assists with creative solutions. It assists anyone, or anything, connected with fire or smoke. At a mental level, it sees the bigger picture. The stone assimilates oxygen, benefiting the circulatory system and skin. It lifts depression. Botswana Agate stimulates the crown chakra, drawing energy into the auric field.

Source: Mount Paku (New Zealand)

Vibration: High

Chakra: Earth star, base, sacral, solar plexus

Physiology: Immune system, kidneys, liver, bladder, sexual organs

Cleansing: All

Source: Botswana

Vibration: Earthy

Chakra: All, especially spleen, soma and crown

Physiology: Lungs. *See* Agate, pages 46–7

Cleansing: All

Black Kyanite

Healer's friend

A powerful healing and detoxifying stone, Black Kyanite keeps physical cells connected to the divine blueprint to maintain optimum health. It encourages fully incarnating into the earth-plane. Facilitating moving into the interlife (the space between physical incarnations) to access the current lifeplan (the learning-plan for present life), Black Kyanite views potential future lives to assess the results of choices made in the present, so that the most constructive future is created. Helpful for those who have lost their way in life or are trying to break a cycle of self-destructive behaviour, Black Kyanite is deeply grounding. It supports environmentalism and evolution of the planet – and soul. ●

Moqui Marbles
(Moqui Balls)

Vitality

Packed with strong Qi and iron, pairs of Moqui Marbles balance male–female energy and stabilize and rejuvenate the body. Held in the hands, positioned either side of the hips or placed top and bottom of the spine, they ground and centre in your core, removing blockages and providing protection. The stones surface parts of the Self hidden in long-ago lives, for healing and reintegration. Moqui Marbles overcome deep-seated fear, particularly of death or spiritual evolution. They take you journeying deep into other worlds, connecting with power animals to assist with soul retrieval. Moqui Marbles clear the planet's meridians and power points. ●

Source: Brazil, USA, Europe, Russia, India, Africa

Vibration: Extremely high

Chakra: Earth star, base

Physiology: Muscular system, cells, throat, urogenital and female reproductive systems, adrenal and parathyroid glands

Cleansing: Avoid water

Source: USA

Vibration: Earthy to high

Chakra: Earth star, Gaia gateway, third eye

Physiology: Immune and digestive system, spine, adrenals

Cleansing: Avoid water

Smoky Quartz

Detoxification

One of the most effective grounding and clearing crystals, relaxing Smoky Quartz improves the tolerance of stress. This stone provides pain relief. A layout of slow-release Smoky Quartz pointing out from the body prevents a healing crisis. It assists with assimilation of minerals, fluid regulation and detoxification of the body or environment, including EMFs. The crystal heals toxic emotional conditions, overcoming fear and lack of trust, instilling a sense of safety and protection. In psychic work, Smoky Quartz facilitates connection to the lower shamanic worlds and the astral plane, shielding against psychic attack and transmuting negative energies. It raises personal vibrations during meditation.

Source: Worldwide

Vibration: Earthy and high

Chakra: Gaia gateway, earth star, base. Aligns all

Physiology: *See* Quartz, pages 38–45

Cleansing: All

Poppy Jasper

Passion reviver

Passionate and potent, Poppy Jasper is gentle and fiery. It activates the base chakra to bring vitality and joy, grounding energy into the body and stimulating libido. Conversely, it calms an over-active base chakra and disperses sexual frustration, soothing an over-stimulated sex-drive. Poppy Jasper balances yin and yang, aligning physical, emotional and mental bodies with the etheric realm. Clearing electromagnetic and environmental pollution, it sustains during stress or prolonged illness, inducing tranquillity and wholeness. Calming emotions, this stone imparts determination, courage and motivation. Poppy Jasper extends sexual pleasure. Re-energizing the body, it also assists birth and rebirthing.

Source: California, USA, China, South Africa

Vibration: Earthy to high

Chakra: Base, sacral. Energizes all

Physiology: *See* Jasper, pages 48–9

Cleansing: All

Carnelian

Creativity

Rejuvenating Carnelian is a powerful motivator with great vitality. Perfect for the base and sacral chakras, it re-energizes the whole energetic system. Paradoxically, it soothes inflammation and over-active conditions, calming where appropriate. Carnelian supports positive life choices, turning dreams into reality. It reverses mental lethargy and transmutes anger or victimhood into empowerment and motivation to get things moving. Stabilizing, Carnelian anchors into the present reality. Removing extraneous thoughts in meditation, it helps you to be fully present. Overcoming abuse and negative conditioning, it encourages you to trust yourself. Carnelian cleanses and re-energizes other stones.

Strawberry Lemurian

Empowerment

If you need an energetic reboot or boost to your self-confidence, Strawberry Lemurian recharges the whole body – instantly. Incredibly energetic and power-full, this is the perfect empowerment crystal. It integrates higher resonances of the heart seed and higher heart into the physical heart. When pink or pale red, it has a gentle feminine energy and heals the matriarchal line. When dark red, it emanates a stronger, more masculine energy. Strawberry embodies the spiritual qualities of a Lemurian Seed crystal, including 'codes' to assist evolution. It grounds that information into the physical body and Earth, ensuring that the information is acted upon with the right timing.

Source: Brazil, Russia, India, Australia, Egypt, Madagascar, South Africa, Uruguay, USA, UK, Czech Republic, Slovakia, Peru, Iceland, Romania

Vibration: Earthy

Chakra: Base, sacral

Physiology: Metabolism, blood and blood-rich organs, liver, spleen, reproductive system, lower back, kidneys, bones, ligaments

Cleansing: All

Source: Brazil

Vibration: Exceedingly high

Chakra: Aligns all

Physiology: Entire physical and etheric bodies

Cleansing: Avoid water

Orange River Quartz
(Hematite Quartz)

Potent power

Orange River dissolves negativity and grounds energy. It harmonizes body, mind and spirit. Drawing earthy Qi into the Gaia gateway, it activates the creativity of the base and sacral chakras, connecting it to the crown and soul star. If you have disconnected from your soul purpose or lost motivation, it realigns your Higher Self and restores your lifepath and capacity for enjoyment, opening to pure pleasure. Orange River overcomes karmic abuse of power – whether as perpetrator or victim. If you gave away power in this or any other life, it reclaims it.

Rubellite
(Pink/Red Tourmaline)

Perfected heart

Rubellite activates and aligns the three-chambered heart chakra, harmonizing heart and mind. It induces emotional balance and calmness, bringing passion to life. Protective Rubellite overcomes abusive situations and destructive relationship patterns, supporting stepping into your personal power. Red Rubellite assists those who struggle to understand love. Pink Rubellite facilitates accepting unconditional love, opening the heart to give and receive. It promotes tactfulness and flexibility, sociability and extroversion, balancing over-aggression or over-passivity. Rubellite detoxifies and infuses vitality into the physical body, unblocking and energizing the sacral and base chakras, increasing creativity on all levels. It induces profound healing. ⓘ

Source: South Africa

Vibration: Earthy and high

Chakra: Base, sacral. Revitalizes all

Physiology: *See* Quartz, pages 38–45

Cleansing: All

Source: Russia, Afghanistan, Brazil, Madagascar, Nigeria, USA

Vibration: Earthy to high

Chakra: Base, sacral, heart, heart seed, higher heart, causal vortex

Physiology: Blood vessels, electrochemical systems. *See* Tourmaline, pages 56–7

Cleansing: All

Yellow Jasper

Companionship

Yellow Jasper infuses body, mind and soul with hope. A stone of the sun, it overcomes depression and anxiety. A useful emotional support for psychosomatic conditions, it assists your earthly journey and keeps you on your soulpath. Yellow Jasper sustains during stressful times and chronic illness. This stone protects and clears the body of environmental toxins and impurities, and emotional angst or outgrown patterns. It cleanses and detoxifies internal organs, including liver, gall bladder and intestines. Yellow Jasper creates a shield, returning gossip and negativity to its source. It overcomes dyspraxia, or accident proneness.

Source: Worldwide

Vibration: Earthy

Chakra: Sacral, solar plexus

Physiology: *See* Jasper, pages 48–9

Cleansing: All

Mookaite Jasper

Versatility

Creating a balance between inner and outer experiences, Mookaite Jasper protects and takes you into a calm centre to wait out any storm. It helps face up to the ageing process, appreciating the wisdom of age rather than the drawbacks. Mookaite acts as a companion for the bereaved or lonely and contacts souls on other planes. It encourages versatility, pointing out all possibilities and assisting in choosing the appropriate one, but encourages facing present circumstances calmly if change is not possible. It is physically stabilizing: mainly red, fortifying the immune system, and yellow, calming it.

Source: Australia

Vibration: Earthy

Chakra: Earth star, base, sacral

Physiology: *See* Jasper, pages 48–9

Cleansing: All

Bumble Bee Jasper

The unfeasible

Bumble Bee Jasper is an excellent healer for sacral and solar plexus chakra dis-ease, food intolerances and allergies. Providing clear focus, it encourages total honesty with yourself as underlying issues surface to be resolved. The stone offers confidence and boosts self-worth. This Jasper represents triumph over the unfeasible, as the bee is not aerodynamically designed to fly and yet does. Bumble Bee Jasper encourages pollination of new projects and is supremely nurturing. Grid it in your garden and around your vegetable patch to call in pollinating insects and ensure continuation of natural food sources. ℹ

Zincite

Rebirther

Zincite is extremely potent as its energy was concentrated by the fiery smelting process of its birth. It synthesizes physical energy and personal power with creativity and manifestation. The crystal removes energy blocks, painful memories, shock and trauma. Re-energizing depleted systems, Zincite anchors the lightbody into the physical realm. It raises kundalini and enhances gut instincts and intuition. Remotivating, Zincite pushes you into your full potential. It embraces necessary change. Zincite overcomes phobias, getting to the root cause and gently releasing it, reprogramming the mind. It releases hypnotic commands and mental imprints. Green-yellow Zincite energetically removes infections.

Source: Australia, Indonesia

Vibration: Earthy to high

Chakra: Base, sacral, solar plexus

Physiology: *See* Jasper, pages 48–9

Cleansing: Avoid water

Source: Poland, Italy, USA and smelting process

Vibration: Earthy to high

Chakra: All, according to colour

Physiology: Kidneys, prostate, skin, hair, immune, reproductive and endocrine systems, organs of elimination and assimilation

Cleansing: Avoid water

Green Ridge Quartz

De-gunker

This heavily iron-coated Golden Healer Quartz is outstanding for its detoxifying effects. Transmuting negative energy, it draws dis-ease out of the body, replacing it with healing light. An effective antidote to EMF pollution, geopathic stress and transgenerational trauma or familial dis-ease, as the crystal pulls out toxicity, the gunky coating falls away to reveal the beauty within. It is a useful support during cancer treatment. Green Ridge Quartz removes ingrained ancestral and shadow material from deep within the family line, sending healing out to the past and forward into future generations. A similar coating may be found on Quartzes from other regions.

Kundalini Quartz

Kundalini raiser

A natural Citrine, Kundalini Quartz safely raises kundalini energy from the base of the spine to the crown, unblocking and cleansing all chakras as it passes through. Transmuting negativity, it opens the soul star and stellar gateway and channels energy back to the ground to begin the circuit once again. Powerfully energizing, it takes you into the heart of creation to become a co-creator. This is the perfect crystal for tantric sex. Kundalini Quartz attracts abundance and creates passion on all levels. It assists flagging libido or loss of motivation. Kundalini Quartz benefits from regular cleansing and recharging.

Source: Green Ridge Mountains (USA)

Vibration: Exceedingly high

Chakra: Re-energizes all

Physiology: *See* Quartz, pages 38–45

Cleansing: Avoid water

Source: Congo

Vibration: Earthy and high

Chakra: Gaia gateway, earth star, base, sacral, solar plexus

Physiology: Reproductive organs. *See* Quartz, pages 38–45

Cleansing: All

Imperial Topaz

Charisma

True Imperial Topaz is rare. Golden Topaz can be substituted but Imperial Topaz has added charisma. Excellent for conscious attunement to the highest forces in the universe, storing information received in this way, the crystal brings joy, generosity, abundance and confidence. It promotes openness and honesty, self-realization, self-control and the urge to develop inner wisdom. Topaz problem-solves and stabilizes emotions. This crystal acts like a battery, recharging spiritually and physically, strengthening faith and optimism. It regenerates cellular structures, strengthens the solar plexus and overcomes nervous exhaustion and insufficient combustion. ◑

Jade

Purity

Serene Jade is cleansing, assisting the body's filtration and elimination organs and facilitating toxic emotional and pernicious core-belief release. Stabilizing the personality, it promotes self-sufficiency, releasing negative thoughts and soothing the mind. Jade stimulates creative ideas, making tasks appear less complex so that they are acted upon immediately. This protective stone keeps the wearer from harm and creates harmony. Integrating mind and body, it releases limiting beliefs, opening the mind to new possibilities. The stone has long been associated with attracting prosperity and good health. It traditionally maintains kidney function. Each colour has additional properties. ◑

Source: Brazil

Vibration: High

Chakra: All

Physiology: Organs and meridians of physical and subtle bodies, cellular structures, endocrine system, gall bladder, nerves, metabolism

Cleansing: All

Source: USA, China, Italy, Burma, Russia, Middle East, New Zealand, Guatemala, Myanmar (Burma), Russia

Vibration: High

Chakra: All, according to colour

Physiology: Kidneys, suprarenal glands, cellular and skeletal systems

Cleansing: All

Chrome Diopside

Analytics

Chrome Diopside revitalizes the chakras and physical body. It supports recovery from surgery, trauma or severe illness. Returning mind and psyche to equilibrium, it balances subtle bodies and soul. The crystal instils deep peace, honouring what you really feel. Chrome Diopside connects your heart to that of Mother Earth, teaching how to care for the planet. The crystal reconnects to healing energies of the plant kingdom. Facilitating remembering forgotten knowledge, it assists learning on many levels, particularly when acquiring fresh skills or studying a language, as it supports assimilating and retaining new information and analysing facts. ❶

Chrysocolla in Quartz

Heartfelt communication

Gentle Chrysocolla in Quartz is often sold as Ajoite Quartz. It shares properties with Ajoite, although at a lower vibrational level. The combination raises consciousness slowly, anchoring divine energy to the earth-plane. The stone combines Chrysocolla with Quartz to access the wisdom of your Higher Self. Enhancing meditation, it brings the divine into everyday awareness. The combination strengthens the heart chakra, opening the emotional intelligence of the heart. The combination is a powerful balancer for the higher heart (thymus) chakra and immune system. It assists whenever the heart has been shut down and needs reawakening with compassion. ❶

Source: Russia

Vibration: Medium

Chakra: Revitalizes all

Physiology: Heart, lungs, circulatory system, glucose metabolism, breakdown of fats and proteins

Cleansing: Avoid water

Source: USA

Vibration: Fairly high

Chakra: Heart, higher heart, throat

Physiology: *See* Quartz, pages 38–45

Cleansing: All

Malacholla

Wholeness

Malacholla has a high vibration that works more gently than Malachite as it incorporates the softness of Chrysocolla. Placed on an area of imbalance, it restores equilibrium, bringing harmony to mind, body and emotions. Place one on the third eye and another on the solar plexus. It surfaces that which has been hidden to be healed with compassionate acceptance. An excellent detoxifier on all levels, Malacholla regenerates and harmonizes the chakra and meridian systems of the physical and subtle bodies. This stone helps you stand in your power. Grid it in areas of environmental unrest. ●

Quantum Quattro

Holistic healing

A stone of ultimate healing, Quantum Quattro strengthens the immune system and switches on beneficial DNA. It prevents a healing crisis or catharsis. Pernicious energies gently drop away. Grounding spiritual vibrations onto the earth-plane, it facilitates information passing freely from all levels of being. Deeply transformative, Quantum Quattro protects against negative energies and pollutants. It draws out deep feelings and psychosomatic causes from this or any other life. Quantum Quattro breaks a cycle of karmic co-dependency, cutting ties and outworn patterns. The stone teaches how to take responsibility for your actions, thoughts and feelings. It clears psychic vision and protects during channelling. ●

Source: Congo, Russia

Vibration: Earthy to high

Chakra: Base, heart

Physiology: Meridians, excretory organs, lungs, blood, joints, muscles, bones, liver, insulin and blood-sugar balance

Cleansing: All

Source: Namibia

Vibration: High

Chakra: All, especially higher heart

Physiology: Intercellular structures, thymus, lungs, pancreas, insulin, thyroid, metabolism, T-cells, liver, kidneys, digestive tract

Cleansing: All

Smithsonite

Inner healing

Smithsonite relieves stress and improves physical immunity. Use when nervous collapse threatens. Perfect for anyone who has had a difficult childhood or felt unloved or unwanted, it gently heals the inner child and alleviates the effects of emotional abuse and misuse without traumatic emotional release. Smithsonite repairs difficult relationships. Creating a secure and balanced life, it imparts harmony and diplomacy, and remedies unpleasant situations. Tranquil, it instils kindness and ensures favourable outcomes. Smithsonite strengthens psychic abilities and connects to the angelic realm. Grid it around the bed to bring healing and protection. ❶

Blue Lace Agate

Ultimate communication

The perfect communication stone, Blue Lace Agate frees up the throat chakra, allowing expression of thoughts and emotions. It clears speech impediments and counteracts feelings of being judged, encouraging a new mode of expression. Feelings that have previously been repressed are calmly given voice. It helps men accept their sensitive, feeling nature. Blue Lace Agate facilitates the expression of spiritual truth. The stone calms stress, neutralizing anger or frustration. It soothes inflammation and fever, releases shoulder and neck problems, and overcomes thyroid deficiencies and throat or lymph infections. Directing vibrations appropriately, Blue Lace Agate enhances sound healing.

Source: USA, Australia, Greece, Italy, Mexico, Namibia

Vibration: High

Chakra: Solar plexus, higher heart, third eye, crown. Aligns all

Physiology: Immune and digestive systems, sinus, bones, veins, muscles

Cleansing: Avoid water

Source: Namibia, South Africa, India

Vibration: Medium

Chakra: Throat, third eye, heart, crown

Physiology: Throat, thyroid. *See* Agate, pages 46–7

Cleansing: All

Que Sera
(Llanoite, Vulcanite)

Synergistic healing

A powerful combination containing Quartz, Feldspar, Calcite, Kaolinite, Hematite, Magnetite, Leucozone and Clinozoisite, Que Sera facilitates standing in your own power, released from self-imposed obligations. If you take the troubles of the world on your shoulders and cannot say no, and especially if you dwell on problems, Que Sera finds constructive solutions. The stone attunes to your Akashic Record, encouraging you to take the most appropriate route for your evolution. A potent healer, Que Sera assists all organs and systems of the physical body. Place it wherever dis-ease or depletion exists. ●

Tanzine Aura Quartz

Alchemical throat healing

Created alchemically from indium, Tanzine Aura Quartz brings about multidimensional balance. It aligns the highest crown chakras and draws cosmic energy into the physical body and to Earth, creating profound spiritual connection and physical equilibrium, redrawing the etheric blueprint. Excellent for restoring thyroid function and returning the pineal and hypothalamus glands to equilibrium, it restores optimal metabolic and hormonal balance, resulting in physical and mental wellbeing. Indium is said to be anti-carcinogenic. The stone overcomes stress, metabolism, mineral assimilation, insomnia, thyroid deficiency and attention deficit disorder. It regularizes the immune system and overcomes depression.

Source: Brazil, USA, South Africa

Vibration: High

Chakra: Earth star, base, sacral, stellar gateway

Physiology: Immune system. *See* Quartz, pages 38–45

Cleansing: All

Source: Artificially created

Vibration: Exceedingly high

Chakra: Throat, third eye, soma, crown, alta major, causal vortex, soul star, stellar gateway

Physiology: Thyroid. *See* Quartz, pages 38–45

Cleansing: All

Lepidocrocite

Bridging

Strongly protective, Lepidocrocite bridges matter and consciousness, facilitating the practical application of spiritual insights. This powerful auric cleanser disperses mental confusion and negativity. It encourages love for yourself, the environment and humanity, teaching how to empower others without entering into power issues. The crystal gives you strength to make commitments to your life journey and work you must do. It alleviates bi-polar disorder, hyperactivity and ADHD, eliminating distraction and confusion. It lessens negative thinking and limiting beliefs and has a strong healing action within the emotional body. Lepidocrocite helps those who always seek control to let go.

Chalcopyrite

Copper power

A major source of copper, Chalcopyrite is a powerful energy conduit, supporting Tai Chi, acupuncture or acupressure. It releases energy blockages and enhances movement of Qi around the body. Linking to the Akashic Record, interlife and ancient civilizations, it accesses past-life causes of present-life difficulties or dis-eases, revealing events you may rather not face. Additional crystals heal such issues. The stone moves between different realities. Creating inner security and self-esteem, Chalcopyrite teaches that abundance is a state of mind. It traditionally heals arthritis, inflammation, infection and fever. ◕

Source: Madagascar, India, Spain

Vibration: High

Chakra: Base, sacral, heart, higher heart

Physiology: Liver, lungs, circulatory system, iris, female reproductive system

Cleansing: Avoid water

Source: USA, France, Chile, Namibia, Zambia, Peru, Germany, Spain

Vibration: Earthy

Chakra: Third eye, crown

Physiology: Veins, joints, hair, excretory organs, RNA/DNA, lungs

Cleansing: Avoid water

Grape Chalcedony
(Grape Agate)

Grace

Sedative and calming, Grape Chalcedony cleanses perception, identifying what is important, helping you sit in stillness and simply be. Activating the karma of grace that says you only have to do enough, its tranquil gentleness dismantles defences and opens your heart. A wonderful emotional support, soothing fears, it heals the inner terrorist that sneakily whispers fear into the heart. Drawing like-minded people together for mutual support, it reminds you that, even when you appear to be totally alone, help is available. A stone of inspiration that encourages trust, Grape Chalcedony facilitates finding your karmic strengths. It decongests the body through lymph flow.

Natrolite and Scolecite

Neuro-stabilizers

Natrolite and Scolecite stabilize neurotransmitters and fine-tune the nervous system after an influx of higher vibrations. Place Scolecite on chakras along the back and Natrolite on the front, to realign the physical body with the lightbody. Scolecite is appropriate if you are new to high-vibration crystals or for a sensitive energy field. It heals auric holes, splits or fragmentation where negative energies or entities could attach. The crystal hooks out remnants of detrimental patterns or beliefs, clearing the etheric blueprint and mental body. Combine with Flint to create a stable earth matrix during profound change, or to reverse polluted earth-energy flows.

Source: Indonesia

Vibration: High

Chakra: All, especially solar plexus and higher

Physiology: Stomach, brain and brain chemistry, lymphatic and nervous systems, ameliorates panic attacks, bipolar disorder or anxiety

Cleansing: Avoid water

Source: USA, Germany, Czech Republic, India, Iceland

Vibration: Earthy and extremely high

Chakra: Third eye, crown, heart seed, soma

Physiology: Nervous system and neurotransmitters, bone, intestines

Cleansing: Avoid water

Moonstone

Intuition

Moonstone enhances intuition and psychic abilities. It calms emotions, reducing instability, and prevents overreactions to situations and emotional triggers. It clears outdated emotional patterning and is the perfect antidote for excessively macho men or overly aggressive females. Moonstone soothes stress at any level. A powerful healer for the female reproductive cycle and menstrual-related dis-ease, it assists birth. Water-attuned, it stabilizes fluid imbalances and resets the biorhythmic clock. Helpful for shock, insomnia and sleep-walking, it calms hyperactive children. Wear in accordance with phases of the moon.

White Calcite

Purification

Delicate White Calcite connects emotions with intellect and assists psychosomatic conditions, clearing pernicious patterns from the etheric blueprint. It has a positive effect if hope or motivation have been lost. Calcite stimulates insights and boosts memory, conferring the ability to put ideas into action. Removing stagnant energy, it cleanses organs of elimination, encourages calcium uptake, dissolves calcification and strengthens the skeleton and joints. White Calcite cleans negative energies from a room. It speeds spiritual development and growth, opens higher awareness and psychic abilities and is excellent for meditation, channelling and out-of-body experiences.

Source: India, Sri Lanka, Australia

Vibration: High to extremely high, according to type

Chakra: Third eye, solar plexus, causal vortex, soma

Physiology: Digestive and reproductive systems, female reproductive cycle, menstrual-related dis-ease, pineal gland, hormonal balance, fluid imbalances, biorhythmic clock, skin, hair, eyes

Cleansing: Avoid water

Source: Worldwide

Vibration: Medium to high

Chakra: Sacral, solar plexus. Realigns all

Physiology: *See* Calcite, pages 50–1

Cleansing: All, if not layered or friable – if so, avoid water

Crystals
for the heart

The heart governs the psyche, consciously or unconsciously, directing the body's reactions to social and physical environments and other people. The heart has emotional intelligence. It deals with gut reactions and intuitions, unconditional love and compassion – and motivation. It encompasses not only relationships but also emotions, attitudes and feelings – and the internal conflicts and multiple agendas arising from past lives and interlife agreements. If noxious emotions and heartbreak are stuck in the emotional body or heart chakra, it leads to psychosomatic dis-ease and challenging relationships. Crystals gently release toxic emotions, instilling a more appropriate feeling.

Emotions and psyche

From the viewpoint of crystal healing, many dis-eases have an emotional basis, being caused not by injury but instead by underlying factors such as stress, emotional repression over a long period, toxic memories, shame, disappointment or spiritual discomfort. Even those that are apparently caused by pathogens may reveal an underlying psychic susceptibility.

'Illness has a purpose; it has to resolve the conflict, to repress it, or to prevent what is already repressed from entering consciousness,' said Georg W. Groddeck (19th-century Swiss physician).

In Chinese medicine, for instance, grief is associated with the lungs. If grief is not fully expressed and let go, or is held onto from other lives, then the lungs cannot function optimally. Similarly, anger or resentment affects the liver and fear affects the kidneys, both filtration systems for clearing toxicity from the body. Previous life attitudes such as hard-heartedness or experiences such as heartbreak play out in the present life as 'a heart condition'. Healing the heart and emotional body releases the underlying condition.

Common causes of emotional dis-ease

- Past experiences: trauma from present or previous lives, shame and distress, personal or familial, lodges itself in the emotional body or heart chakra.
- Defence mechanism: 'un-wellness' avoids confrontation with the challenges of life or dealing with inner emotional problems. Clearing the chakras, especially the base and earth star, resolves this.
- Powerlessness: being unable to take control of life and an inability to extend compassion to yourself due to a blocked heart chakra leads to psychosomatic dis-ease.
- Holding onto the past: living in the past, or bringing conditions forward, personal or familial, creates emotional dis-ease and is held in the karmic and ancestral bodies and past-life or causal vortex chakras, as well as the heart.

Releasing stuck emotions

Anger, resentment, jealousy, guilt, shame and the like are self-destructive emotions. Feelings may be held onto consciously or unconsciously, repressed deep in the psyche until they turn on the body or mind through the physical and psychic immune system. Placing a crystal on relevant chakras, or gridding them around the body, gently releases this emotional dross, and positive feelings such as self-worth and confidence take their place.

Exercise

Heart healing

A simple Star of David grid heals the heart and clears heartbreak, jealousy and so on. It can be placed over the actual heart or positioned close to a bed or where it will be seen often.

Suitable crystals: *Clearing* – Smoky Quartz, Peridot and Rhodonite. *Love-infusing* – Rose Quartz, Garnet and Rhodochrosite. *See also* the crystal portraits on pages 68–307.

1   Lay a downward-facing triangle with appropriate clearing crystals and join up.
2   Lay an upward-facing triangle with love-infusing crystals and join up.

LEFT Selenite above the head and Ruby over the higher heart chakra give emotional support.

Chakric heart connections

Three chakras in particular have a profound effect on your heart and emotional wellbeing.

Solar plexus

The solar plexus chakra holds emotions and deep ancestral patterning. Unrecognized emotions seriously damage the body, or a current relationship, when unconsciously triggered. Keeping the solar plexus clear ensures you are able to experience emotions and feel feelings, no matter how unacceptable you may have been taught that they are, and then let them go. Suppressing and rejecting perfectly natural feelings creates psychosomatic distress. This suppression may have occurred in previous lives and been carried forward. Traditionally yellow crystals such as Citrine, Topaz or Yellow Jasper cleanse the solar plexus. When doing so, place a Smoky Quartz, Flint, Hematite or Obsidian at your feet to ground and absorb toxicity released.

Three-chambered heart chakra

The three-chambered heart chakra comprises the heart seed, heart and higher heart chakras. When all three parts of the chakra are activated, cleansed and integrated, the soul makes its presence felt more strongly on the earth-plane. If you are aware of the effect your emotions have upon your body and your progress in life, then compassion for yourself and others becomes a natural state of being. Opening and integrating, the three-chambered heart is facilitated by having the soul star and stellar gateway chakras connected to the earth star and Gaia gateway.

Exercise

Three-chambered heart-chakra integration

Suitable crystals: Tugtupite, Pink Petalite, Green Aventurine, Rose Quartz, Danburite, Mangano Calcite, Smoky Quartz. *See also* the crystal portraits on pages 68–307.

1 Place a heart-seed activator such as Tugtupite or Pink Petalite at the base of the breastbone. Breathe gently into the point until it tingles.
2 Place a Green Aventurine, Rose Quartz or other heart crystal on the breastbone, level with the nipples.
3 Place a higher heart-chakra activator such as Danburite or Mangano Calcite midway up the breastbone.
4 With a crystal wand or the power of your mind, trace a figure of eight to join up the crystals, crossing over the heart-crystal point. Feel the three-chambered heart chakra opening and integrating to receive your soul.
5 Place a Smoky Quartz or other grounding stone at your feet.
6 With a crystal wand or the power of your mind, trace an extended threefold figure of eight around the three-chambered heart chakra, connecting it to the earth star chakra at your feet. Feel the subtle-energy bodies integrating to ground your soul.

OPPOSITE LEFT Three-chambered heart integration.

OPPOSITE RIGHT To clear the spleen chakra, hold an appropriate crystal below the left armpit.

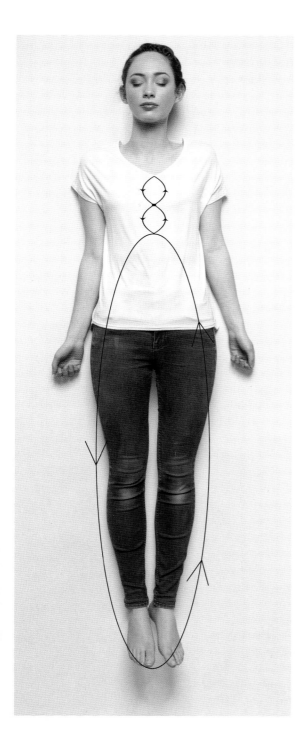

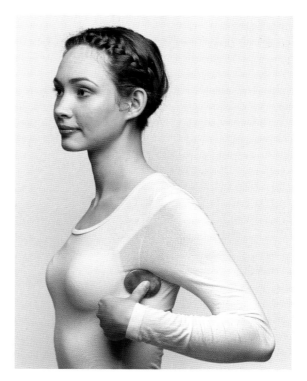

Spleen chakra

The spleen chakra is beneath the left armpit. Old – and current – relationships hook in here to deplete energy and block new relationships. A constant ache indicates the chakra is stuck open and a psychic vampire is drawing an energy fix, or a previous partner has not let go. When the chakra is blocked, emotional energy, especially anger, becomes stuck and this depletes you.

Exercise

Clearing the spleen chakra

Suitable crystals: Green Aventurine, Raw Charoite, Flint, Jade and Lemurian Seed. *See also* the crystal portraits on pages 68–307.

1 Simply hold an appropriate crystal below the left armpit.

Healing sexual or emotional abuse

Sexual relationships, or a lack of them, have a marked effect on wellbeing. The base and sacral chakras contain remnants of previous sexual partners, including memories of sexual abuse. The solar plexus and heart hold emotional abuse cords, and the spleen chakra is linked to energy vampires. All chakras may have been infiltrated by controlling authority figures. The base and sacral chakras are the site of libido and stored kundalini power which, when released, empowers. If libido is low, then a passionate stone such as Ruby or Red Jasper stimulates it. If libido is over-active, then a calming one such as Green Kyanite or Green Aventurine restores balance.

Exercise

Clearing hooks from the higher heart, or other, chakra

Free your spleen, heart, base, sacral or solar plexus chakra hooks by spiralling out an appropriate crystal to pull out hooks or inappropriate energetic connections. (Note: the same basic process described below and in the illustrations opposite applies to each of the chakras).

Suitable crystals: Quartz point, Flint, Raw Charoite, Jasper or Rainbow Mayanite shard. *See also* the crystal portraits on pages 68–307.

1 Touch the chakra with the crystal.
2 Take your hand up, out and away from the chakra.
3 With a spiralling motion continue until the crystal is at arm's length. Now cleanse the crystal (*see* page 27).
4 Bring the crystal back to your heart, breathing in its energy as you do so.

Hold or tape a Tantalite, Green Aventurine, Green Fluorite or Jade crystal over the chakra after hook-clearing. Feel it creating a three-dimensional protective pyramid around the chakra and sealing your aura.

If, having removed hooks from the spleen chakra, a pain occurs under the right armpit, the energy vampire has become frustrated at having the power source cut off. Tape a piece of Gaspeite, Tugtupite or Bloodstone over the site and leave in place until the message is received that you will not give away any more of your energy.

OPPOSITE The 'clearing hooks' exercise can help you to pull out 'hooks' or inappropriate energetic connections.

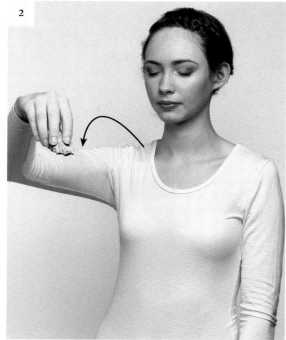

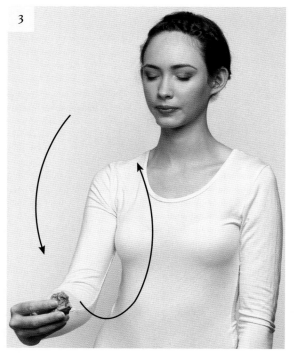

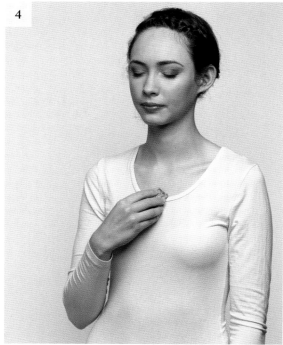

Ruby in Fuchsite or Kyanite

Grief healer

Source: Tanzania, India, Zambia

Vibration: Earthy and high

Chakra: Crown, throat, heart, base, past life, causal vortex

Physiology: Heart and circulation

Cleansing: All

An emotional balancer and a profoundly healing crystal for the heart.

Characteristics

An emotional balancer, Ruby carried in a matrix of Fuchsite or Kyanite is a profoundly healing crystal for the heart. Perfect for releasing grief or heartbreak, it dissolves abuse or trauma issues stemming from incidents or situations in any timeframe. The combination creates an altered state of consciousness that facilitates accessing soul memory and integrating spiritual learning. Either crystal is extremely helpful in soul healing and past-life work. Powerfully amplifying the biomagnetic field around the body, it heals energy bodies and removes outdated mental patterning or emotional congestion, settling a new positively loving vibration into the body. The combination promotes individuality while retaining interconnectedness with the rest of humanity at an emotional level. The stone reassures that it is safe to love again, and keeps an open heart chakra functioning optimally so that love is received and radiated out appropriately. ❶

Heart protection

The combination stone focuses psychic ability and activates self-empowerment. Acting as a magnet for Qi, it reveals what is needed in order to move forward and courageously follow new paths in life. Highly protective, it shields the heart from all that is negative and traumatic. If you come under psychic attack or ill wishing, wear it over your higher heart chakra.

MAIN Ruby in Kyanite
ABOVE Ruby in Fuchsite
LEFT Ruby in Fuchsite

Rose Quartz

Unconditional love

Source: South Africa, Brazil

Vibration: Extremely high

Chakra: Heart, higher heart, heart seed

Physiology: Adrenals. *See* Quartz, pages 38–45

Cleansing: All

Rose Quartz promotes the self-love that is essential before love is accepted from others.

Characteristics

Compassionate Rose Quartz carries unconditional love and acceptance, bringing deep emotional healing and promoting the self-love that is essential before love is accepted from others. The stone teaches that unconditional love does not mean sacrificing yourself, being walked on or abused, while saying, 'It's okay, I still love you no matter what you do to me.' It creates appropriate boundaries, allowing someone else the space to be who they are without trying to force change, but not being overwhelmed when they are less than perfect. Dispersing illusions around what is truly love in action, Rose Quartz helps you to say a firm but loving 'No'. Hold one whenever you practise tough love – the art of standing firm. It is helpful for overcoming addictions, obsessions or a tendency to self-harm in any way.

Healing heartbreak

Rose Quartz heals heartbreak or disappointment. It attracts mutually loving relationships rather than co-dependency or abuse, as might have previously been the case. Place one by your bed to attract a twinflame or soulmate. A powerful stone for healing grief and loss, Rose Quartz strengthens empathy and sensitivity, enhancing all interactions with others. It encourages self-forgiveness and absolution for those who have, apparently, wronged you, revealing their role in your soulplan. The beautiful stone invokes self-trust and enhances self-worth.

Neighbourly peace

If you suffer from noisy or disruptive neighbours, place a large Rose Quartz on the party wall. It settles disputes and is an excellent shield against EMF smog and geopathic stress.

MAIN Rose Quartz heart
RIGHT Raw Rose Quartz
FAR RIGHT ABOVE Rose Quartz
FAR RIGHT BELOW Rose Quartz tumbled stone

Nzuri Moyo

Good-heart

Soothing Nzuri Moyo activates metaphysical abilities
and encourages a loving relationship. Meaning 'beautiful
spirit' in Swahili, Nzuri Moyo is a complex combination
of minerals that draws unconditional love into the body to
heal individual cells and open the heart. A joy-full stone, it
releases emotional blockages and anger from all three heart
chakras, opening the higher-dimensional three-chambered
heart chakra and clearing the emotional body. Answering
those who ask the great questions of life, it promotes
calmness and clarity of mind during troubled times or
challenging energy shifts, enabling you to live with
the answers.

Black Obsidian

Deep soul-cleanser

A deep healer, Obsidian offers insight into causes of dis-
ease. It removes blockages and debris from past lives and
reverses previous misuse of power, addressing power issues
on all levels. The stone blocks psychic attack and removes
negative spiritual influences. It anchors the spirit into the
body. Obsidian brings deep-seated emotions and issues to
the surface, accessing your shadow and integrating positive
qualities hidden there. It works extremely fast, but you
may need other crystals to deal with issues arising from it.
The stone clarifies the mind and clears confusion. It assists
the body's structures to energetically detoxify, blocking
geopathic stress and environmental pollution.

Source: East Africa, Namibia

Vibration: Earthy and high

Chakra: Heart, higher heart, heart seed,
third eye, soma

Physiology: Immune and nervous system, lungs,
tumours, joints, bones, muscles, anxiety

Cleansing: All

Source: Mexico, Central America, Canada, USA

Vibration: Earthy

Chakra: Earth star, base, sacral

Physiology: Digestion, detoxification, arteries, joints,
circulation, prostate

Cleansing: All

Rainbow Obsidian

Cord-cutter

Cutting the cords of old love, Rainbow Obsidian gently releases hooks that previous relationships have left in the heart, replenishing heart chakra energy. One of the softer-acting Obsidians, Rainbow Obsidian nevertheless has strong protective properties. It absorbs negative energy from energy fields and draws stress from the body. This stone facilitates past-life healing, gaining insight into how the past is affecting the present, especially at the level of health and wellbeing. It gently teaches about evolution of your spiritual nature, pointing out what must be let go before you make a shift into expanded consciousness.

Boulder Opal

Fire-in-the-heart

Opal in a matrix of grounding ironstone, Boulder Opal is aligned to the fire and earth elements. Energizing a depleted heart, it stabilizes emotions and attracts true love. Resistant to cracking, Boulder Opal helps put tough love into practice, when appropriate. The vibrant flashes of colour alleviate depression and ease suffering. Encouraging clarity of thought and balancing conscious and subconscious minds, this stone reveals your true desires and motivation when you gaze into it. Boulder Opal encourages practical people to develop their spiritual side, and assists spiritually minded people to succeed in the everyday world. *See also* Yowah Nut, page 200.

Source: Mexico

Vibration: High

Chakra: Heart

Physiology: *See* Black Obsidian, opposite

Cleansing: All

Source: Queensland (Australia)

Vibration: Earthy and high

Chakra: Earth star, base, sacral. Energizes all

Physiology: *See* Opal, pages 54–5

Cleansing: Avoid water

Hessonite Garnet

Loyalty

Hessonite Garnet is regenerative and revitalizing, dissolving ingrained behaviour patterns and boosting the entire system. It inspires love, devotion and commitment, balancing libido and alleviating emotional disharmony. Instilling courage and hope into seemingly hopeless situations, wearing Hessonite Garnet sharpens perceptions, bestowing self-confidence and courage. In Indian astrology it is linked to Rahu, the north node that holds your soulplan and spiritual destiny, imparting exceptionally potent powers. Hessonite endows the user with longevity, good health, prosperity and happiness. The stone is geared towards creativity and personal expression. It stimulates expanded awareness and past-life recall. ●

Rhodolite and Raspberry Garnet

Inspiration

Rhodolite and Raspberry Garnet both bring inspiration to heart and mind. Healing the emotional body, they open you to receive emotional abundance without going over the top. Increasing self-worth, they alleviate feelings of inadequacy or worthlessness. Under the influence of either of these stones, you recognize your own gifts and share them with others without ego. These gentle Garnets are helpful where sexual healing is required, as they dissolve guilt and shame, encouraging you to have compassion for yourself. These stones dissolve noxious emotional patterns relating to abuse, clearing the memory and developing healthy sexuality. ●

Source: India, USA, Brazil, China, Kenya, Madagascar, Myanmar (Burma), Namibia, Sri Lanka, Tanzania

Vibration: High to extremely high

Chakra: Base, sacral, heart

Physiology: Bladder, intestine, sexual organs, spleen

Cleansing: Avoid water

Source: North Carolina, USA, Mexico, Argentina, Myanmar (Burma)

Vibration: High

Chakra: Base, sacral, heart, crown

Physiology: Blood, heart, lungs, metabolism, digestive tract, sexual organs

Cleansing: Avoid water

Cinnabar in Jasper

Alchemical catalyst

This highly energetic combination turns your world upside down and inside out and gives you a whole new perspective on your lifepath. Highlighting experiences that polished your soul, it teaches that everything is perfect exactly as it is. Cinnabar in Jasper transmutes anger and resentment or psychological impotence into dynamic assertion that powers life and manifests whatever you need. Calming short-fused people, it protects from other people's anger. Placed a hand's breadth beneath the right armpit, it de-energizes anger cords implanted in any lifetime. Carry it if you feel physically or mentally exhausted and unable to face challenges. ⬤

Rhodonite

Trauma-soother

Rhodonite soothes the nervous system. An excellent first-aid remedy for trauma or shock, it is an effective wound-healer. It calms and supports mind, body and soul in challenging situations. Revealing all sides of an issue, it is beneficial in cases of emotional self-destruction or physical self-harming, co-dependency or abuse, healing the heart trauma that results. Rhodonite dissolves memories of abuse and emotional scars gathered over many lifetimes, replacing them with love and forgiveness. It also helps you to achieve your highest potential. It builds confidence and opens the heart to unconditional love. The stone assists lovers reach tantric union.

Source: Philippines, Spain, USA, Slovenia, Egypt

Vibration: High

Chakra: Base, sacral

Physiology: Energy and circulatory systems, sexual organs, blood, liver, spleen

Cleansing: Avoid water

Source: Russia, Canada, Australia, Brazil, Sweden, Peru, England, USA

Vibration: High

Chakra: Solar plexus, heart, higher heart, heart seed

Physiology: Nervous system, lungs, ears, bones, joints

Cleansing: All

Eudialyte

Personal empowerment

Eudialyte clears depression and dissatisfaction, releasing negative emotions such as jealousy, anger, guilt, resentment and animosity. Promoting self-forgiveness and healthy self-love, it expedites profound change. Drawing together soul-companions, Eudialyte reveals the reason behind the reunion. If you meet an unwilling soulmate or are attracted to someone, but question whether a sexual relationship is appropriate or whether there is another purpose to the meeting, meditating with Eudialyte reveals the answer. Imbued with strong lifeforce, it aligns chakra flow to connect spirit and mind with the emotional body, bringing about profound reorientation. Eudialyte ends a relationship with graceful ease.

Ruby

Follow your bliss

A powerful shield against psychic attack and vampirism of heart energy, potent Ruby is an emotional protector. A warning stone, it darkens when danger or illness draws near. Ruby encourages passion for life and enhances a flagging libido. It imparts vigour, but may overstimulate sensitive or irritable people. Ruby improves motivation and sets realistic goals. This stone helps you to follow your bliss, promoting positive dreams and clear visualization. Attracting abundance, it facilitates retaining wealth. Ruby brings up anger or negative energy for transmutation and facilitates the removal of anything negative from your energy bodies or your path in life. ❶

Source: Greenland, Russia, Canada, Madagascar, USA

Vibration: High

Chakra: Earth star, base, heart. Aligns all

Physiology: Cellular and nervous systems, energy management, brainwaves, optic nerve, neurotransmitters

Cleansing: All

Source: India, Madagascar, Russia, Sri Lanka, Cambodia, Kenya, Mexico, Zimbabwe, Tanzania

Vibration: High

Chakra: Base, sacral, heart

Physiology: Immune system, energy management, detoxification, blood, lymph, heart, circulatory system, adrenals, kidneys, reproductive organs, spleen

Cleansing: All

Kammerite

Instant detox

Chlorite and chromium-based, Kammerite is an excellent cleanser and healer. It detoxifies on many levels, including the spiritual. Uniting heart, mind and spirit, the crystal helps you to be more open to alternative belief structures and to recognize truth. It clears negative emotions such as guilt, anger and fear that impede spiritual progress, and expands the mind to reach higher consciousness. Assisting with spirit and implant release, the crystal provides a bridge to the angelic realms or mentors in multidimensions. Combined with a grounding stone, it brings your Higher Self closer to your physical body.

Cobalto-calcite
(Roselite)

Love on a rock

Cobalto-calcite symbolizes unconditional love and forgiveness. Excellent for emotional healing, it soothes intense feelings and releases toxic emotional patterning and blockages, facilitating emotional maturation. The stone assists you to love yourself and others and to feel good about your life. Facilitating self-discovery, connecting heart with mind, this beautiful crystal harmonizes intellect with emotions. It facilitates the recognition of innate talents and life purpose. Supporting those who carry pain for other people, or for the planet, and ameliorating loneliness, Cobalto-calcite is excellent for distance healing. It helps you, or those you love, become all that you might be.

Source: Iceland, Greenland, Turkey, Scotland, India, Scandinavia

Vibration: High

Chakra: Higher heart, third eye, crown. Cleanses aura

Physiology: All organs and systems

Cleansing: Avoid water

Source: Democratic Republic of the Congo (Zaire), Morocco, Italy, Australia, USA

Vibration: High

Chakra: Heart

Physiology: Heart. *See* Calcite, pages 50–1

Cleansing: Avoid water

Rhodochrosite

Selfless love

Rhodochrosite encourages the spontaneous expression of feelings, including passionate and erotic urges. Removing denial, it teaches the heart to assimilate painful feelings without shutting down. Identifying ongoing relationship patterns, it reveals the purpose behind an experience. It is the stone par excellence for healing sexual abuse, and is wonderful for people who feel unloved. A powerful heart healer, it brings lightness into life. This compassionate stone lifts a depressed mood and imparts a dynamic attitude to life. It integrates spiritual with material energies. Rhodochrosite attracts a soulmate, but this may not be a blissful experience as soulmates assist with all forms of karmic lessons, even harsh ones.

Source: Argentina, Colorado (USA), South Africa, Russia, Uruguay

Vibration: Earthy and high

Chakra: Solar plexus, heart

Physiology: Reproductive, respiratory and circulatory systems, kidneys, eyes, blood pressure, heartbeat, thyroid

Cleansing: All

Mangano Calcite

Gentle forgiveness

A stone of forgiveness, Mangano Calcite offers unconditional love and acceptance, gently softening the hardest and most defended of hearts. Encouraging you to feel love for yourself, the compassionate energy dissolves resistance and releases ancient fears, grief and resentments that keep the heart trapped in the past. It brings repressed memories to the surface for healing. Mangano Calcite is helpful for anyone who has suffered trauma or assault in any timeframe, as it heals the inner child, drawing deep childlike happiness and joy into your life. The stone enhances self-worth and self-acceptance, lifting tension and anxiety. It heals nervous conditions and prevents nightmares.

Source: Brazil, Peru, Belgium, UK, Czech Republic, Slovakia, Iceland, Romania, USA

Vibration: High

Chakra: Three-chambered heart

Physiology: Heart. *See* Calcite, pages 50–1

Cleansing: All

Pink Muscovite

Reflection

Pink Muscovite acknowledges flaws in humanity without judging, offering unconditional love and acceptance. It mirrors back projections – parts of ourselves that we find unacceptable and push 'out there'. The crystal recognizes that things we do not like in another are really unacknowledged characteristics within ourselves. Muscovite transforms and integrates these qualities, finding the gift. It stimulates the heart chakra, opening intuition and psychic vision. The crystal ameliorates the effects of too rapid a psychic opening. Pink Muscovite releases tension within the physical and emotional bodies, aligning subtle bodies and meridians with the physical body, creating balance.

Tugtupite

Emotional intimacy

Tugtupite bridges heart and mind, anchoring unconditional love in the world. The stone facilitates emotional honesty and intimacy. If you have forgotten how to love, Tugtupite gently clears blockages, opening your heart and enfolding it in universal love. Love blossoms in your life. Tugtupite teaches the power of self-love, without which you cannot value yourself or another, give or receive love or know intimacy. Opening the three-chambered heart chakra, it instils passion and fertility. Tugtupite deepens relationships, so that love is expressed through every thought and deed. It sends unconditional love to the world and healing to war zones and sites of ethnic conflict.

Source: Switzerland, Russia, Austria, Czech Republic, Brazil, New Mexico (USA)

Vibration: High

Chakra: Heart

Physiology: Blood sugar, pancreatic secretions, fluid balance, kidneys

Cleansing: Avoid water and earth

Source: Greenland

Vibration: Exceedingly high

Chakra: Three-chambered heart

Physiology: Liver, blood, heart, metabolism and hormone production, blood pressure

Cleansing: Avoid water. Heat re-energizes

Pink Opal

Emotional healing

The gentle, yet high frequency of Pink Opal heals the emotional body and repairs its connection to the three-chambered heart chakra. An effective heart-healer, Pink Opal disperses wounds and anxiety and gently dissolves painful memories blocking the heart. This tranquil Opal suits highly sensitive people who need to approach crystal work slowly, letting go long-suppressed pain. It heals issues carried forward from past lives, replacing them with compassion for your Self. Dissipating stress, this is excellent for anyone who has lost the sweetness in life. It can help balance blood-sugar levels.

Morganite
(Pink Beryl)

Love-attractor

Morganite attracts unconditional love, encouraging loving thoughts and actions towards your Self and others. Assisting in becoming aware of disregarded needs of the soul, Morganite releases karmic emotional pain and facilitates recognizing unfulfilled emotional needs and unexpressed feelings. It dissolves conscious or unconscious resistance to healing, clearing victim mentality and opening the heart to receive unconditional love and healing. The stone holds the emotional body stable while psychosomatic changes take place, and creates a holding space for cellular and DNA changes to occur. It is helpful for soul retrieval, realigning energetic and physical bodies with the soul. ⓘ

Source: Peru

Vibration: Medium high

Chakra: Heart, higher heart, spleen, alta major

Physiology: Pancreas. *See* Opal, pages 54–5

Cleansing: Avoid water

Source: Brazil, Madagascar, Afghanistan, China, Mozambique, Namibia, Russia, Zimbabwe, USA

Vibration: Extremely high

Chakra: Three-chambered heart

Physiology: Heart, circulation, sexual organs, cellular structures, nervous system

Cleansing: All

Thulite

High heart Qi

Thulite explores the dualities of the human condition, combining love with logic. It encourages free expression of passion and sexual feelings. Teaching that lust, sensuality and sexuality are a perfectly normal part of life, it encourages the constructive expression of feelings. Thulite is strengthening and regenerating, helpful in cases of extreme weakness and nervous exhaustion. It strengthens libido, especially in women. Imbued with Qi, it stimulates healing and revitalizes the body. Use Thulite wherever there is resistance to be overcome. It brings out your extrovert qualities, encouraging curiosity and inventive problem-solving, and is excellent for actors.

Danburite

Emotional healer

Danburite facilitates emotional healing and fills the heart with unconditional, universal love. The crystal integrates the three-chambered heart chakra. It dissolves heartbreak, bringing inner peace and helping you live with love and acceptance. This crystal facilitates connection to the angelic realm and beyond. It draws enlightenment and spiritual light, instilling serenity and eternal wisdom. In meditation it takes you to a high state of consciousness and accesses inner guidance. Danburite is a karmic cleanser, perfect for accompanying the dying on their journey beyond death. Physically, it clears allergies and chronic conditions and has a strong detoxifying action.

Source: Greenland, USA, Norway, Austria

Vibration: High

Chakra: Three-chambered heart

Physiology: Calcium absorption, stomach, reproductive organs

Cleansing: Avoid water

Source: Japan, Madagascar, Mexico, USA, Myanmar (Burma)

Vibration: Extremely high

Chakra: Three-chambered heart, third eye, crown, soul star, stellar gateway

Physiology: Circulatory, muscular and motor systems

Cleansing: Avoid water

Sunstone

Vitality

Sunstone revitalizes the body and lifts dark moods.
If you have lost your enthusiasm for life, Sunstone
remotivates, facilitating self-empowerment and instilling
awareness of your own value. It dissolves co-dependency,
and supports independence. This highly energetic stone
overcomes procrastination, giving the impetus to move
forward. It detaches from feelings of being sabotaged
or discriminated against, encouraging optimism and
enthusiasm. The crystal acts as a spiritual compass and
heightens intuition. Removing hooks located in the
chakras or energy bodies, it is extremely beneficial for
tie-cutting with energy vampires or previous partners. ●

Yellow Kunzite

Self-containment

Yellow Kunzite connects the heart centre to the solar
plexus and mind, showing how feelings affect thoughts
and how those thoughts affect emotional wellbeing.
It overcomes depression, obsession and the urge to self-
harm. Clearing resistance, the crystal effects compromises
between personal needs and those of others, adjusting to
the pressure of life. It dispels attached entities and mental
influences from the energy bodies and chakras, and
protects against mental overwhelm and transgenerational
imperatives. Kunzite imparts the ability to be self-contained
within a crowd. Clearing environmental smog and
deflecting radiation and microwaves from the auric field,
Kunzite blocks geopathic stress. ●

Source: Australia, Canada, China, Congo, India,
Mexico, Norway, Russia, Sri Lanka, Tanzania, USA

Vibration: High to extremely high

Chakra: Base, sacral, solar plexus

Physiology: Cartilage, muscles, joints, immune and
autonomic nervous systems, all organs, throat

Cleansing: Avoid water

Source: USA, Madagascar, Brazil, Burma,
Afghanistan

Vibration: High

Chakra: Solar plexus, heart chakra, throat, third eye

Physiology: Immune, nervous and circulatory
systems; heart muscle, joints, brain chemistry, DNA,
cellular blueprint, calcium–magnesium balance

Cleansing: Avoid water

Tanzurine
(Emerald and Cherry Quartz)

Heart harmonizer

The two colours of Tanzurine complement each other and their soft energy harmonizes the heart and immune system. Tanzurine restores the rhythm of life, resetting physiological and subtle-energy systems. If polarity has been reversed, a pair of stones restores normality. They act on the electrical system of the heart, regulating it. A natural pacemaker, Tanzurine calms an over-active heartbeat and stimulates a sluggish one. The combination expands the heart chakra, creating a greater capacity for giving and receiving unconditional love. Tanzurine releases outdated ties and resentment and encourages speaking about hurts incurred. Once release has taken place, the stones stimulate forgiveness.

Watermelon Tourmaline

Super-activator

An activator for the heart chakra, opening the three-chambered heart chakra and connecting it to the Higher Self, Watermelon Tourmaline fosters love, tenderness and friendship and teaches tact and diplomacy. Gentle Watermelon Tourmaline creates inner security, alleviating depression and fear. Highlighting the inner dynamics of situations, this stone treats emotional dysfunction, releasing pain held anywhere in the subtle bodies. Facilitating the clear expression of intentions, it supports relationships and finds joy in situations. Watermelon Tourmaline dissolves any resistance to becoming whole once more. ❶

Source: Tanzania

Vibration: Earthy and high

Chakra: Higher heart

Physiology: Sleep patterns. *See* Quartz, pages 38–45

Cleansing: All

Source: Brazil, Sri Lanka, Tanzania, Nigeria, Kenya, Madagascar, Mozambique, Namibia, Afghanistan, Pakistan, Malawi

Vibration: High

Chakra: Three-chambered heart

Physiology: *See* Tourmaline, pages 56–7

Cleansing: Avoid water

Gaspeite

Spleen and liver protection

Gaspeite fortifies the heart and soul and grounds spiritual energy into the body. It assures you that, if help is needed, you only have to ask. Wear protective Gaspeite over the spleen chakra if you are vampirized by an energy pirate or undermined by a needy person. Place it under your right armpit for protection against another person's anger or resentment. Gaspeite assists when feeling resentful or bitter about life, especially hurtful or destructive actions. It dissolves anger, distress or pain and opens the higher heart chakra, bringing calm emotions. Gaspeite bridges emotional and physical levels of being and ameliorates psychosomatic effects.

Source: Canada, Australia

Vibration: Earthy

Chakra: Spleen, liver, heart, higher heart

Physiology: Liver, gall bladder

Cleansing: All

Green Kyanite

Heart consciousness

Green Kyanite is a tranquillizing crystal filled with universal love. The heart has its own intuitive intelligence and Green Kyanite creates energetic pathways to your deepest Self. It transfers information from the soma or third-eye chakras so that the heart assimilates and acts upon it. This crystal improves emotional balance, health and performance, relieving stress and distress. It discerns the truth of a matter and recognizes ulterior motives and hidden agendas. Physically, Green Kyanite restores the flow of Qi around the body. It also facilitates earth-healing and connects with nature spirits.

Source: Nepal, Pakistan, Austria, Brazil, India, Kenya, Russia, Serbia, Zimbabwe, USA

Vibration: Extremely high

Chakra: Gaia gateway, heart, higher heart, third eye, soma, alta major, causal vortex. Aligns all

Physiology: Heart, adrenals, throat, brain; immune, nervous and hormonal systems

Cleansing: Avoid water

Peridot

Cleansing power

Peridot teaches that holding onto people, or the past, is counter-productive. A powerful cleanser, Peridot neutralizes toxins on all levels, alleviating jealousy, resentment, spitefulness and anger. It enhances confidence and self-assertion without aggression. Peridot purifies the subtle and physical bodies and mind, releasing 'old baggage'. Looking back to the past to find the gift in your experiences, it shows how to forgive yourself and move on. Mistakes are acknowledged and learned from. Past-their-sell-by-date contracts, promises, burdens, guilt or obsessions are cleared, so that a new frequency is accessed. This visionary crystal helps you to understand your spiritual purpose.

Eye of the Storm

Calm centring

Eye of the Storm helps you to stay grounded and centred within the turbulence of the bigger picture. Showing where you have hyped-up problems, it offers a wider view. You remain in a calm, objective space beyond fear or panic. Reminding you that the bigger picture is fluid and ever-changing, depending on actions taken, Eye of the Storm reprogrammes a sense of lack into abundance. For people who feel that the world owes them a living, it shows the value of fair reward. For those with no sense of entitlement, it offers a fundamental sense of worth.

Source: USA, Hawaii, Brazil, Egypt, Ireland, Russia, Sri Lanka, Lanzarote

Vibration: Medium to high

Chakra: Heart, solar plexus

Physiology: Soft tissues, metabolism, skin, heart, thymus, lungs, gall bladder, spleen, intestinal tract, eyes

Cleansing: Avoid water

Source: Brazil

Vibration: Earthy and high

Chakra: All

Physiology: Blood pressure, adrenals, kidneys

Cleansing: All

Emerald

Successful love

Emerald brings domestic bliss and loyalty, enhancing unity and unconditional love. The stone keeps a partnership in balance. Colour change is said to signal unfaithfulness. Opening the heart chakra, it calms emotions. This life-affirming stone has great integrity. It ensures physical, emotional and mental equilibrium, eliminating negativity. Emerald gives the strength of character to overcome the misfortunes of life and inspires deep inner knowing, broadening vision. A wisdom stone, promoting discernment, truth and eloquent expression, it brings to the surface what is unconsciously known. Emerald is beneficial to mutual understanding within a group, stimulating cooperation. ❶

Malachite

Ultimate detoxification

Breaking outworn patterns and unwanted ties especially with energy vampires or previous partners, Malachite releases toxic emotions and inhibitions, encouraging free expression of feelings. It may induce a catharsis and require additional stones, such as Smoky Quartz, to calm the abreaction (the release of a previously repressed emotion). Malachite alleviates shyness and supports friendships. The stone strengthens the ability to process information, helping to understand difficult concepts. Malachite is a soul-cleanser. It attunes to angelic and spiritual guidance, and has a strong affinity with nature and devic forces. The stone facilitates scrying, or inner or outer journeying, as it enhances intuition and insight. ❶

Source: Colombia, Brazil, Zambia, Pakistan, Afghanistan, Russia, Australia, USA

Vibration: High

Chakra: Heart, higher heart

Physiology: Sinuses, lungs, heart, spine, muscles, eyes, liver, pancreas

Cleansing: All

Source: Russia, Democratic Republic of the Congo (Zaire), Australia, Namibia, South Africa, Germany, Romania, Chile, Mexico, USA

Vibration: Earthy and high

Chakra: Earth star, Gaia gateway, base, sacral, heart, solar plexus

Physiology: Joints, muscles, optic nerve, DNA, cellular structure, immune system, liver, pain receptors

Cleansing: All

Hiddenite
(Green Kunzite)

New beginnings

Hiddenite grounds spiritual love and support into the body. Gently releasing feelings of failure, it assists people who put on a brave face to receive comfort and support from others – and the universe. Facilitating transfer of knowledge from higher realms, it supports new beginnings and births the unknown. Aware of collective responsibility for the care of Earth, this crystal encourages growth and evolution. It expands spiritually, intellectually and emotionally. Hiddenite focuses on the present, relinquishing injustices of the past or anxieties for the future. It is helpful for overcoming obsessions or the urge to self-harm. ◑

Bowenite
('New Jade')

Fidelity

Protective Bowenite shields from enemies and destructive forces via the aura. Releasing blocked or repressed emotions, this stone is a powerful heart healer that stimulates kundalini rise. It provides psychic protection against ill-wishers and negative forces. Said to encourage fidelity and bond relationships, Bowenite connects to the Higher Self for guidance. Whenever you are stuck or have an intractable problem, it finds a solution through your dreaming mind. Place it under the pillow and ask for an insightful dream. Tell yourself that you will remember the solution when you wake.

Source: USA, Afghanistan, Pakistan

Vibration: Extremely high

Chakra: Higher heart, heart, third eye. Heals aura

Physiology: Heart, thymus, chest

Cleansing: Avoid water

Source: New Zealand, Pakistan, USA, Afghanistan, South Africa, China

Vibration: High

Chakra: Heart, higher heart, solar plexus, spleen

Physiology: Pancreas, head, scalp

Cleansing: All

Chrysoprase

Divine wholeness

Chrysoprase helps you to feel part of the divine whole. It promotes hope and offers personal insights. Encouraging fidelity in business and personal relationships, it draws out talents and stimulates creativity, bringing openness to new situations. Healing co-dependence, Chrysoprase supports independence while encouraging commitment. It reviews egotistical motives and the effect on personal development, aligning ideals with behaviour. Overcoming compulsive or impulsive thoughts and actions, it turns attention to positive events. Chrysoprase opposes judgementalism, stimulating acceptance of your Self and others. It assists forgiveness and compassion. Hold the stone to prevent speaking out unthinkingly in anger. It averts nightmares, especially among children.

Source: USA, Russia, Brazil, Australia, Poland, Tanzania

Vibration: Earthy

Chakra: Sacral

Physiology: Infertility, eyes, skin, heart, thyroid, hormonal balance, digestive system

Cleansing: Avoid water

Chrysocolla

Heartfelt communication

Facilitating verbal expression, Chrysocolla empowers both sexes to communicate in a clear, loving way. Gentle Chrysocolla transmutes negative energy, healing scars on the emotional body. It alleviates guilt and brings joy, easing judgementalism, especially of your own Self, and encourages compassion to all. Chrysocolla helps you to love yourself – vital if you are to accept love from others. An aid to meditation, it opens psychic vision and accepts with serenity changing situations, especially those over which you have no control. It encourages self-awareness and inner balance, invoking inner strength to speak your truth.

Source: Israel, Democratic Republic of the Congo (Zaire), Chile, England, Katanga, Mexico, Peru, Russia, New Mexico (USA)

Vibration: Earthy

Chakra: Sacral, solar plexus, heart, throat, third eye

Physiology: Metabolism, pancreas, thyroid, throat, female reproductive system, digestive tract, liver, kidneys, intestines, bones, blood

Cleansing: Avoid water, unless tumbled

Hemimorphite

Personal responsibility

Hemimorphite facilitates self-development in the fastest way possible. It teaches how to take personal responsibility for your own happiness or dis-ease, showing how reality is created through thoughts and attitudes you hold. The stone indicates where you fall under outside influences that are not in accord with your soul-view, and where you carry outdated soul contracts that require reframing. Developing inner strength, Hemimorphite manifests your highest potential. A protective stone, particularly against malicious thoughts, Hemimorphite raises the body's vibrations and facilitates communication with the highest spiritual levels. It reframes the past and releases noxious emotions.

K2 Stone

As above, so below

K2 grounds, centres and rebalances, giving more control over your emotions and mind. It facilitates sharing with others at the deepest level, understanding their point of view – although not necessarily adopting it. K2 promotes group harmony and working together to attain a goal. This stone of peace and reconciliation, inner and outer, heals personal or collective conflict. It teaches that peace in the world can only be attained when there is peace in your own heart. K2 accesses the Akashic Record and facilitates soul retrieval and past-life readings. It clears psychic blockages and prohibitions and obsessive compulsive disorder (OCD).

Source: England, Mexico, USA, Zambia

Vibration: High

Chakra: Higher heart

Physiology: Blood, heart, cellular structures

Cleansing: Brown rice, sound, essences

Source: Karakoram Range (Pakistan)

Vibration: Earthy and extremely high

Chakra: All

Physiology: Head, pain receptors, bones

Cleansing: All

Crystals
for the mind

Over-thinking, too much mind-chatter, closed-mindedness, limiting beliefs and mental control by others all lead to dis-ease – as does the strong, but largely unrecognized, effect on the mind of emotions such as excessive worry and shame. Fortunately crystals quickly switch off the chattering mind, clarifying thought and embracing the dynamic mindfulness of the present moment, rather than obsessively worrying about past or future. They enhance mental function at all levels, reprogramming thought patterns where appropriate, assisting memory and bringing brain hemispheres back into balance.

Communication and the mental chakras

Although it could be assumed that the mentally orientated chakras are those in the head, such as the third eye, crown and alta major, good communication and clear thinking actually depend on connections being established between those chakras and the throat, heart and solar plexus energy centres, plus your Higher Self (*see* page 159). 'Clear thinking' means having an independent mind that is capable of weighing up evidence, seeing all sides of an issue and coming to an informed opinion based on what currently is, rather than the past or an imagined future. It does not mean slavishly following what you are told is right or being influenced by repressed fears and unacknowledged emotions. If you are attuned to your Higher Self, you automatically harmonize your heart and soul into a congruent whole. You communicate from your centre, unaffected by what others think, as you have no need of their approval. Fortunately crystals can have a profound effect on your mind, releasing mental and emotional influences on how you think and feel.

Addiction

Addiction takes two forms. The physical, in which the body becomes biologically dependent on a substance or act, and the psychological, in which the mind compulsively uses a substance or action to quell underlying stress, emotions such as shame or a sense of inferiority, or traumatic memories. Crystals assist in breaking the cycle of dependency, facilitating stress release and instant mindfulness. Mindfulness means being aware in the moment, focused on the present, not somewhere back in the past or projected into the future. It's not mindlessness, which acts by rote, or meditation, but rather a dynamic, yet soft attentiveness. It's about living each moment in your daily life to the full, and then flowing onto the next.

Exercise

Taking time out

Crystal mindfulness only takes a few moments, but makes an enormous difference to your life.

Suitable crystals: Anything banded, such as Banded Agate; or calming, such as Amethyst, Auralite 23, Amazez, Eye of the Storm, Selenite.

1   Keep a suitable calming crystal in your pocket.
2   Every so often, especially when stressed, take it out, hold it close to your eyes and focus on it until it fills your mind.
3   Breathe deeply and slowly ten times, making the out-breath longer than the in-breath.
4   Return the crystal to your pocket.

OPPOSITE Gazing into a crystal such as
Amethyst or Auralite 23 quickly encourages
a state of mindfulness.

Calming the mind

It is easy for the mind to get stuck in a loop. The same old thoughts go round and round, following outdated beliefs imprinted into your mental conditioning by authority figures in this or any other lifetime. The continuous Vesica Piscis layout harmonizes all parts of the brain, calming the mind and synchronizing activity of the hemispheres. It dissolves all the 'oughts and shoulds' with which you have been programmed, facilitating the speaking of truth from your centre and soul.

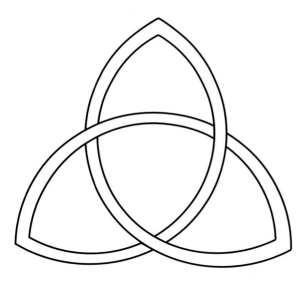

Exercise

Dissolving ingrained patterns and limiting beliefs

Suitable crystals: Amazez, Auralite 23, Prairie Tanzanite or Blue Lace Agate. *See also* the crystal portraits on pages 68–307.

Prairie Tanzanite grid

1 Lie down comfortably where you will not be disturbed.
2 Place a suitable mental harmonizing or belief-releasing crystal on the crown chakra above the head.
3 Lay two crystals just above ears.
4 Place a communication crystal on the throat.
5 Lay two crystals either side of throat on top of the shoulders.
6 Trace the continuous Vesica Piscis symbol, using a wand or the power of your mind to join up the crystals.
7 Breathe gently and evenly, feeling the crystals, harmonizing your brainwaves and releasing limiting beliefs and ingrained thought patterns.
8 Lie still for 5 to 15 minutes, allowing the crystals to do their work and attune you to your inner truth.
9 Gather up the crystals and thank them for their work.
10 Stand up slowly and stamp your feet.

ABOVE LEFT A continuous Vesica Piscis grid.

OPPOSITE Laying crystals around your head clarifies the mind.

Dissolving a thought form

Thought forms may appear to be solid and 'real' and yet have no actual substance. But they have a profound effect on how you function mentally. Typical thought forms are the critic, the saboteur and the perfectionist. Created by powerfully negative or controlling mental input, thought forms may be the product of your own mind or arise from other people's expectations or authoritarian dictates. They lodge themselves in the mental subtle body as an internal thought form or lurk in the ancestral or past-life subtle bodies. Internal thought forms are usually experienced as a derogatory inner voice or obsessive thoughts. They emanate subtle feelings of disapproval or command. External thought forms inhabit the lower astral realms close to Earth, and may speak as an inner voice, although often appearing as separate entities such as guides or metaphysical communicators.

How to recognize a thought form

- A nagging voice gives negative messages such as 'that's a bad thing to do', 'you're not good enough', 'it's all your fault', 'you'll never be/get what you want', 'you don't deserve', 'you're too clever for your own good'.
- It feels subtly wrong.
- It may resemble someone you know, especially if they have passed on.
- It has little substance or resonance to it.
- The 'guidance' is fallible and may be malicious.
- It seems to be stuck in a loop.

Clearing thought forms

To remove an external thought form, dedicate a large thought-form dissolving crystal such as Iolite and leave it in a room to do its work. Internal thought forms tend to be stored in the third-eye chakra or just behind the ears. Use a Selenite wand to detach them or place a thought-form dissolving crystal over the site. Aegerine is excellent for mental obsession if you can't get someone or something out of your mind. Place it under the pillow at night. Remember to cleanse the crystal frequently.

LEFT Aegirine
ABOVE Iolite

ABOVE **Place an appropriate crystal (this one is Labradorite) over your third eye to dissolve thought forms or mental imperatives.**

Amethyst

Addiction-breaker

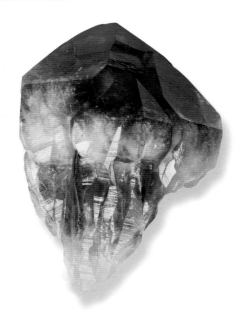

Source: Worldwide

Vibration: High to extremely high

Chakra: All, depending on type

Physiology: All, depending on type, cells, hormonal and immune system, intestines

Cleansing: All

Stilling the mind, Amethyst takes it to a mindful space.

Characteristics

Amethyst heals subtle dis-ease. Stilling the mind, it takes it to a mindful space. An excellent stress reliever, Amethyst enhances memory and decision-making and improves motivation. Relieving the compulsions, obsessions and neediness that underlie addictions, it dispels anger, fear, rage and anxiety and comforts grief. Protective Amethyst guards against psychic attack, enhances higher states of consciousness and facilitates meditation and spiritual awareness. Repelling negative energies of all kinds, it screens out EMF smog or geopathic stress.

Chevron Amethyst

Amethyst and White Quartz creating a V-shaped or banded pattern, Chevron Amethyst assists you to look deep inside yourself. Gently releasing resistance to opening up, it is profoundly metaphysical. Excellent for the third eye, it enhances physical and intuitive vision and accesses multidimensions of consciousness. Gazing into its bands facilitates journeying out of the body. The bands create a powerful healing field around the user, cleansing and repairing auric bodies. Chevron Amethyst harmonizes the energies of the autonomic and sympathetic nervous systems.

Smoky Amethyst

Smoky Quartz with Amethyst grounds spiritual energy into the body and contacts the highest possible spiritual energies. Clearing negative energies and entity attachment, especially at the third eye, it calls in beneficial influences. Smoky Amethyst protects against psychic attack and alien invasion, and disconnects those who are intertwined at the higher spiritual chakras. It amplifies and directs sound-healing.

Vera Cruz Amethyst

With extremely high vibrations, delicate Vera Cruz Amethyst instantly takes you into a beta brainwave state, facilitating meditation and shamanic journeying. This beautiful Amethyst awakens spirituality and transformation. Activating the positive potential of junk DNA and epigenetics, it facilitates deep soul memories rising into conscious awareness for release.

MAIN Amethyst point
RIGHT Chevron Amethyst
FAR RIGHT Vera Cruz Amethyst or matrix

Crystal Cap

With exceptionally high vibrations, Crystal Cap connects to expanded consciousness and multidimensional realms, retaining full awareness of all you experience during journeying. Taking you to dimensions not as firmly corporeal as our present reality, it connects to Lemuria (an ancient civilization now lost) and lives beyond the stars, bringing back wisdom and skills developed there. Working from the etheric blueprint to the physical, Crystal Cap heals dis-eases of the soul and subtle causes of addictions, eating or brain-based 'dis-orders'. It harmonizes brain hemispheres, encouraging integration and equilibrium, and activating neurotransmitters and fresh neural pathways.

Amethyst Elestial

An extremely powerful healer, protective Amethyst Elestial stimulates the pineal gland. Activating the highest chakras, it opens a connection to interplanetary beings, guides and mentors. Dispersing negative energy, it provides calm reassurance and stress reduction. Assisting multidimensional cellular healing and integrating brainwaves, Amethyst Elestial ameliorates the effects of drugs or alcohol.

See also Auralite 23 (*see* pages 134–5), Amazez™ (*see* page 149) and Brandberg Amethyst (*see* pages 218–21).

FAR LEFT Prasiotrine (Green Amethyst)
LEFT Smoky Amethyst Elestial Quartz
ABOVE Crystal Cap Amethyst
RIGHT Twin Brandberg Amethyst Elestial

Amethyst Herkimer

An Amethyst Herkimer is a rare crystal with wonderfully refined vibrations that induce clarity of mind and spirit. Place on the third eye to induce spiritual visions, and above the head to open the high-vibration chakras and assimilate cosmic energy.

Amethyst repels negative energies of all kinds.

LEFT Amethyst Herkimer
BELOW Amethyst Geode

Auralite 23

Ultimate mind-clearer

Source: Canada

Vibration: Extremely high

Chakra: Throat, third eye, soma, past life, causal vortex, alta major, soul star, stellar gateway. Balances all

Physiology: Brain and brain chemistry, DNA, cleanses and aligns all organs and energy bodies

Cleansing: All

Auralite 23 offers space to breathe and relax.

Characteristics

Auralite 23 shuts down the constant mind-chatter that so plagues people, taking you into a place of perfect serenity, especially if racing thoughts prevent you sleeping. It synchronizes brain hemispheres and creates conscious connection with higher dimensions. This synergistic crystal deepens meditation and enhances metaphysical abilities. It offers space to breathe and relax, enjoying inner solitude and experiencing profound stillness. Its gently soothing waves of energy remove stress and encourage you to put down burdens. If you need to plan a course of action, effortlessly switching off the ticking clock of time, Auralite 23 utilizes what you know to begin the process and then let go and stop worrying. Call on this crystal for comfort and to maintain your cool during times of shock or distress.

Generic properties

A layout or grid of Auralite 23 cleanses and balances the chakras and accelerates spiritual development. Smoky Quartz and Hematite components of the crystal ground the energies into the body and planet. A deep soul-cleanser, it facilitates remembrance of past lives, stimulating the insights needed to release karmic patterns and heal the relevant etheric blueprint (the subtle-energetic grid from which the physical body develops and is maintained).

MAIN Aurelite 23 point
LEFT Aurelite 23 slice
RIGHT Aurelite 23
BELOW LEFT Aurelite 23 point
BELOW RIGHT Hematite-coated Aurelite 23 point

Chinese Writing Stone

Reaffirmation

A crystal of recommitment, Chinese Writing Stone realigns your goals towards a higher purpose and reaffirms relationships and loyalties, while adjusting to any changes required. The stone accesses the Akashic Record to read the purpose for the present incarnation and facilitates taking responsibility for choices made. It opens up creativity and guides towards the most productive way to express this. Excellent if you suffer from writer's block, Writing Stone counteracts sloppiness. It unlocks the dreaming mind. Use it to guide your dreams – and to bring your dreams into everyday reality.

Snowflake Obsidian

Emergence

Snowflake Obsidian gently surfaces toxic emotions, detrimental thought patterns and traumatic memories. Revealing destructive life patterns, it reframes them in a more beneficial way. It also surfaces unexpectedly positive secrets. This serene stone provides balance during times of stress and change, and shields against negativity. In past-life work, Snowflake Obsidian heals ingrained karmic patterns and reveals sources of harmful thought patterns. It teaches you to be receptive and value mistakes as well as successes, showing the gift in each. Snowflake Obsidian turns loneliness into at-oneness.

Source: China, California

Vibration: Earthy

Chakra: Base, earth star, alta major, causal vortex, past life

Physiology: Eyes, spine, muscles, legs

Cleansing: All

Source: USA

Vibration: Earthy

Chakra: Base, sacral

Physiology: Veins, skeleton, circulation, skin, eyes, joints

Cleansing: All

Pinolith

Soothing

A mix of Magnetite and Dolomite, Pinolith is a stress-reliever that eases feelings of hurt, loneliness, sorrow or anxiety. Instilling an optimistic approach to life, it reminds you that all life is a spiritual experience. It overcomes petulance, bigotry and narrow-mindedness. Detoxifying mind and body, Pinolith places unconditional love into circumstances where a partner faces issues such as addiction, reminding you not to become an enabler. It opens the heart chakra to loving yourself and wholeheartedly loving another, while setting boundaries. Bringing peace of mind, Pinolith stimulates visualization and creativity. ◑

Nellite
(Honey Stone)

Bridging

Combining Pietersite and Blue-gold Tiger's Eye, Nellite is found at the joining point of the two. It bridges two realities. As with all stones that occupy liminal space, it assists shamanic journeying, facilitating psychic visions and connecting to spiritual guidance. The stone suggests a new direction when the way forward is blocked, sliding around obstacles. It helps you to live from your truth without compromise and supports you if you feel isolated as a result. A stone of insight, it recognizes what motivates others and accepts them without judgement. ◑

Source: Austria

Vibration: Medium

Chakra: Earth star, base, sacral, heart

Physiology: Detoxification, teeth, bones, magnesium assimilation, cells, muscles, vascular system, stomach, intestines, gall bladder, kidneys

Cleansing: All

Source: Namibia, South Africa

Vibration: Medium

Chakra: Third eye, soma, alta major

Physiology: *See* Pietersite, page 225, and Tiger's Eye, page 199

Cleansing: All

Nunderite

Memory

Supporting memory and truthful recall, Nunderite facilitates all healing processes and clarifies the mind. Grounding and calming, it supports during times of change and necessary upheaval, adjusting to the result. Perceptive Nunderite helps you to view yourself, your characteristics and energy bodies objectively. Dissolving emotions such as sorrow and sadness, it alleviates self-pity, installing spiritual awareness of the higher purpose of events instead. The stone encourages joining like-minded groups. Nunderite facilitates remote viewing, making you invisible during the process, and keeping your secrets safe from prying eyes.

Plume Agate

Focus

Plume Agate facilitates creative visualization, clarifying exactly what you want and creating a potent image that actualizes goals. A stone of focus, it assists job-hunting or uncovering hidden agendas. Plume Agate encourages staying focused in the present reality and thinking pragmatically. It facilitates making important decisions and acting on them. A stone of truth, Plume Agate encourages self-analysis and confidence. It is a record keeper for environments rather than an individual, giving access to the wider past. Plume Agate overcomes fear and anxiety, providing stress relief.

Source: New South Wales (Australia)

Vibration: Medium

Chakra: Throat, third eye, soma, crown

Physiology: Brain, nervous system

Cleansing: All

Source: USA

Vibration: High

Chakra: Third eye, soma, alta major

Physiology: Blood vessels. *See Agate, pages 46–7*

Cleansing: All

Triplite

'Frenemy'-detector

Overcoming energetic depletion and kick-starting creativity, Triplite boosts the flow of kundalini and Qi, integrating it at physical, emotional, mental and etheric levels. It helps face situations calmly, finding solutions and applying them resolutely. Triplite assists you to manifest whatever you most need for your spiritual development. On the dantien, it repels invasive energies and identifies frenemies (inner or outer) – the person who is friend to your face and yet criticizes or sabotages you behind your back is revealed, so that you resolve the situation with grace, parting if appropriate.

Zircon

Virtue

Overcoming prejudice, Zircon teaches the brotherhood of humanity and clears the effects of discrimination from the emotional body. Enhancing clear thinking, it separates the significant from the insignificant. Zircon promotes constancy and removes negative attitudes such as jealousy, possessiveness, victimization, homophobia, misogyny or racism. A stone of union, it instils stamina and tenacity. Traditionally, Zircon protects against robbery, lightning, bodily harm and disease. It tests celibacy. Promoting unconditional love and letting go of previous partners, Zircon harmonizes the spiritual nature with the environment. It brings all systems of the physical and subtle bodies into alignment. ●

Source: Pakistan, USA, Germany, Finland, Namibia

Vibration: High

Chakra: Base, sacral, solar plexus, heart, dantien

Physiology: Metabolic function regulator, circulatory system, liver, spleen, blood pressure, physiological processes, bone development, soft-tissue repair and assimilation of minerals

Cleansing: All

Source: Sri Lanka, Cambodia, Myanmar (Burma), Vietnam, Australia, Nigeria, Madagascar, Canada, Ukraine

Vibration: High

Chakra: All, according to colour

Physiology: Bones, muscles, liver, female reproductive system (may cause dizziness in pacemaker wearers or epileptics – if so, remove immediately)

Cleansing: All

Lithium Quartz

Perfect equilibrium

A balancing crystal that returns you to perfect equilibrium, Lithium Quartz is a natural antidepressant. It gently reaches back into past lives to dissolve roots of emotional or mental dis-ease pervading the present life. Reprogramming the subconscious mind, it releases ancient anger and grief. Giving comfort to the dying and those who are bereaved, Lithium Quartz brings awareness that death is part of an ongoing natural cycle. It facilitates smooth transition, particularly from a terminal illness. Said to resonate with every note on the musical scale, it enhances sound-healing.

Porcelain Jasper
(Exotic Jasper)

Peace

Porcelain Jasper is extremely calming, encouraging persistence and inner peace. Excellent for the emotional and mental etheric bodies, it cleanses wounds and reintegrates universal love into the subtle bodies. Slow-acting, it encourages the healthy regeneration of tissue. Porcelain Jasper grounds to earth, forming a shield around the whole body that blocks negative energy invasion, EMFs and pathogens. It gently unblocks the heart chakra and activates the heart seed. Clearing karmic debris, toxic emotions and ingrained mental patterning, it protects against worry and stress. Porcelain Jasper stimulates appropriate responsibility in relationships.

Source: Worldwide

Vibration: High

Chakra: Past lives, crown, causal vortex, alta major

Physiology: *See* Quartz, pages 38–45

Cleansing: All

Source: Sonora Mountain (Mexico)

Vibration: Earthy

Chakra: Heart, heart seed, solar plexus

Physiology: Heart, soft tissue, spleen, abdominal organs, kidneys, gall bladder, liver, digestive tract, veins, arteries, female reproductive organs

Cleansing: All

Orange Kyanite

Creative activator

This vibrant Kyanite grounds plans so that they actually get carried out. Orange Kyanite delves deeply into your psyche to identify and release causal connections behind mental karmic blockages. It activates your passions and your pleasures. The stone stimulates creativity, bringing success to all creative endeavours. Orange Kyanite reverses low self-esteem and feelings of inferiority that lie behind cruelty, pomposity, jealousy or apathy. Infertility or sluggishness may indicate that hooks from other people, especially from sexual encounters, are blocking the sacral chakra. Orange Kyanite heals the site.   ❶

Septarian
(Dragon Stone)

Public speaker

Harmonizing mind and emotions, Septarian assists public speaking. It instils confidence and clarity, holding an audience with the power of words. Releasing outdated mental patterns and mores, it instils new behaviours and beliefs. The stone increases creativity, facilitating feeling more in control of your life. Correcting mental and emotional imbalance, it deepens meditation and spiritual exploration, opening new pathways for kundalini energy to rise. Septarian facilitates memories of former lives. It connects to elemental dragon energy.

Source: Tanzania

Vibration: Extremely high

Chakra: Earth star, base, sacral, past life

Physiology: Brain, cerebellum, throat, adrenal glands, uro-genital system, liver, blood pressure, motor function

Cleansing: All

Source: Madagascar, USA

Vibration: Earthy and high

Chakra: Earth star, base, heart, throat, third eye

Physiology: Immune system, joints, intestines, nervous system, pancreas

Cleansing: All

Golden Danburite
(Agni Gold™)

Universal-mind connector

Golden Danburite connects to the universal mind, opening your heart to the highest guidance. It facilitates deep karmic soul-healing, releasing outdated soul imperatives and emotions that prevent your soul living its plan for the current lifetime. Releasing miasms (predisposition to a disease) and intellectual imprints carried forward, this stone dissolves mental hooks located in the subtle bodies. It accesses the soulplan for the current lifetime and points the soul in a new direction. Assisting allergies and chronic conditions, its strong detoxifying action works best at the psychosomatic level of healing.

Green Calcite

Mental cleanser

Dissolving rigid beliefs and outdated mental programming, Green Calcite restores balance and clarity to the mind. It lets go the familiar and comforting that are outgrown and which no longer serve. The stone facilitates communication on all levels and helps children to hold their own in debates. A powerful stimulator for the immune system, it rapidly absorbs negativity and rids the body of bacterial infections. Green Calcite soothes nausea, pain and inflammation. It increases fertility and attracts abundance – drawing prosperity into a home. It is useful in grids, but cleanse it frequently.

Source: USA, Mexico, Myanmar (Burma), Russia, Madagascar

Vibration: Extremely high

Chakra: Third eye, crown, higher crown

Physiology: Brain function, liver, gall bladder, muscular and motor function

Cleansing: Avoid water

Source: Worldwide

Vibration: Earthy to high

Chakra: Dantien, navel, solar plexus, spleen

Physiology: Stomach. *See* Calcite, pages 50–1

Cleansing: All

Infinite Stone

Stress release

Infinite Stone releases physical, emotional and mental stress and is a great 'worry stone'. Alleviating negative thoughts and expectations, and helpful for those who continually seek praise and approval, it removes survival-based blockages from lower chakras and boosts self-esteem. Healing loss, grief, separation and betrayal, it connects to angelic realms for comfort and guidance. Accessing and integrating past, present and future, Infinite Stone facilitates other exploration, promoting compassion for your Self. The stone takes you into the interlife to complete healing that was not undertaken after a former life. Place under the pillow for restful sleep.

Source: South Africa

Vibration: High

Chakra: Past life, causal vortex, base, sacral, solar plexus, heart

Physiology: Joints, muscles, connective tissue, immune system

Cleansing: All

Fluorite

Organizer

Excellent for processing information so that the mind becomes sharper, Fluorite overcomes any disorganization or stress, physical or mental. It improves coordination and counteracts mental disorders. No matter which colour, this stone dissolves fixed ideas and illusions and reveals the truth behind a situation. Helpful when you need to act objectively, it gives you inner strength and stability to withstand internal or external influences and pressure. Fluorite cleanses and stabilizes the aura, grounding and integrating spiritual energies. It heightens intuitive powers and enhances trance states. ❶

Source: Worldwide

Vibration: Medium to high

Chakra: Heart, higher heart, third eye, soma, alta major

Physiology: Brain, joints, bones, teeth, muscles and acts as an anti-inflammatory

Cleansing: Avoid water

Indicolite and Blue Quartz

Spiritual clarity

Stimulating spiritual freedom and self-expression, Indicolite is Blue Tourmaline, often included in Quartz. Inspiring hope, Blue Quartz calms the mind, assuages fear and facilitates understanding your spiritual nature. It reaches out to like-minded others. Overcoming mental disorganization, Indicolite instils clarity and self-discipline and fires creativity. Indicolite Quartz stimulates out-of-body-experiences and facilitates journeys through multidimensional consciousness. Offering an overview of your lives, it indicates why you have chosen to incarnate again. Encouraging those who constantly give to learn to receive, it supports fidelity, ethical behaviour, tolerance and a love of truth. ◑

Lapis Lazuli

Heaven on earth

Lapis Lazuli is a powerful stress releaser. It encourages self-expression and taking charge of your own life, facilitating self-awareness so that you see the bigger picture. Lapis Lazuli brings objectivity and clarity to the mind and teaches the value of active listening. A stone of deep spiritual insight, it stimulates psychic abilities and clairvoyance, and facilitates spiritual journeying to contact spirit guardians and mentors. The stone blocks psychic attack. Placing it on psychic or past-life chakras reverses curses and clears dis-ease caused by not speaking out in the past. ◑

Source: Brazil, Sri Lanka, USA, Bulgaria, Madagascar, Nigeria, Mozambique

Vibration: High

Chakra: Third eye, past life, crown

Physiology: *See* Quartz, pages 38–45, and Tourmaline, pages 56–7

Cleansing: All

Source: Afghanistan

Vibration: Extremely high

Chakra: Throat, third eye, soma, crown, past life, alta major, causal vortex

Physiology: Immune system, respiratory and nervous systems, throat, larynx, thyroid, ears, internal organs, bone marrow, blood

Cleansing: All

Apatite

Interface between consciousness and matter

A stone of manifestation attuned to the future and yet connecting to past lives, Apatite balances the physical and subtle-energy bodies and overcomes nervous exhaustion. The stone develops your psychic abilities and enhances spiritual development. Apatite deepens meditative states and raises kundalini energy. Clearing blockages in the base chakra, Apatite ameliorates frustration and supports expressing passion without guilt. Encouraging a humanitarian attitude and dispelling apathy, it induces openness and social ease, dissolving aloofness and alienation. Drawing off negativity about yourself and others, it calms hyperactive and autistic children.

Azurite

Third-eye activator

Azurite accelerates psychic development, raising consciousness to the highest level and deepening meditative states. Challenging your view of reality, it facilitates safe journeys out of the body, releasing limiting belief systems so that you move through the unknown without fear. This stone understands the effect of mind on the body, and amplifies energy flow through the nervous system. Excellent for mental processes, Azurite assists anyone who talks too much out of nervousness. Clearing emotional debris and ancient fears, it cleanses the emotional body and creates inner peace. The stone facilitates deep multidimensional intercellular reprogramming. ●

Source: Canada, USA, Mexico, Norway, Russia, Brazil

Vibration: High

Chakra: Third eye, base

Physiology: Energy system, bones, cells, calcium absorption, cartilage, teeth, joints, rickets, metabolic rate, glands, meridians, organs, hypertension

Cleansing: Avoid water unless tumbled

Source: USA, Australia, Chile, Peru, France, Namibia, Russia, Egypt, Italy, Germany

Vibration: High

Chakra: Third eye, soma

Physiology: Memory, brain structure, detoxification, throat, joint, spine, kidney, gall bladder, spleen, liver, thyroid, bones, teeth, skin, embryonic development. If palpitations occur, remove immediately

Cleansing: All

Blue Topaz

Writer's friend

Excellent for written communication and expressing yourself more fully, Blue Topaz enhances mental abilities, encouraging clear thought and focused concentration. Helpful for public speaking, it clears the throat and third-eye chakras. If you need to make decisions about matters in your life, such as the ideal job or how to implement your lifepath, meditate with Blue Topaz. It connects to the angels of truth and wisdom, facilitating living according to your own aspirations and recognizing whether you have strayed from your truth. If so, Blue Topaz gently assists you to let go of limiting beliefs embracing spiritual independence. ●

Sapphire

Wisdom

According to a medieval lapidary, Sapphire is a cure for 'foulness and envy', comforting the body and limbs and breaking bonds of witchcraft. A seeker after spiritual truth associated with love and purity, Sapphire is the wisdom stone. Releasing unwanted thoughts and mental tension, it keeps you on the spiritual path. Creating serene peace of mind, Sapphire aligns physical, mental and spiritual planes and restores balance within the energy body. It ameliorates depression and confusion and assists concentration. Raw Sapphire is effective for Earth and chakra healing. ●

Source: India, Pakistan, Sri Lanka, South Africa, Japan, Australia, Mexico, USA

Vibration: High

Chakra: Third eye, throat

Physiology: Eyes, throat

Cleansing: All

Source: Myanmar (Burma), Czech Republic, Slovakia, Brazil, Kenya, India, Australia, Sri Lanka

Vibration: High

Chakra: Throat, higher heart

Physiology: Body systems, glands, eyes, blood, veins

Cleansing: All

Sodalite

Mental integration

Healing a disordered mind, restoring normal functioning of intuitive perception and encouraging rational thought, Sodalite facilitates reception and integration of new information. It releases control mechanisms that are holding you back from being who you truly are, enhancing self-esteem, self-acceptance and self-trust. Uniting logic with intuition, it opens spiritual inner-sight, bringing information from the higher mind to the physical level. It stimulates the third eye and deepens meditative states. Sodalite relieves the symptoms of dyslexia and dyspraxia. Bringing emotional balance, it calms panic attacks. The stone creates harmony in group work. ●

Sunset Sodalite

Positive solutions

Combining Sodalite and Feldspar, Sunset Sodalite finds positive solutions to problems. This creative stone stimulates the mind and connects it to Source energy, a universal or divine energy that permeates the whole cosmos and everything in it, so that creative ideas flow with ease. Easing writer's block, it supports academics, students and teachers, disclosing the hidden significance behind what is learned or experienced. This crystal builds confidence and self-esteem. A stone of honesty, it links the throat to the solar plexus so that emotions are expressed with ease. Sunset Sodalite enhances, strengthens and expands spiritual awareness and psychic gifts, opening a connection to cosmic consciousness, which it grounds on the earth-plane. ●

Source: Brazil, Italy, Greenland, British Columbia (Canada), Portugal, Romania, Myanmar (Burma), Russia

Vibration: High

Chakra: Throat, third eye

Physiology: Metabolism, lymphatic system, internal organs, immune system, throat, digestive system

Cleansing: All

Source: Brazil

Vibration: High

Chakra: Throat, solar plexus, third eye, crown

Physiology: Metabolism, lymphatic system, internal organs, immune system, throat, digestive system

Cleansing: All

Blue Calcite

Stilling mind-chatter

A communication enhancer, soothing Blue Calcite clarifies the mind, quietening mental chatter and lifting thoughts to a higher vibration to accelerate spiritual maturation. Excellent for opening psychic gifts, the crystal assists clear communication of thoughts and feelings, especially hurt or dissent. Blue Calcite filters negative energy, transmutes it and returns it to benefit the sender and receiver. This gentle stone assists recuperation and relaxation. Soothing nerves and lifting anxieties, it releases noxious emotions and facilitates adapting to necessary change. The crystal lowers blood pressure and dissolves pain.

Source: Mexico

Vibration: High

Chakra: Throat, third eye

Physiology: Eyes, throat. See Calcite, pages 50–1

Cleansing: Avoid water

Blue Chalcedony

Speaker's aid

Opening the mind to assimilate new ideas, Blue Chalcedony stimulates learning new languages. It improves memory, encouraging mental flexibility and enhancing verbal dexterity and listening skills. Measuring your words before you speak, it facilitates holding back what you may later regret. The stone encourages reflection and imparts the ability to look forward optimistically, facilitating acceptance of change and improving self-perception. Excellent for clearing illnesses associated with weather and pressure changes, it wards off psychic attack and protects during political unrest. Useful for the eyes, it promotes inner-sight and insight.

Source: USA, Austria, Czech Republic, Slovakia, Iceland, Mexico, England, New Zealand, Turkey, Russia, Brazil, Morocco

Vibration: High

Chakra: Throat, third eye, soma

Physiology: Mucous membranes, eyes, immune and lymphatic systems, blood pressure

Cleansing: All

Blue John

Storage facility

A wisdom stone, Blue John absorbs information from the environment, acting as a storage facility. It accelerates learning and uses precise, focused energy to find solutions where this seems impossible. It brings organization to the mind and stabilizes mental health. Blue John cuts through clutter and negativity, sharpening perception and integrating what has already been learned with what is being acquired. Bringing structure to the inner and outer life, Blue John recognizes where outdated behaviour patterns must change and where something formerly held as absolute truth needs to evolve into something higher.

Source: Derbyshire (England)

Vibration: High

Chakra: Third eye, soma, crown

Physiology: Respiratory system, fluid balance, bones, brain. *See* Fluorite, page 143

Cleansing: Avoid water

Amazez™

Interconnection

Peaceful Amazez™ raises vibrations and strengthens the aura, releasing residual stuck energy. It facilitates out-of-body and multidimensional journeys, offering protection and guidance and opening metaphysical abilities. It celebrates individual uniqueness and promotes unity, encouraging inter-dependency and cooperation at the highest level, helping you to step out of the small Self. However, Amazez ensures that you do not lose yourself in another. Excellent for anyone engaged in dispassionate service, at core soul level it asks, 'What meets your deepest need?' Amazez releases communication blocks while quietening the chattering mind.

Source: Madagascar

Vibration: Exceedingly high

Chakra: Causal vortex, alta major, knee

Physiology: Ears, eyes, bone density, digestion, teeth, calcium balance

Cleansing: All

Ametrine

Spiritual clarity

Connecting the physical realm with higher consciousness, Ametrine stimulates creativity and supports taking control of life. It imbues mental clarity, harmonizing perception and action and resolving apparent contradictions. Protecting against stress and creating inner wellbeing, Ametrine heightens concentration. It facilitates thinking things through, encouraging exploration of all possibilities. Enhancing acceptance of others, it overcomes prejudice. Protective during journeying, Ametrine guards against psychic attack. It brings insight into underlying causes of emotional distress, raising deep-seated issues to the surface. Its powerful cleansing properties disperse negativity from the aura and toxins from the body.

Stichtite

Companionship

Compassionate Stichtite has a calming influence on the environment. Useful if you live alone, it supports manifesting your true Self, living in accordance with your soul-contract (between you and another person or between you and your Higher Self) for the present life and clearing outdated vows and promises. Facilitating keeping your mind and opinions open and emotional awareness acute, it highlights how emotions and ingrained attitudes affect wellbeing and resolves issues. Stichtite is the perfect tool if you, or your child, need to take a different path in life, assisting ADHD or 'new age' children (*see* page 193) who suffer from hyperactivity or similar spiritual dis-eases. Stichtite raises kundalini through the chakra system.

Source: Bolivia

Vibration: High

Chakra: All

Physiology: Blood, metabolism, immune and autonomic nervous systems, DNA/RNA, oxygenation

Cleansing: All

Source: USA, Tasmania, Canada, South Africa

Vibration: High

Chakra: Earth star, base, heart, third eye, crown

Physiology: Skin, teeth, gums

Cleansing: All

White Agate

New life

Pure White Agate creates a holding space during soul retrieval, providing a receptacle for soul-parts that require healing before reintegration. It teaches love and respect for one's Self. Centring and grounding, it calms over-stimulation and panic attacks, and creates inner sacred space. White Agate facilitates peacefulness and is excellent for meditation. There is perfect resonance with higher crown chakras, assisting in integrating downloads of spiritual information into the earth-plane. During conception and pregnancy, White Agate encourages bonding between mother and baby. After birth, it supports high-quality nurturing.

Beryl

Distraction filter

A useful scrying tool, Beryl protects against outside influences and manipulation. It supports during stress, giving courage to shed unnecessary baggage. It filters out distractions, teaching how to do only that which you need to do. Assisting you to actualize potential, it tunes into Higher Self guidance as to what you should be doing. A powerful detoxifier, it clears pollutants on all levels. A medieval lapidary cites water in which Beryl has steeped as an excellent cure for hiccups, as well as nourishing love between a man and woman who have become weary.

Source: Worldwide

Vibration: High

Chakra: Past life, alta major, causal vortex, soma, crown, soul star, stellar gateway

Physiology: Electrical systems. *See Agate, pages 46–7*

Cleansing: All

Source: USA, Brazil, China, Ireland, Switzerland, Australia, Czech Republic, France, Norway

Vibration: High

Chakra: Third eye, soma, crown (according to colour)

Physiology: Pulmonary and circulatory systems, liver, heart, stomach, spine, throat, detoxification

Cleansing: All

Crystals for the spirit

Holding divine light and unity consciousness, crystals have a natural affinity with the realm of soul, spirit and Higher Self. Ideal for soul-healing and connecting to the soulplan for the present lifetime, they create the perfect mode of communication at metaphysical levels, opening expanded awareness and higher consciousness and linking it deep into Mother Earth.

Spiritual connection and higher chakras

Two pairs of earth and higher crown chakras hold you balanced between planet and cosmos, enabling your soul to be comfortable in incarnation while evolving through assimilation of cosmic energies. The Gaia gateway and earth star chakras beneath your feet are linkage points for your soul connection to Earth's soul and the subtle-energy grid that surrounds the planet. These chakras mediate inflow of sacred earth energy to stabilize and assimilate higher spiritual frequencies, while you remain grounded in your physical body, connected to your soul and Higher Self. They energetically link to higher crown chakras, the soul star and stellar gateway, portals for channelling spiritual light into the physical body, raising its vibrations accordingly. The soma chakra links the etheric and lightbody to the physical self, and the causal vortex provides an access point for the Akashic Record and your soulplan. When these chakras are in harmony, your spiritual purpose is clear and you communicate with your highest spiritual mentors. Place appropriate crystals on chakras to make the connection.

Exercise

Integrating the higher chakras

Blue Kyanite is a useful stone for opening and integrating the higher chakras around the head.

1 Place Blue Kyanite on the appropriate chakra with a grounding crystal such as Flint, Smoky Quartz or Hematite at your feet.
2 Dizziness may occur, in which case breathe slowly and easily, pushing the energy down to your feet until it stabilizes.

RIGHT Kyanite

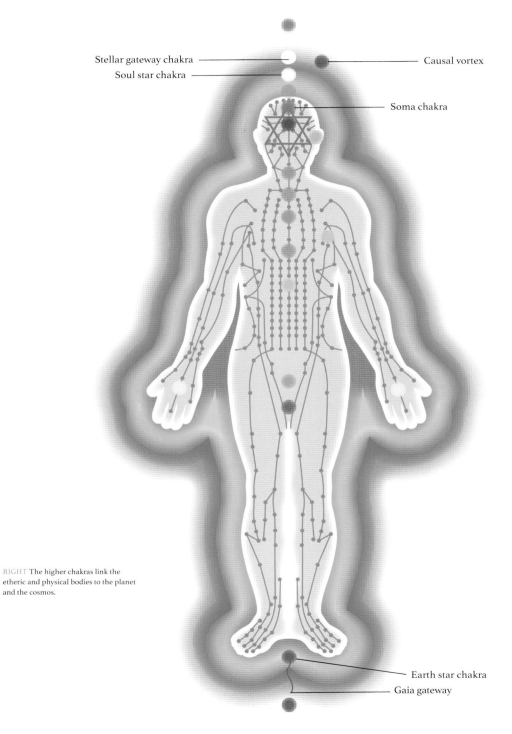

Stellar gateway chakra

Soul star chakra

Causal vortex

Soma chakra

RIGHT The higher chakras link the
etheric and physical bodies to the planet
and the cosmos.

Earth star chakra

Gaia gateway

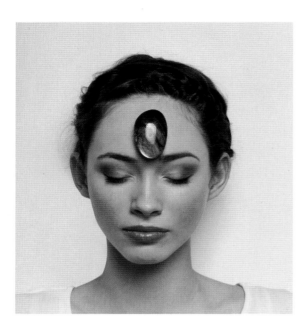

ABOVE Labradorite opens the third eye.

Inner sight

When the higher crown chakras are connected to the earth chakras, it grounds your inner sight, located in the third eye, which is facilitated by the use of crystals.

Exercise

To open the inner eye

1 Place a grounding stone such as Flint, Hematite, Shungite or Smoky Quartz at your feet.
2 With your eyes closed, look up to your inner screen, between and slightly above your eyebrows.
3 Place a third-eye crystal such as Apophyllite or Labradorite mid-forehead.
4 Absorb the crystal energy so that it opens your third eye.
5 If there is resistance or a headache develops, replace the crystal with Rhomboid Selenite or Bytownite, pulling energy down into your belly and to the crystal at your feet until the blockage clears.

Exercise

Integrating soul and psyche

The figure of eight or lemniscate layout integrates 'above' with 'below' and facilitates profound soul-healing. The layout draws spiritual energy down into the body and melds it with earth-energy drawn up from the feet to create perfect balance and core energy solidity.

1 Place high-vibration stones from the waist to above the crown and down again.
2 Place grounding stones from the waist to below the feet and up again.
3 To complete the grid, place an integration stone at the crossover point.
4 Complete the circuit back to the first stone.

RIGHT A lemniscate layout using Anandalite to draw on cosmic energy to heal the soul and Red Jasper to anchor it into the physical level. A Yowah Nut over the centre functions as an integrator, and Flint acts as a grounding stone at the feet.

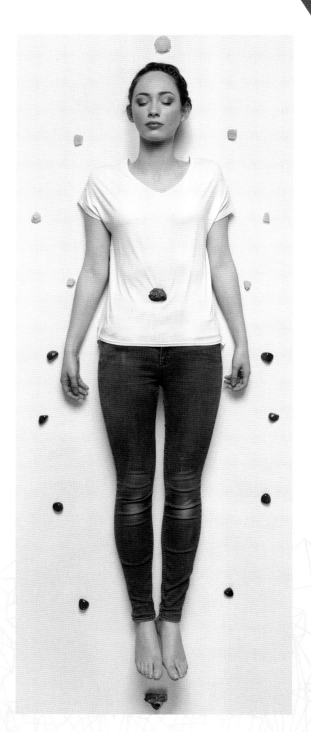

LEFT **Iridescent Anandalite**
OPPOSITE ABOVE **Clear Selenite**
OPPOSITE BELOW **Bytownite**

Contacting the Higher Self

A vehicle for soul consciousness, the Higher Self's vibration is less dense than that of the physical body, extending beyond the purely physical realm and therefore seeing much further. Crystals assist in raising your physical vibrations sufficiently for your Higher Self to manifest on the earth-plane. A simple visualization makes contact.

Exercise

Higher Self contact

Suitable crystals: Selenite, Anandalite, Kyanite, Bytownite or other Higher Self crystals. *See also* the crystal portraits on pages 68–307.

1 Settle yourself comfortably, placing a grounding stone at your feet, such as Flint, Hematite, Smoky Quartz.
2 Take a big breath and sigh out any tension you may be feeling.
3 Hold your crystal over the heart seed chakra. Feel the chakra opening like the petals of a flower, connecting the heart and higher heart and opening the three-chambered heart chakra.
4 Take your crystal up to the crown chakra. Feel the chakra opening. The higher crown chakras above your head expand and a string-like sensation pulls you up as you take the crystal to the highest point you can reach. Allow your vibrations to rise.
5 Invite your Higher Self to move down through the higher crown chakras until it fills your crown chakra. From the crown chakra, it moves into the three-chambered heart.
6 Experience the love that your Higher Self has for you, drawing that love deep into your being. Welcome it, learning to trust and feeling safe.
7 When you are ready to end the exercise, ask your Higher Self to remain connected to your heart.
8 Close the chakras above your head, folding them in like flowers closing for the night. Close the crown and third eye chakras.
9 Leave the three-chambered heart open, making sure that your earth star chakra is holding you firmly in incarnation – that is, in your physical body and not floating a foot off the planet.
10 Slowly bring your attention back to your physical body and the room around you.

Anandalite™ (Aurora Quartz)

Light being

Source: India

Vibration: Exceedingly high

Chakra: Soul star, stellar gateway, soma

Physiology: *See* Quartz, pages 38–45

Cleansing: All

Anandalite reaches the highest possible spiritual dimensions.

Characteristics

Iridescent Anandalite™ reaches exceptionally high dimensions. This shamanic crystal strips you down to the bare bones of your soul before rebuilding your energy bodies. Disharmony created when subtle bodies fail to integrate higher consciousness causes spiritual or physical dis-ease. Anandalite™ activates the body's natural healing mechanism, constructing an energetic grid that passes healing vibes through the biomagnetic field, etheric and physical bodies to de-energize and deconstruct older, detrimental energy structures. It facilitates kundalini awakening, releasing emotional blockages standing in the way of spiritual awakening.

Properties

Integrating dualities, Anandalite™ expands consciousness and harmonizes new frequencies so that the whole body benefits from a quantum uplift, whereby the physical frequencies are raised to a higher rate. Anandalite™ takes you travelling through the cosmos and beyond, transcending even metaphysical senses to move beyond the limits of time and space into a quantum field of consciousness that is non-local, everywhere and nowhere at once. It immerses you in a multidimensional holographic universe, facilitating mystical inter-connectedness that is bliss or unity consciousness, becoming one with spirit or source.

Chakra sweep

Anandalite™ purifies and aligns the whole chakra system to higher frequencies, when swept from the earth star chakra to the crown and then down the back of the body, and over again to ground the energies. Then sweep from side to side.

MAIN Anandalite
ABOVE Anandalite flower
BELOW LEFT Anandalite cluster
BELOW RIGHT Anandalite stalactite

Labradorite

Interface

Source: Madagascar, Italy, Greenland, Finland, Russia, Canada, Scandinavia

Vibration: High

Chakra: Higher heart, throat, third eye, soma. Aligns all

Physiology: Brain, eyes, metabolic and hormonal systems

Cleansing: Avoid water

This highly mystical crystal is a bringer of light.

Characteristics

This highly mystical crystal is a bringer of light, containing esoteric knowledge. Raising consciousness and connecting with universal energies, it takes you into another world or other lives. Protective Labradorite creates an interface between your own personal energy field and that of another person. Deflecting unwanted energies from the energy bodies and preventing energy leakage, it is excellent for screening yourself while allowing awareness of what is happening in another field. You do not take on thoughts and feelings, but remain objectively aware. Labradorite aligns the physical and etheric bodies and accesses soul purpose, raising consciousness and grounding spiritual energies into the physical body. This crystal opens intuition and activates psychic gifts. It draws messages from the unconscious mind to the surface, facilitating understanding internal conflicts and multiple agendas. Labradorite banishes fears and insecurities. It strengthens trust in your Self and the universe. ❶

Properties

Placed on the third-eye or past-life chakras, Labradorite clears psychic debris from previous disappointments and removes other people's projections and expectations, including thought forms that have hooked into the energy bodies.

Bytownite and Spectrolite

Bytownite (Yellow Labradorite) and Spectrolite are forms of Labradorite that are particularly useful for opening a third eye that has been 'locked shut' in previous incarnations, resulting in karmic blockages. Place over the site and lie quietly until the eye opens – it may appear on your inner screen as an actual eye opening or you may feel twitching and pulling slightly above and between your eyebrows. Remove the crystal when the sensation ceases.

MAIN Labradorite
LEFT Raw yellow Labradorite (Bytownite)
ABOVE Spectrolite

Tektite

Extraterrestrial contact

A meteorite from outer space, Tektite reveals past lives, especially those lived on other stars, planets or elsewhere in the multidimensions of consciousness. Encouraging contact with star beings and extraterrestrial communication, it enhances spiritual growth through higher knowledge. Tektite helps you to let go of undesirable experiences, remembering soul lessons learned but dissolving trauma. It takes you deep into the heart of a matter, promoting insight into the true cause and necessary action. This stone strengthens the aura around the body and balances male–female energies. It was traditionally worn as a fertility talisman.

Astrophyllite

No limits

Astrophyllite facilitates out-of-body experiences, acting as guide and protector when travelling through other realms. It facilitates standing outside yourself to take an objective view and realign your soul purpose. The stone introduces your full potential, recognizing that you have no limits. Eliminating without guilt anything outgrown in your life, it teaches that as one door closes, another opens. This stone increases your capacity for self-knowledge and activates your dreams, enabling you to 'dream true' to see the path your soul requires you to tread. It increases sensitivity of touch and improves awareness of other people's needs.

Source: No limits

Vibration: Earthy and high

Chakra: All

Physiology: Capillaries, circulation, muscles, feet

Cleansing: All

Source: USA, Greenland, Canada

Vibration: Extremely high

Chakra: Soul star, stellar gateway, palm

Physiology: Reproductive and hormonal systems, cellular structures, large intestine, fatty deposits

Cleansing: All

Shiva Lingham

Potency

A stone of balance and integration, Shiva Lingam releases
you from psychological patterns and beliefs you have
outgrown, particularly around sexual matters and those
inherited from ancestors. It opens creativity at every level.
The stone energetically stimulates potency and fertility and
heals the effects of abuse. Traditionally, a Shiva Lingam
embodies the wisdom of the deities brought to Earth.
It awakens kundalini power and embodies a balance of
masculine and feminine energy. Use one to cut subtle ties
with former partners lodged in the base and sacral chakras.

Source: India

Vibration: Earthy

Chakra: Base, sacral, earth star

Physiology: Electrical circuits, reproductive organs

Cleansing: All

Fulgarite

Lightning strike

A shaman's stone that retrieves soul-parts left at a past-life
death, trauma, disappointment or other event, Fulgarite
assists journeys to the interlife to ascertain why a soul
has not fully incarnated in the present. Fulgarite brings
the soul-parts home for reintegration. Energy tightly
focused into a tiny space blasts out ingrained patterns
and pernicious thoughts. Fulgarite facilitates letting go
of anything blocking progress, opening the way for new
behaviours that serve your soul. Bringing thought into
form, Fulgarite teaches how to hold the highest of intents.
Embodying your divine self, it creates natural harmony.

Source: USA, Sahara, Gobi Desert

Vibration: High

Chakra: All, as required

Physiology: Soul

Cleansing: Avoid water and earth

Merlinite

Magical

Merlinite holds the combined knowledge of shamans, alchemists, magician-priests and workers of magic to support spiritual evolution. It blends spiritual and earthly vibrations, accessing multidimensional shamanic realms. Merlinite reads the Akashic Record, inducing journeys to heal previous-life trauma into the present for shadow work or into future lives to gain insight on creating a positive future. Helpful if you are undergoing the dark night of the soul, Merlinite brings harmony into the present life, balancing yin–yang, masculine and feminine energies, conscious and subconscious, intellect and intuition.

Herderite

Consciousness-raiser

Herderite opens psychic awareness and raises consciousness to the highest possible level. It creates awareness of the multidimensional spiritual Self and induces a deep connection to Gaia, enabling you to walk lightly but purposefully on Earth. Herderite assists adaptation of the physical brain to accommodate heightened awareness and energies from the universal mind. It repatterns the etheric blueprint so that brain injuries or blockages are returned to the optimum. The crystal improves concentration and memory. Attuning to Herderite facilitates restructuring physical and energy bodies at every level.

Source: New Mexico

Vibration: Extremely high

Chakra: Third eye, past life, causal vortex

Physiology: Heart, nervous, respiratory and circulatory systems, intestines, heart, karmic blueprint

Cleansing: All

Source: Brazil, South Africa, USA, Germany, Russia

Vibration: High

Chakra: Third eye, Gaia gateway, stellar gateway, soul star, alta major, causal vortex, soma

Physiology: Head, brain chemistry. Multidimensional

Cleansing: Avoid water

Spectrolite

Spirit meets matter

Protective and perceptive, Spectrolite creates an interface between spirit and matter, or two energy fields. It protects the auric field against subtle-energy leaks. Opening metaphysical abilities, it connects to the Higher Self for guidance and to multidimensional consciousness, taking you into other lives. Spectrolite facilitates initiation into the mysteries, and prepares body and soul for spiritual evolution, banishing fears and insecurities about the process. The perfect stress reliever, it goes to the root of the matter, showing the intent behind thoughts and actions, and is a useful companion through change.

Source: Finland

Vibration: Extremely high

Chakra: Third eye, soma

Physiology: *See* Labradorite, pages 162–3

Cleansing: Avoid water

Orange Sphalerite

Cosmic grounding

Orange Sphalerite heals tiredness arising from intensive interaction with extremely high-vibration crystals. The physical body may struggle to assimilate these new frequencies. Orange Sphalerite gently expands spaces between cells in physical and energetic bodies so that frequencies penetrate between cell walls. This facilitates outdated energy to release, and higher vibrations to switch on positive genetic potential. The crystal builds a new energetic structure – attuned to what the individual needs, rather than 'one size fits all'. Bringing cells together again, it incorporates the new structure into the core energy field and provides spiritual grounding. ❶

Source: Bulgaria, Canada, Democratic Republic of Congo (Zaire), Mexico, Namibia, Spain, USA

Vibration: Extremely high

Chakra: Base, sacral, dantien, navel, solar plexus

Physiology: Cellular structures

Cleansing: Avoid water

Rainbow Mayanite

Soul of the sun

Rainbow Mayanite speaks truth and accesses power. It activates joy and purpose. Rapidly dissolving cords, attachments, hooks, patterns and implants from any timeframe or dimension, it replaces destructive cellular memory and auric imprints, creating core soul-healing. Releasing past-life and ancestral patterning, removing karmic encrustations and toxic dross absorbed from others or the environment, it builds new soul-supportive energy structures. This crystal takes you into the depths of yourself to discover your own treasures. Linking to mentors, you can see situations from both sides, recognizing how your soul manoeuvres your pathway and how apparently detrimental situations offer soul gifts.

Diaspore
(Zultanite™)

A different perspective

Diaspore delivers an energetic boost or sedates, as required. Viewed from different directions, Diaspore changes colour, enabling you to see things in a fresh light. Taking the unexpected perspective, it 'sees round corners' to discover what is to come. Strengthening mind and intuition, and facilitating absorbing knowledge, Diaspore enhances metaphysical abilities. Opening higher crown chakras, it grounds high-vibration energy to Earth. On the forehead, it promotes lucid dreaming and wearing it enhances psychic connections when reading for other people. On the solar plexus, it fills the body with golden light. ●

Source: USA

Vibration: Extremely high

Chakra: Aligns all

Physiology: Cellular system. *See* Quartz, pages 38–45

Cleansing: Avoid water

Source: Turkey, Russia, New Zealand, USA, Brazil, Argentina, UK, China

Vibration: High

Chakra: Crown, soul star, stellar gateway, alta major, causal vortex, soma, solar plexus

Physiology: Acid–alkaline balance, soft tissue, T-cells, immune system, bone development

Cleansing: Avoid water

Libyan Gold Tektite

Earth calling

Created when a meteorite catapulted molten rock and sand high into the stratosphere, creating a glass-like substance, multidimensional Libyan Gold Tektite helps those who do not feel connected to the planet to ground themselves. Carrying abundant life-force, it is a traditional amulet for any journey – physical or metaphysical – taking you beyond the boundaries of the known and across frontiers of consciousness. It has powerful links to the wisdom of ancient Egypt. Dissolving restrictions placed in another life, it cuts away all that is outgrown. Harnessing phenomenal force, Libyan Gold creates a new life.

Bytownite
(Yellow Labradorite)

Third-eye unblocker

Accessing the highest levels of consciousness, Bytownite stimulates metaphysical gifts and visualization, opening a blocked third eye and expanding spiritual vision. Assisting trance, clairvoyance and channelling, it reconfigures the mental body and attunes to higher wisdom. Helping to manage your personal power, it detaches from undue influence by others and overcomes indecision. Releasing from co-dependency, it assists resistance to enabling behaviour – being unable to let someone learn their own lessons in life, or unconsciously wanting to prolong dependency. Bytownite works on the etheric blueprint to assist the physical body.

Source: Libya

Vibration: Extremely high

Chakra: Solar plexus, third eye, soma, higher crown

Physiology: Kidneys, bladder, gall bladder

Cleansing: All

Source: Mexico, China, Mongolia, USA

Vibration: High

Chakra: Third eye, soma

Physiology: Stomach, spleen, liver, gall bladder, adrenal glands

Cleansing: All

Angel Aura Quartz

Angelic guidance

Serene Angel Aura Quartz is created by fusing platinum, silver or gold onto Quartz to create a highly supportive spiritual energy of exquisite purity. The iridescence shines like the wings of angels – hence the name – and contacts guardian angels and angelic guidance. This crystal facilitates remembering soul lessons from past incarnations and attuning to present-life soul purpose. It clears the throat chakra and encourages loving communication. Angel Aura aligns all chakras and harmonizes subtle bodies with the physical. It can relieve dis-eases such as autism or Asperger's syndrome, and soothes anxiety, panic attacks and phobias.

Seraphinite

Angelic cleanser

Cleansing and self-healing due to its high chlorite content, Seraphinite's transcendent, ethereal energy assists spiritual enlightenment, grounding expanded awareness into the physical plane. It contacts angels, the Divine Feminine and nature spirits. Seraphinite aligns the etheric bodies with the spinal cord, from where kundalini energy rises and radiates into the whole physical body. Releasing emotional patterns and tendencies that no longer serve soul and spirit, Seraphinite smoothes social contacts and facilitates understanding between different cultures.

Source: Artificially created

Vibration: High

Chakra: Throat

Physiology: Nervous system. *See* Quartz, pages 38–45

Cleansing: Avoid water or abrasives

Source: Siberia

Vibration: High

Chakra: Gaia gateway, stellar gateway, base

Physiology: Blood, cellular structures, liver, kidneys, heart, lungs

Cleansing: Avoid water

Moldavite

Time traveller

Moldavite fuses extraterrestrial energies with Mother Earth, taking you way beyond your limits and bringing you into contact with your Higher Self and star beings. Moldavite integrates the divine blueprint and accelerates spiritual growth, downloading information from the Akashic Record into the lightbody. It assimilates information so that you become fully conscious. Detaching from security issues such as money and worries for the future, it takes you forward to see the results of actions taken in the present, or to learn what is needed now to create a positive future. ●

Shattuckite

Spiritual energy conduit

Shattuckite heightens frequencies and amplifies thought, facilitating clear metaphysical vision, communicating what is seen. Shattuckite dissolves ancient curses and commands to secrecy. It is helpful where past-life experience has blocked metaphysical abilities, as it removes hypnotic commands and edicts. An excellent energy conduit, Shattuckite insists that the purest source is contacted during channelling. Developing automatic writing and telepathy, its powerful energy ensures that a communicating entity does not take over the physical body. It is helpful for genetically transmitted diseases and radiation damage.

Source: Czech Republic, Slovakia, Bavaria, Moldavia

Vibration: Extremely high

Chakra: Third eye, soma, higher crown

Physiology: Etheric bodies

Cleansing: Avoid water and earth

Source: USA

Vibration: High

Chakra: Heart, higher heart, throat, third eye, crown

Physiology: Tonsils, intercellular structures

Cleansing: All

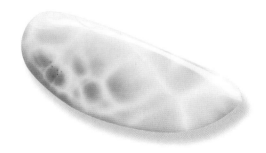

Larimar

Spiritual equanimity

Larimar dissolves self-sabotaging behaviour, alleviates guilt and removes fear, bringing about emotional balance and taking control of life. During stress and change, it enables challenges to be met with equanimity. Larimar radiates love, peace and tranquillity, healing heart trauma. Holding the stone induces a deeply meditative state in which the soul is guided onto its true pathway. Larimar facilitates communication with other realms and attunes to the energy of Mother Earth. It is excellent for healing past-life relationships and assists those seeking a soulmate, although karmic contracts may need dismantling.

Turquoise

Protector

Promoting spiritual attunement and facilitating communication with angelic realms, protective Turquoise enhances intuition and meditation. It explores past lives and shows without judgement how the creation of seeming 'fate' is an ongoing response to previous actions that were neither 'good' nor 'bad'. They simply were. This strengthening stone is excellent for exhaustion, depression or panic attacks. It calms nerves when speaking in public, dissolves self-sabotage, facilitates creative expression and stabilizes mood swings. Turquoise is anti-inflammatory, benefiting gout, rheumatism, cramps, arthritis and similar dis-eases. A pain reliever, it protects against airborne pollutants and allergies. ●

Source: Dominican Republic

Vibration: Extremely high

Chakra: Heart, heart seed, throat, third eye, soma, crown, alta major, causal vortex

Physiology: Arteries, joints, meridians, head, chest and neck

Cleansing: Avoid water

Source: Afghanistan, India, USA, Mexico, Iran, Chile, China, Tibet

Vibration: High

Chakra: Throat, third eye

Physiology: Immune system

Cleansing: All

Ajoite and Ajo Quartz

Compassionate being

Ajoite is increasingly rare but Ajo Quartz with a somewhat lower vibration can be substituted. This stone of compassionate peace wraps your soul in universal love and attunes to angelic realms, while retaining contact with Mother Earth. Ajoite facilitates profound spiritual revelation and creates inner serenity, recognizing the multidimensionality of your being. It draws karmic wounds or implants and noxious emotions out of the body, no matter in which timeframe they originated. Gently infilling the resulting space with unconditional love, it reframes cellular memory. Resolving conflict through forgiveness, Ajoite offers compassion to your Self and others. ⬤

Aquamarine

Courage

Aquamarine reduces fear or stress and removes extraneous thoughts, filtering information reaching the brain and clarifying perception. It dissolves self-defeating programmes, allowing the soul to be heard. Having an affinity with sensitive people, Aquamarine invokes tolerance of others. Overcoming judgementalism, it supports those overwhelmed by responsibility, and encourages responsibility for your Self. Counteracting the forces of darkness and procuring favour from the Spirits of Light – angels and higher beings – it brings unfinished business to a conclusion and ensures closure on all levels. Aquamarine clears blocked communication and assists self-expression and understanding underlying emotional states. ⬤

Source: South Africa, USA

Vibration: Exceedingly high

Chakra: Higher heart, heart, soma, causal vortex, alta major

Physiology: Cellular memory. *See* Quartz, pages 38–45

Cleansing: All

Source: USA, Mexico, Russia, Brazil, India, Ireland, Zimbabwe, Afghanistan, Pakistan

Vibration: High

Chakra: Throat, third eye. Aligns all

Physiology: Throat, glands, thyroid, pituitary, hormonal system, cleansing organs, eyes, jaw, teeth, stomach, immune and auto-immune systems

Cleansing: All

Mount Shasta Opal

Vortex energy

From a major energy vortex, Mount Shasta Opal puts you in touch with spiritual protection afforded by archangels and ascended beings and connects to the phenomenal energy of the site. A powerful shamanic stone, Mount Shasta Opal facilitates travelling stealthily during metaphysical workings and lower-world journeys, assisting soul retrieval. This Opal connects to the wisdom of Lemuria, opening a cosmic portal through which ancient knowledge passes. Before opening such a portal, programme the crystal to ensure that only beings with the highest good in mind are granted access to Earth.

Blue Kyanite

Ultimate healing

Amplifying high-frequency energies, Blue Kyanite aligns chakras and subtle bodies, clearing pathways and meridians. It encourages speaking your highest truth, cutting through fears, illusions and blockages and increasing capacity for logical thought. Kyanite is tranquillizing, inducing deep meditative states, and yet stimulates psychic abilities. Facilitating detaching from the idea of blind fate or implacable karma, Blue Kyanite reveals measures required to balance out the past. Grounding and mediating the flow of spiritual energy, Kyanite restores Qi to the physical body and is a natural pain reliever. It restabilizes the energy bodies and soul after transformation. ●

Source: Mount Shasta (USA)

Vibration: High

Chakra: Purifies all

Physiology: Throat. *See* Opal, pages 54–5

Cleansing: Avoid water

Source: Switzerland, Brazil

Vibration: Extremely high

Chakra: Throat, third eye, crown, alta major, causal vortex, stellar gateway, soul star

Physiology: Muscles, temperature control, thyroid, adrenal glands, throat, brain

Cleansing: Avoid water

Rhomboid Blue Selenite

Third-eye unlocker

Rhomboid Blue Selenite is a specific shape and type of Selenite that unlocks the third eye when it has been 'nailed shut' in other lifetimes or in childhood. So often, adults tell a child they are imagining things when they speak what they see or intuit, and a child quickly learns to shut down inner sight. More deeply embedded, psychic manipulation and prohibitions against 'second sight' in other lifetimes also block the third eye. Rhomboid Selenite releases migraines resulting from a blocked third eye, assisting the assimilation of higher-vibration energy into the psychic eye and opening inner sight.

Source: UK

Vibration: Earthy and high

Chakra: Third eye

Physiology: *See* Selenite, page 184

Cleansing: Avoid water or abrasives

Angelite

Angelic connection

Deepening attunement and heightening spiritual perception, Angelite facilitates angelic contact. It enhances telepathic communication and out-of-body journeys. Angelite opens psychic channelling from the highest sources, connecting to universal knowledge and raising awareness of multidimensional realms. It facilitates speaking your truth and being more compassionate, accepting that which cannot be changed. Preventing psychic overwhelm, Angelite creates a protective auric shield and balances etheric and physical energies. A useful stress and tension reliever, it overcomes fear and anger and fosters forgiveness.

Source: Peru

Vibration: High

Chakra: Throat, third eye, crown

Physiology: Thyroid, meridians, soft tissue, blood vessels, fluid balance

Cleansing: All

Celestite

Reintegrating the soul

Celestite assists angelic communication and remembers the divine nature of your soul. Connecting to your guardian angel, it stimulates clairvoyance and promotes dream recall and out-of-body journeys. Supporting your spiritual development at the highest level, this crystal teaches trust in the infinite wisdom of the universe. It facilitates conflict resolution and instils balance in times of stress. Carry one if you are a 'worry-guts'. Celestite's gentle vibes cool fiery emotions and the crystal quietens and sharpens the mind, promoting mental clarity and fluent communication. ❶

Idocrase

Opening prison doors

Linking to the Higher Self, Idocrase heals the part of the soul that is embedded in incarnation. It releases feelings of being trapped on Earth. Healing past-life experiences of being a prisoner or in extreme danger, or of mental or emotional restraint, it gently dissolves anger and alleviates fear. The crystal creates a strong sense of inner security. Idocrase opens the mind and clears negative thought patterns so that the mind functions clearly. It also stimulates the urge to discover, linking this into creativity and the possibility of inventing a new life.

Source: USA, Canada

Vibration: High

Chakra: Throat, third eye, crown, soul star, stellar gateway

Physiology: Eyes, ears, throat, muscles, elimination systems

Cleansing: All

Source: USA

Vibration: High

Chakra: Third eye, soma, past life

Physiology: Tooth enamel, nutrient assimilation

Cleansing: All

Iolite

The compass

A vision stone, Iolite clears thought forms and facilitates visualization. It stimulates intuitive insight and inner knowing. A journeying facilitator, Iolite releases causes of addiction or obsession. Bringing about inner balance and reorientation, it supports expressing your true Self, freed from expectations by those around you. As it encourages taking responsibility for your Self, it overcomes co-dependency within a partnership or parental relationship. It dissolves discord that has occurred. In contact with the auric field, Iolite gives off an electrical charge that re-energizes the field and aligns the subtle bodies.

Smoky Amethyst Elestial Quartz

Intense protection

Smoky Amethyst Elestial calls in the highest beneficial influences and grounds them. Protecting against psychic attack and alien invasion, it repels negative energy, attracting positive vibrations. Clearing entities, it assists spirit release or death-midwifery, assisting people who are dying to move out of this world and into the next – grid it around the room in which such work is carried out. Contacting guides and angelic helpers, it assists in disconnecting those who have previously made a mystic marriage and are intertwined at higher spiritual chakras. Smoky Amethyst Elestial amplifies and directs sound-healing.

Source: USA, Australia, Brazil, Myanmar (Burma), Canada, India, Madagascar, Namibia, Sri Lanka, Tanzania

Vibration: High

Chakra: Third eye

Physiology: Detoxification, liver, pituitary, sinus, respiratory system, fatty deposits

Cleansing: All

Source: Madagascar (Africa)

Vibration: Earthy and high

Chakra: Earth star, aligns all

Physiology: *See* Quartz, pages 38–45

Cleansing: All

Tanzanite

Violet flame

A heat-transformed crystal that changes hue depending on the direction from which it is viewed, Tanzanite facilitates altered states of consciousness and a profoundly deep meditative state. Stimulating metaphysical abilities, it links to angelic realms, spirit guides and ascended masters. Accelerating spiritual growth, it downloads information from the Akashic Record, dissolves outdated karmic dis-ease and creates space for new patterns to be integrated. The crystal facilitates contact between universal mind and physical realms, intuition and intellect. Tanzanite communicates insights received, putting them into practice. ●

Source: Tanzania

Vibration: Extremely high

Chakra: Heart, throat, third eye, higher crown

Physiology: Head, throat, chest

Cleansing: Avoid water

Amphibole Quartz

A place of love

Amphibole creates a connection to the highest level of spiritual experience, opening a ladder to the Higher Self and multidimensional awareness, calling in guardian angels and higher beings. Amphibole accesses numerous lifetimes of the soul and breaks outdated patterns, reconnecting to ancient wisdom in your soul memory. Facilitating introspection and insight, it attunes to the wisdom of the universal mind. Encouraging a detached perspective on life, Amphibole recognizes that there are many valid pathways. It subtly shifts workplace energies, bringing about cooperation and harmony.

Source: Brazil

Vibration: High

Chakra: All

Physiology: Etheric bodies. *See* Quartz, pages 38–45

Cleansing: All

Rutilated Quartz
(Angel Hair)

Energy integration

Rutilated Quartz is an efficient vibrational healer. A perfect balance of cosmic light and grounded energy, it illuminates the soul, promoting spiritual growth. The crystal assists out-of-body journeying, scrying and channelling, contacting spiritual guidance. Its Rutile content draws off negative energy, releasing the past and cleansing the aura. Protecting against psychic attack, and ideal for therapists or counsellors, Rutilated Quartz filters negative energy from a client, supporting their energy field during emotional release and confrontations with darker aspects of the psyche. It draws off karmic dis-ease and reframes events still affecting the present.

Faden Quartz

Reintegrator

Faden Quartz unifies the Self, encouraging fragmented soul-parts to reintegrate. Connecting the 'silver cord' that tethers the etheric body to the physical, it protects during journeying and reels the soul back to the body. Accessing the interlife, it provides an overview of soul lessons and root causes of dis-ease. Faden Quartz heals broken trust and facilitates emotional autonomy and intimacy, encouraging loving yourself. This crystal harmonizes a group or family, overcoming conflict and healing breaks. Faden Quartz connects healer and patient working at a distance, and grids areas of unstable earth or physical energy to restore equilibrium.

Source: Worldwide

Vibration: High

Chakra: All

Physiology: Respiratory tract. *See* Quartz, pages 38–45

Cleansing: All

Source: Worldwide

Vibration: Medium

Chakra: Crown, past life

Physiology: Bones. *See* Quartz, pages 38–45

Cleansing: All

Herkimer Diamond

High-vibe protection

Herkimer Diamond attunes to the highest levels of
spiritual connection and your own inner Self. It stimulates
metaphysical abilities. Transmuting noxious energies, it
opens energetic channels around the physical and subtle
bodies to accommodate high-vibration energy, activating
the lightbody. Meditating with it accesses your soul's
purpose for the current lifetime, reframing past-life issues
that are still creating difficulties in the present. Herkimer
Diamond is strongly protective, especially against EMFs.
Gridded around a house or bed, Herkimers block geopathic
stress. The crystal assists insomnia.

Apophyllite

Third-eye activator

Creating a conscious connection between physical and
spiritual realms, Apophyllite accesses multidimensions.
This metaphysical stone opens the third eye, particularly
if this was blocked in previous lives, stimulating intuition
and clairvoyance. Facilitating journeys into past lives and
enhancing telepathy and channelling, the crystal promotes
introspection into your own behaviour, highlighting the
part you played in what was created and the consequences.
It brings about recognition of one's true Self. A stress
reducer, Apophyllite releases suppressed emotions and
overcomes anxiety, worries and fears. It neutralizes allergies
and has been found to assist during asthma attacks.

Source: USA

Vibration: Exceptionally high

Chakra: Aligns all

Physiology: Cellular structures, metabolism, electrical
systems. *See* Quartz, pages 38–45

Cleansing: All

Source: India, Germany, Canada, Norway, Scotland,
Ireland, Brazil, Japan, USA

Vibration: High

Chakra: Heart, heart seed, third eye, crown, soma,
soul star, stellar gateway

Physiology: Eyes, mucus membranes, skin,
respiratory system

Cleansing: Avoid water

Azeztulite™

Light-bearer

The Azez are appearing in crystals around the world. A race of star beings using crystals to bring higher frequencies to Earth, they expand consciousness and spiritual evolution. The vibrational shift that Azeztulite™ induces is powerful and may have unpleasant side effects until fully assimilated (combine with Orange Sphalerite). Outdated patterns must be dissolved and emotional cleansing completed before the shift occurs. Azeztulite instantly induces a state of 'no mind', creating a protective spiral around the physical body. It stimulates kundalini rise. It also tunes into spiritual guidance from the future, aiding important decisions.

Source: Worldwide

Vibration: Extremely high

Chakra: Third eye, crown, stellar gateway, soul star, causal vortex, alta major

Physiology: Spiritual level

Cleansing: All

Himalayan Quartz

Teacher

Quartz from the high Himalayas is found in several forms. It grounds spiritual energy deep into the planet while establishing a powerful connection to higher guidance. Imbued with the wisdom of the ancients, ethically mined Himalayan Quartz crystals are power stones. They amplify energy and intention, raising your thoughts towards enlightenment. Himalayan Quartz provides a shield against negativity or psychic attack, especially those with black inclusions. These crystals assist in reading the Akashic Record, accessing past and future lives with ease. (*See also* Nirvana and Ice Quartz, pages 182 and 233.)

Source: Himalayas

Vibration: High

Chakra: All

Physiology: *See* Quartz, pages 38–45

Cleansing: All

Lemurian Seed

Ladder of consciousness

Lemurian Seed crystals open a portal to stellar experiences, anchoring ancient wisdom into the present. Attuning to previous spiritual training, they reawaken inherent skills. Teaching that we are many-dimensioned beings with a small part in physical incarnation, they pierce illusions of separateness, reminding us of our spiritual ancestry. Lemurian Seeds insist that we do personal inner work as well as facilitating the evolution of others. The etched markings are ascended like a ladder, accessing inter- and multidimensional consciousness. Lemurians teach that time is an illusion, showing how to move beyond its boundaries into true reality, taking an objective viewpoint of prior lifetimes.

Source: Brazil, Russia, Tibet, Arkansas (USA), Zambia

Vibration: Exceedingly high

Chakra: All, especially third eye

Physiology: *See* Quartz, pages 38–45

Cleansing: All

Nirvana Quartz

Crystallized divine consciousness

Left behind by receding glaciers and standing at the interface of consciousness and matter, Nirvana Quartz is spiritual alchemy embodied. Amplifying the flow of ascension energy into the physical realm, Nirvana Quartz integrates the lightbody. It facilitates a shift into inner nirvana: a pure illumined mind combined with unconditional love. This crystal removes barriers to spiritual or psychological growth and awakens potential as the soul sheds its karma, soul imperatives and deepest illusions to attune to its true purpose. Teaching that we truly create our reality, Nirvana Quartz vastly expands our vision of what that reality could be.

Source: Himalayas

Vibration: Extremely high

Chakra: soul star, stellar gateway

Physiology: Beyond the physical

Cleansing: All

Petalite

Spiritual evolution

Petalite rapidly accelerates spiritual evolution, accessing downloads of cosmic consciousness. It creates a safe space in which to open spiritual contact and accesses the angelic realm and ascended masters, linking you to the highest levels of spiritual knowing. It enhances meditation and conscious attunement, rapidly moving beyond your present level of metaphysical abilities. This crystal gently tie-cuts previous relationships or family members that drain your energy. It reframes outdated contracts and vows. Pink Petalite dissolves feelings of abandonment and alienation.

Phenacite

Higher Cconsciousness

Phenacite opens metaphysical abilities and stimulates spiritual contact, connecting to ascended masters for mentoring. It activates the lightbody and enhances inner knowing. A multidimensional crystal of higher consciousness, Phenacite downloads information from the Akashic Record so that karmic dis-disease is dispersed. It activates healing from the karmic etheric body to the physical, repairing the etheric blueprint as a prerequisite for physical healing. The crystal facilitates grounding spiritual downloads in everyday life. Petalite dispels stress, depression or anxiety, and heals hysteria, hallucinatory dissociation or manic states. ●

Source: Brazil, Australia, Namibia, Manitoba (Canada), Zimbabwe

Vibration: Extremely high

Chakra: Heart seed, third eye, soma, crown, stellar gateway, soul star

Physiology: Eyes, lungs, muscles, intestines, endocrine and metabolic systems

Cleansing: All

Source: Brazil, Russia, Norway, Zambia, Zimbabwe, Sri Lanka, Tanzania, USA

Vibration: Extremely high

Chakra: Third eye, soma, crown, stellar gateway, soul star

Physiology: Etheric bodies

Cleansing: All

Sacred Scribe

Crystal wormhole

Sacred Scribes are shaped Russian Lemurians. They often display an almost technological absence of feeling – cold, rational 'mental' energy. Excellent for people who are overly emotional or mentally out of control, they insist on sharp focus. It's impossible to hide the truth in their presence. Sacred Scribes assist with balance, seeing things from all sides. Creating a still point for the mind, tuning into a silence in which esoteric information is downloaded without thought or the need to know what or why, the crystal enables you to see what's at the other end of the wormhole.

Source: Russia

Vibration: High to extremely high

Chakra: Soma

Physiology: Beyond the physical

Cleansing: All

Selenite

Crystallized divine light

Inhabiting the space between light and matter, translucent Selenite anchors the lightbody into the Earth vibration, and downloads divine light into the physical body. It creates a safe, peaceful space that does not allow outside influences to penetrate. Selenite detaches entities from the aura and prevents anything external from influencing the mind. It reaches into other lives, or the future, and checks progress made with the current lifeplan, pinpointing lessons and issues being worked upon. Bringing about a conscious understanding of what is occurring at the subconscious level, it shows how it can best be resolved.

Source: USA, Mexico, Russia, Austria, Greece, Poland, Germany, France, England

Vibration: Extremely fine

Chakra: Crown, stellar gateway, soul star, alta major, causal vortex

Physiology: Spinal column, teeth, bones

Cleansing: Avoid water

Trigonic Quartz

Soul midwife

Trigonic facilitates a theta-brainwave state that creates deep healing and restructuring of body, beliefs and realities. A 'supercomputer' that communicates, no matter where the separate parts may be, Trigonic accesses multidimensional awareness. Its stated aim is elimination of war and conflict in all its manifestations, personal and collective, inner and outer. However, Trigonics bring up unresolved conflicts for resolution as part of the process. The triangles are cosmic DNA soul-encoding. Trigonics insist you release all blockages from chakras, and toxicity from physical and auric bodies, prior to shifts occurring. The process cannot be short-circuited or evaded.

Scottish Greenstone

Faerie-realm connector

A mystical stone that connects to the sacred Celtic past and faerie realm, Scottish Greenstone is an amulet for protection and healing, effective against 'poisons and the dark arts'. It returns the body to a time unhindered by the stresses and pollution of modern times. It is creating a home for the advanced beings now inhabiting the crystal skulls that wish to share their wisdom to assist the evolution of Earth. Clearing clutter and creating a strong innerworld connection, Scottish Greenstone imparts a sense of worthiness and invincibility to the Self.

Source: Brazil and elsewhere

Vibration: Extremely high

Chakra: Higher heart, soma, soul star, stellar gateway

Physiology: Soul and light bodies. *See* Quartz, pages 38–45

Cleansing: All

Source: Scottish Highlands and Islands

Vibration: Earthy and high

Chakra: Harmonizes all

Physiology: Subtle-energy fields, skins, pain receptors, energy management

Cleansing: All

Crystals for children

Children are instantly drawn to crystals, loving their bright sparkly energies, but kids are just as happy with rough pieces of rock as with faceted gems, which makes them perfect for putting in pockets or under pillows (*see* Precautions, page 188). Rose Quartz is an excellent healing crystal for anyone from a newborn baby finding it difficult to adjust to having arrived on the planet, to the stroppiest teenager battling with the hormonal and emotional challenges of puberty, especially those with an urge to self-harm. (Rose Quartz, and other versatile crystals that are equally effective for children, can be found in other sections of the book.)

Childhood ailments

Crystals can be very soothing in childhood, not only at an emotional level but also for physical ailments. Appropriate crystals can be gridded around a bed (*see* pages 32–3), placed in bathwater or on the body. They can be spritzed around the energy field as an essence or applied directly onto the body (*see* pages 30–1).

Precautions

- Crystals for young children should be placed out of reach.

- Use tumbled, not sharp, crystals.

- Use only crystals that are large enough not to be swallowed.

- Crystals should only be placed on or around children under the constant supervision of an adult.

- Do not allow children to handle potentially toxic crystals (indicated with the Caution symbol ⊘).

Acne or Eczema: Carnelian, Halite, Ocean Jasper, Rose Quartz, Selenite, Snakeskin Agate

Asthma: Banded Agate, Blue Aragonite, Blue Crackle Quartz, Green Aventurine, Nzuri Moyo

Burns and sunburn: Dumortierite, Quartz, Rose Quartz

Chicken pox/shingles/cold sores: Black Tourmaline, Blue Lace Agate, Chrysoprase, Dalmation Stone, Green Tourmaline, Fluorite, Kyanite, Lapis Lazuli, Quartz, Rhodochrosite, Rose Quartz, White Agate (and *see* Itching)

Colds, flu, viral and bacterial infections: Bloodstone, Chalcopyrite, Fluorite, Jade, Malachite, Que Sera, Quantum Quattro, Shungite, Turquoise

Colic: Dumortierite

Coughs: Chrysotile, Quantum Quattro, Que Sera, Shungite

Earache: Ammonite, Ammolite, Peanut Wood

Earache when flying: Blue Euclase, Pink Crackle Quartz

Eyes: Blue Chalcedony, Emerald, Malachite

Fractures: Cradle of Life, Green Quartz, Magnetite, Faden Quartz, Selenite

Headache: Amethyst, Aquamarine, Lapis Lazuli, Quartz, Selenite

Immune-system support: Amethyst, Bloodstone, Blue Lace Agate, Black Tourmaline, Botswana Agate, Chrysoprase, Citrine, Emerald, Epidote, Garnet, Infinite Stone, Jade, Lapis Lazuli, Lepidolite, Malachite, Moki Marbles, Moldavite, Mookaite Jasper, Moss Agate, Obsidian, Opal, Picture Jasper, Quantum Quattro, Quartz, Rhodochrosite, Rhodonite, Rubellite, Rutilated Quartz, Shungite, Smithsonite, Topaz

Insect bites: Klinoptilolith, Rose Quartz, Shungite

Insomnia: *See* nightmares

Itching: Azurite, Chrysocolla, Green Aventurine, Hematite, Malachite, Rose Quartz

Measles: Dalmatian Stone (and *see* Itching)

Nausea/motion sickness: Bloodstone, Blue Apatite, Chlorite Quartz, Citrine, Dioptase, Emerald, Gaspeite, Green Aventurine, Green Calcite, Green Fluorite, Green Garnet, Hematite, Jade, Yellow Jasper

Nerves: Charoite, Indicolite, Kambaba Jasper, Seraphinite

Nightmares: Amethyst, Chrysoprase, Charoite, Moonstone, Prehnite

Pain: Amber, Amethyst, Cathedral Quartz, Celestite, Charoite, Chevron Amethyst, Flame Agate, Fuchsite, Green Calcite, Hematite, Hematoid Quartz, Herkimer Diamond, Howlite, Infinite Stone, Lapis Lazuli, Pearl Spa Dolomite, Peridot, Tiger Iron

Sore throat/tonsillitis: Blue Lace Agate, Fluorite, Indicolite Quartz, Quantum Quattro, Shungite (place on base chakra and throat)

Sprains and bruises: Bloodstone, Magnetite, Magnesite, Rose Quartz, Selenite

Teething pain: Blue Euclase, Cathedral Quartz, Quantum Quattro

Temperature regulation: Crackled Fire Agate, Dinosaur Bone, Nuummite, Pyrite in Magnesite, Quartz (place large piece beside left ear)

ABOVE Always use suitably-sized crystals for children and place them appropriately.

Childhood challenges

Crystals are the perfect antidote to issues that many young children and teenagers face. A crystal carried in the pocket gives confidence and protection and heals underlying emotional issues. Stones such as Snakeskin Agate and Nuummite were used by shamans for thousands of years to confer invisibility. They help protect a child from bullies. Gridding crystals around or under the bed also assists. Children enjoy creating their own layouts, so encourage them to choose crystals and express their creativity.

ADHD: Brandenberg Amethyst, Lepidocrosite, Stichtite, Tantalite, Tanzine Aura Quartz

Anorexia: Ametrine, Golden Calcite, Lepidolite, Malachite, Orange Kyanite, Rhodochrosite, Rose Quartz, Stibnite, Topaz

Body dysmorphia: Dianite (Blue Jade), Muscovite

Bulimia: Rose Quartz, Stibnite

Bullying: Carnelian, Freedom Stone, Nuummite, Red Jasper, Snakeskin Agate, Sugilite

Dyscalculia (number blindness): Epidote in Prehnite

Dyslexia: Fluorite, Pyrite, Scapolite, Sugilite, Tantalite

Dyspraxia/accident proneness: Black Moonstone

Self-confidence: Agate, Citrine, Lapis Lazuli, Rhodonite, Rose Quartz, Ruby, Tourmaline, Variscite

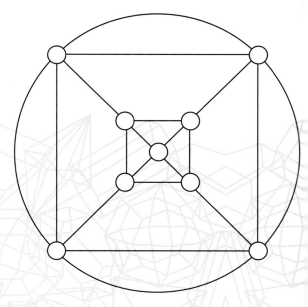

Exercise

Expanded square layout

Suitable crystals: Sugilite, Fluorite, Flint, Herkimer Diamond, Rose Quartz. *See also* the crystal portraits on pages 68–307.

1 Place a suitable keystone in the centre of the square.
2 Place crystals on each point of the inner square.
3 Place anchor crystals on the outer points.
4 Place other crystals as feels appropriate.
5 Leave the grid in place where it will not be disturbed. Cleanse regularly (see page 27).

OPPOSITE An expanded square grid.

BELOW Flint, Herkimer Diamond and Fluorite surround a Rose Quartz heart in this layout, to join heart and mind and encourage communication and clarification of confused feelings.

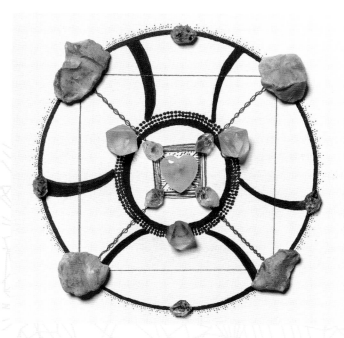

Sugilite (Luvulite)

Love

Source: Canada, South Africa, Japan, India, New South Wales (Australia), Tajikistan, Italy

Vibration: High

Chakra: Heart

Physiology: Heart, brain, lymphatic and immune systems, fluid balance

Cleansing: All

Sugilite assists sensitive souls to adapt to Earth's vibration and is excellent for 'new age' children.

Characteristics

Sugilite contains lithium, a natural tranquillizer. It calms and centres, gently releasing emotional turmoil, alleviating despair and protecting the soul from shocks and disappointments, bringing light and love into the darkest situations. Sugilite assists sensitive souls adapt to Earth's vibration and is excellent for 'new age' children (those who have incarnated with a slightly different, raised vibratory frequency and find it difficult to settle into the heavy Earth vibration). Drawing off negative energy, the stone lends loving support. Ideal for children who have dyslexia or dyspraxia to keep in their pocket, it encourages positive thoughts and reorganizes brain patterns. Fostering forgiveness and eliminating hostility, Sugilite assists a child who is being bullied to walk away. Conflict is dissolved without confrontation. One of the major love stones, offering spiritual love and wisdom, Sugilite opens all chakras to the flow of love, bringing them into alignment. The stone teaches how to live from your truth and reminds the soul of its reasons for incarnating. It answers great questions of life such as 'Why am I here?', 'Where did I come from?' 'Who am I?' and 'What else do I need to understand?'

Sociability

Sugilite resolves group difficulties and encourages loving communication. It supports 'misfits' of any kind, anyone who does not feel Earth is their home, or who experiences social anxiety, paranoia or schizophrenia. Excellent for autism, it grounds the soul more fully into the present reality. Sugilite promotes understanding the effect of the mind on the body and its place in dis-ease. ●

MAIN Sugilite
ABOVE Sugilite triangle
RIGHT Carved Sugilite flower

Dalmatian Stone

Into the body

Source: Mexico

Vibration: Earthy

Chakra: Base, sacral, earth star

Physiology: Cartilage, nerves, reflexes

Cleansing: All

Dalmation Stone is excellent for connecting children to their physical body.

Characteristics

Dalmatian Stone imparts physicality to the soul, grounding it in the earth star chakra and creating a link to Mother Earth. It reminds you that you are a spiritual being on a human journey and so is excellent for connecting children to their physical body and their reason for incarnating. Grounding and centring in the body, the stone helps come to terms joyfully with being in incarnation, no matter what age you may be.

This stone attunes to the innocent child within everyone, fortifying the spirit. It awakens a sense of fun and is a useful pick-me-up for depression or energy depletion. Containing Tourmaline, Dalmatian Stone quickly transmutes negative energy and outworn patterns. If you are prone to over-intellectualization or excessive thinking, Dalmation Stone gets you out of your head and into your body. It moves you forward in life, but also suggests that reflecting on possible actions and planning with care may be appropriate in certain circumstances.

Antithesis to bullying

Protective Dalmatian Stone is traditionally said to sound a warning when danger is near. It strengthens composure under all circumstances and prevents fantasizing about potential revenge scenarios that would be hurtful to yourself.

Physically, it supports athletes, protecting against injuries, and guards against nightmares, keeping the monsters at bay. ◉

This stone attunes to the innocent child within everyone.

MAIN Dalmation Stone roundel
BELOW Dalmation Stone

Pyrite

Fool's gold

Pyrite is toxic and should never be ingested. An excellent energy shield that blocks out negative energy and pollutants, traditionally it wards off infectious diseases. Worn around the neck, it protects auric bodies, deflecting harm and danger. Pyrite overcomes feelings of inadequacy and inertia, anxiety and frustration, boosting self-worth and confidence. It assists boys who feel inferior as it strengthens confidence in their masculinity. It may be too strong for 'macho' teens, though, initiating aggression. Cubic Pyrite expands and structures mental capabilities, balancing instinct with intuition, creativity with analysis. ●

Spiderweb Jasper

Reweaving the web

As the name suggests, Spiderweb Jasper connects to the energetic webs of life, including Earth's energy meridians and the multiverses. It attunes you to awareness of how these energies interact: changing, reweaving and integrating the web of life. This is the spider magic of the Moirai (Fates) apparently spinning our destiny. But Spiderweb Jasper sees past that illusion to what really is and facilitates taking control for your Self. Healing a frayed nervous system, it unites loose strands of energy and instils stamina. Protective for the aura, it guards during shamanic journeying.

Source: UK, North America, Chile, Peru

Vibration: Earthy

Chakra: Base, sacral

Physiology: Bones, brain, cell formation, DNA, meridians, digestive tract, circulatory and respiratory systems, lungs

Cleansing: Avoid water

Source: Mexico, Arizona, California, Idaho, Nevada, Oregon, New Mexico (USA)

Vibration: Earthy

Chakra: Gaia gateway, earth star, base

Physiology: Nervous system, neurological connections, bones, teeth, gums, muscles, heart, liver, gall bladder, stomach

Cleansing: All

Apache Tear

Grief counsellor

This gentle form of Black Obsidian suits children, as it slowly brings negativity to the surface to be transmuted. An excellent detoxifier, Apache Tear absorbs negative energy and protects the aura. It cleanses the earth star chakra, creating a root into Mother Earth. Apache Tear is believed to shed tears in times of sorrow and it comforts grief. It provides insight into sources of distress and relieves long-held grievances, including those carried from other lives. This stone stimulates analytical capabilities and promotes forgiveness. An Apache Tear removes self-imposed limitations and increases spontaneity.

Source: USA

Vibration: Earthy

Chakra: Earth star, Gaia gateway, base, sacral

Physiology: Assimilation of vitamins, detoxification, muscles

Cleansing: All

Black Moonstone

Coordinator

Black Moonstone assists with puberty and PMS. Less volatile at full moon than White Moonstone, it calms emotions and ameliorates over-sensitivity to situations and emotional stress. Perfect for when a new baby arrives, Black Moonstone brings out nurturing feminine energy, supporting inner knowing. Calming hyperactive children, it assists dyspraxics to be aware of the space that their physical and etheric bodies take up, making them less clumsy. A psychic stone, it provides protection during involuntary night journeys out of the body, screening clairvoyant contact and telepathy so that only beneficial messages are received.

Source: Madagascar

Vibration: Extremely high

Chakra: Third eye, soma

Physiology: Hormonal and fluid balance, breasts, female reproductive organs

Cleansing: Avoid water

Tourmalinated Quartz

Grounded protection

An effective grounding stone, Tourmalinated Quartz clears the aura of negativity, transmuting it into positive. It creates a protective energy shield against harm or pollutants at any level, and is effective against EMF emissions and geopathic stress. Tourmalinated Quartz releases children who become addicted to gaming on their computer or phone, gently easing them away from the source of their obsession. The crystal eliminates ingrained destructive patterns and actualizes the strength needed to alleviate negative or hostile relationships and situations. The crystal facilitates shadow integration work. ⓘ

Ammonite

Turning inwards

Ammonite assists a child to look within, going deep down into the core of being and from there to recognize how feelings and emotions affect the external environment. The shape symbolizes universal energy and the sacred geometry that underpins our world. It represents the continually ebbing and flowing cycles of time and energy to which that world is subject. Filled with stabilizing Qi, Ammonite acts as a filter, clearing the auric field of negativity and removing all that is outgrown so that the new emerges. Its soothing energy is helpful for ear infections and similar problems.

Source: Brazil

Vibration: Earthy

Chakra: Earth star, base

Physiology: *See* Quartz, pages 38–45 and Tourmaline, pages 56–7

Cleansing: All

Source: Worldwide

Vibration: Earthy

Chakra: Earth star, base

Physiology: Female reproductive system, ears, lungs

Cleansing: All

Coprolite
('Dino Poo')

Ancient remains

Children are fascinated by Coprolite. After all, who would have expected dinosaur poo to be around today? It symbolizes just how long that which has apparently been eliminated hangs around. The stone enhances memory and facilitates past-life regression. It gets to the bottom of survival issues, providing courage to continue what may be a difficult journey through life. Coprolite strengthens intelligence and increases intellectual stability, assisting the assimilation of new information, mental flexibility and dexterity of thought processes. Perfect for exam time, Coprolite opens the mind to new ideas.

Tiger's Eye

Lightening

Tiger's Eye alleviates depression and lifts dark moods. It instils trust in the future, showing how to set realistic goals. Assisting in decision-making, it promotes clarity of intention. Tiger's Eye gently heals issues of self-worth, self-criticism and blocked creativity. It supports an obsessive or fearful personality to make changes. Tiger's Eye creates a high-vibrational yet grounded state, supporting children born with new energetic frequencies that do not fit well into the earth-plane as yet. Tiger's Eye teaches integrity and the correct use of power. It deflects negative energy and protects against ill-wishing and bullying. ❶

Source: UK, USA

Vibration: Earthy

Chakra: Earth star, base, sacral

Physiology: Skeletal and digestive systems, nutrient assimilation, detoxification

Cleansing: All

Source: South Africa, Australia

Vibration: Medium

Chakra: Solar plexus, third eye

Physiology: Eyes, digestion, throat, bones

Cleansing: Avoid water

Dragon's Blood Jasper

Inner dragon

Dragon's Blood Jasper is a fascinating stone that tames the inner dragon. Children love its magical energy and its ability to connect to these mythical creatures, who, as all children instinctively know, are nowhere near as scary as those portrayed in fairytales. They are helpful mentors. The stone assists children to separate fact from fiction: what they know in their heart to be true as opposed to what they are told. It creates a wide protective barrier around the body, strengthening the physical level of being as well as the energetic, and imparts courage to overcome obstacles.

Yowah Nut

Polarity-balancer

A combination of strong, protective Ironstone and delicate, cherishing Opal, a Yowah Nut balances polarities. It holds dualities such as mother and father, male and female, positive and negative, yin and yang in equilibrium, giving each an appropriate amount of power and influence. It balances the inner parental voices with the inner child's need. The Nut has a powerful connection to Mother Earth and her nurturing powers, reminding that we are all her children. During shamanic journeying, it takes you safely into the lower world for soul retrieval and integration work. On the dantien, it raises kundalini.

Source: South Africa

Vibration: Earthy and high

Chakra: Heart, earth star

Physiology: Brain, liver, gall bladder, small intestine, thyroid, immune system

Cleansing: All

Source: Queensland (Australia)

Vibration: High

Chakra: Gaia gateway, earth star, base, soul star, stellar gateway, causal vortex, alta major, dantien

Physiology: *See* Opal, pages 54–5

Cleansing: All

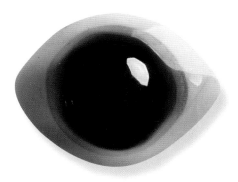

Shiva Agate Eye

The all-seeing eye

These beautiful stones wash up on an Indian riverbank and are carved into shape. A Shiva Agate Eye helps children to distinguish fantasy from reality. It provides protection against ill-wishing and bullying, enhancing intuition, imagination and concentration. With an abundance of Qi, it assists children who are apathetic to face challenges. The Eye encourages seeing what is necessary and making a commitment to future goals. Carrying one in the pocket stimulates creative solutions. The stone directs the course of dreams, resolving problems. It facilitates reading the Akashic Record and sacred texts, finding both inspiration and insight.

Source: India

Vibration: Earthy

Chakra: Third eye, soma

Physiology: Eyes

Cleansing: All

Crazy Lace Agate

Laughter-bringer

Crazy Lace Agate is a happy stone that promotes inner stability, outward composure and maturity. Its gift of laughter absorbs emotional pain and protects against further hurt. The protective qualities encourage security and self-confidence. A stone of focus, Crazy Lace Agate assists with difficult decisions, promoting mental agility, liveliness and flexible thinking. It brings shy children out of their shell and assists communication. This stone overcomes fear of spiders and crawling insects. It protects against sudden fears or negative vibes and is a useful amulet when travelling, being especially effective against traffic accidents.

Source: Mexico

Vibration: Medium

Chakra: Base, sacral, dantien

Physiology: *See Agate, pages 46–7*

Cleansing: All

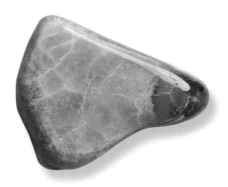

Youngite

Inner child

Youngite reconnects to the joyous, innocent child within everyone, releasing the creative power that child offers. Combining Brecciated Jasper and Drusy Quartz, the colour currently available is redder than previously, giving added impetus. Healing wounds from childhood and beyond, it assists soul retrieval and reintegration as it coaxes back childish soul fragments that split off through trauma, joy, projection or wishful thinking, no matter in what timeframe that occurred. This shamanic stone accesses different planes of consciousness, taking you to a space without thought, where souls meet and merge, linking multidimensions, supra-consciousness and All That Is.

Pink Carnelian

Parent–child harmony

The gentle energy of Pink Carnelian improves the parent–child relationship, making it more compassionate and loving on both sides. The stone restores trust in your Self after abuse or emotional manipulation. Releasing negative emotions such as envy, rage or resentment, it promotes a renewed love of life. Pink Carnelians assist anyone trapped in abusive situations, bolstering independence and faith in your own judgement. The stone reduces jealousy and possessiveness in romantic or parent–child relationships. It helps teens who face anguish over their sexuality. Pink Carnelian may assist with overcoming eating disorders.

Source: USA

Vibration: Medium

Chakra: Base, sacral, navel

Physiology: Non-physical

Cleansing: All

Source: Worldwide

Vibration: Medium

Chakra: Base, sacral, navel

Physiology: *See* Carnelian, page 79

Cleansing: All

Pink Moonstone

Gentle nurturer

This Moonstone, which is pinkish peach in colour, has a gentle, nurturing vibration attuned to divine feminine and goddess energy. It assists children finding it hard to bond with their mother, especially if there was separation at birth due to anaesthesia, birth challenges or adoption. On the navel, it eliminates feelings of abandonment and separation, reconnecting a nourishing etheric cord between child and parent, if appropriate. It assists mothers who had difficulty bonding with their child due to post-natal depression or complications of pregnancy and birth, or who over-compensate for a separation. This stone promotes emotional healing on both sides.

Pink Agate

Soul cleanser

The power of Agate lies in its ability to transmute noxious emotions, such as jealousy, bitterness and resentment carried from previous lives, creating unrest in the soul. Pink Agate heals this with a gentleness that makes it suitable for children. With its powerful cleansing effect, Agate highlights and releases anything standing in the way of wellbeing, especially traumatic experiences. Promoting self-acceptance and forgiveness, Pink Agate increases receptivity to spiritual promptings from the soul. Carrying a Pink Agate gives the courage to hold fast to your truth, especially if a child is being bullied.

Source: India, Australia, Austrian Alps, India, Burma, Poland, Norway

Vibration: High

Chakra: Navel

Physiology: *See* Moonstone, page 91

Cleansing: Avoid water

Source: Worldwide

Vibration: Medium to high

Chakra: Base, sacral, solar plexus, navel, past life

Physiology: *See* Agate, pages 46–7

Cleansing: All

Tangerine Aura Quartz

Creative metaphysics

Playful Tangerine Aura Quartz activates profound metaphysical abilities. Created by alchemy from vaporized gold, iron oxide and copper on Quartz, it stimulates the sacral chakra, making you feel more at home within your environment. It removes blockages so that creativity flows freely and effortlessly. A stone of psychological resilience, it promotes high self-worth and increases self-confidence. Carrying or wearing Tangerine Aura supports anyone trying to overcome self-esteem issues, as it stimulates love for one's Self. The crystal connects to your own unique gifts and talents.

Source: Manufactured

Vibration: High

Chakra: Base, sacral, solar plexus

Physiology: *See* Quartz, pages 38–45

Cleansing: Avoid water

Orange Natrolite

An angel on your shoulder

A stone of angelic communication, Orange Natrolite cleanses the crown chakra and anchors that connection on the earth-plane. It assists children – and adults – to connect to their personal guardian angel. Soothing worry and fear, Natrolite lifts cares and 'the weight of the world' off your shoulders and offers support when life is challenging or scary. It brings comfort and healing to past or present wounding, especially where there has been emotional and mental abuse. It eases fearful memories or anticipation. Orange Natrolite prevents nightmares and soothes a child suffering from night terrors.

Source: Canada

Vibration: High

Chakra: Crown and higher crown chakras

Physiology: Female reproductive and hormonal systems

Cleansing: Avoid water

Fuchsite

Independence

Helpful for a child who cannot be separated from an electronic device, Fuchsite shields from EMF output and calms the addiction. It accesses knowledge with practical value. The crystal assists a child interact with other people, especially socially. Perfect for a parent who over-caretakes a child, constantly doing things for them instead of letting the child be independent, or the parent who makes a martyr of themselves 'for the child's sake', it releases someone who is dependent on a child for their identity, restoring self-worth and a sense of being a separate self.

Green Tourmaline
(Verdelite)

Belonging

Calming Green Tourmaline supports hyperactive children and assists sufferers from claustrophobia or panic attacks. Detoxifying, it assists ailments such as constipation and diarrhoea. An excellent healer for the physical heart, this nurturing crystal brings balance and joie de vivre to life. It promotes compassion, tenderness and patience, instilling a sense of belonging and assisting a child who feels like an outsider within the family or school. Transforming negative to positive energy and dispelling fear, Green Tourmaline promotes openness and patience. The stone overcomes problems with father and authority figures. ●

Source: Brazil, India, Zimbabwe, Russia, Switzerland

Vibration: High

Chakra: Higher heart

Physiology: Red and white blood-cell ratio, carpel tunnel, spine, musculoskeletal system

Cleansing: Avoid water

Source: Brazil, Tanzania, Nigeria, Kenya, Madagascar, Mozambique, Namibia, Afghanistan, Pakistan, Sri Lanka, Malawi, USA

Vibration: High

Chakra: Heart

Physiology: Eyes. See Tourmaline, pages 56–7

Cleansing: Avoid water

Prehnite

All-round healing

Prehnite assists all childhood ailments. It stabilizes hyperactive children, releasing karmic causes of the condition. Prehnite alleviates nightmares, phobias and deep-seated fears. Aligned to Earth's meridian grid, the crystal seals the auric field in a protective shield. It brings peace and protection to the environment, teaching how to be in harmony with nature and elemental forces, revitalizing your surroundings. Prehnite connects to Archangel Raphael and multidimensional beings, assisting children who do not feel comfortable in the dense earth-vibration to contact their home planet. It also assists those who hoard possessions, or love, because of inner lack. ❶

Blue Howlite
(Turquenite)

A friend in your pocket

Children love this bright stone with its wonderfully calming properties. Blue Howlite reduces anxiety, tension and stress. It calms frustration and rage, quickly halting temper tantrums, aggressiveness, rudeness or emotional upsets. The stone releases attachments or cords linking emotional pain from this or a previous life to the present, so it is excellent for a child who carries over unhealed traumatic memories or inherits transgenerational trauma. The stone boosts children – or adults – who suffer from low self-esteem and who are crippled by self-criticism or shyness. It helps them to feel comfortable as they are.

Source: South Africa

Vibration: High

Chakra: Heart, higher heart

Physiology: Kidneys, bladder, thymus, shoulders, chest, lungs, connective tissue

Cleansing: All

Source: Canada (dyed)

Vibration: Low

Chakra: Crown, throat

Physiology: Bones, teeth

Cleansing: All

Charoite

Here and now

Charoite converts dis-ease into physical and emotional wellbeing and replenishes energy when exhausted. It bestows deep, refreshing sleep with insightful dreams, and overcomes insomnia. Relieving autism and manic depression, it calms stress and worry, bringing about a relaxed attitude. Charoite overcomes resistance and puts things into perspective. Bestowing drive, vigour and spontaneity, it facilitates acceptance of others. Stimulating perceptive analysis, it releases deep fears and dissipates compulsions and obsessions, releasing from other people's programming. The stone overcomes a sense of alienation or frustration and accepts the present moment as perfect.

Purple Fluorite

Order out of chaos

Protective Fluorite discerns when outside influences are at work and shuts off manipulation and undue mental influence. Guarding against computer and electromagnetic stress, it assists children who are addicted to electronic gadgets detach from them. Anti-viral, Fluorite cleanses and reorganizes anything within the body that is not in perfect order, overcoming any form of disorganization or chaos. It increases self-confidence and dexterity, assisting learning by integrating new information. Fluorite calms a hyperactive child, focusing the mind. It brings order and stability to groups, linking them into a common purpose, and helps a child to fit in. ❶

Source: Russia

Vibration: High

Chakra: Heart, crown, knee, causal vortex

Physiology: Autonomous nervous system, energy utilization, yin–yang, blood pressure, eyes, heart, liver, pancreas

Cleansing: All

Source: USA, UK, Australia, Germany, Norway, China, Peru, Mexico, Brazil

Vibration: Earthy to high

Chakra: Throat, third eye, crown

Physiology: Balance and coordination, teeth, cells, bones, DNA, skin, mucus membranes, respiratory tract, joints

Cleansing: Avoid water

Scapolite

Releasing scapegoating

Scapolite assists a child who has become the family scapegoat – blamed for ills the family suffers. The stone calls back projections, so each member of the family deals with their own issues and challenges. It silences the inner critic and self-blame that destroys self-confidence. Rejigging the emotional blueprint, Scapolite clears outdated emotional trauma. A stone of self-discipline stimulating independence, it sets achievable goals and creates conscious change. Freeing the left side of the brain, it overcomes dyslexia and hyperactivity. Blue Scapolite cuts through confusion, and Yellow rejects emotional manipulation and destructive thoughts such as 'I'm not good enough.'

Snow Quartz

Tact

Snow Quartz's effect is slower and gentler than Clear Quartz, making it suitable for children. It supports a child learning lessons that may feel overwhelming, or one who has had to take on more responsibility than is age-appropriate. Young carers are helped by this Quartz, which moves children – or adults – beyond perceived limitations. It releases a sense of martyrdom or victimhood or anyone who needs to be needed, answering the question 'Why me?' from a soul level. The gentle stone helps you to think before you speak, especially psychic children who blurt out what they are seeing.

Source: Madagascar, USA, Norway, Italy, Mexico

Vibration: High

Chakra: Base, sacral, navel, past life

Physiology: Intercellular memory, calcium assimilation, veins, bone, shoulders, eyes, bladder

Cleansing: Avoid water

Source: Worldwide

Vibration: Earthy

Chakra: All

Physiology: *See* Quartz, pages 38–45

Cleansing: All

Crackle Quartz

Damage limitation

Children are delighted by the light, bright energies of fun-loving Crackle Quartz. Although it has been superheated and colour-infused, it carries life-enhancing energy-expanding qualities. Promoting joy, it appeals to the inner child in everyone. The full colour range creates a useful chakra set for children. Pink Crackle Quartz heals an abused or emotionally damaged child, drawing out pain and replacing it with love. It teaches that no longer worrying about what others think creates emotional independence. The stone insists that you take responsibility for your feelings and actions. It soothes ear pain during flying.

Source: Heat-amended

Vibration: Medium to high

Chakra: All, according to colour

Physiology: Brittle bones. *See* Quartz, pages 38–45

Cleansing: All

White Muscovite

Clearing projections

White Muscovite is helpful for children who over-eat from a need for comfort or to quell feelings of inferiority or inadequacy. It supports during exploration of painful feelings and facilitates taking back projections, recognizing that everyone has flaws, but that overcoming these is part of the soul's learning programme. Dispersing insecurity, anger and self-doubt, it assists transformation and integration of unloved qualities. Stabilizing the brain, White Muscovite overcomes clumsiness, dyspraxia and left–right confusion. By allowing us to see ourselves as others see us, Muscovite changes the image presented to the outside world.

Source: Switzerland, Russia, Austria, Czech Republic, Brazil, New Mexico (USA)

Vibration: High

Chakra: Third eye, higher crown, navel

Physiology: Hair, eyes, weight

Cleansing: Avoid water

Crystals for karmic clearing

The influence of the past is ever-present. Your soul carries imprints of previous lives and past experiences – and karma. The subtle-energy bodies and chakras hold memories of traumas and dramas that occurred way back in the past, in addition to soul contracts made without regard to just how long 'forever' could be. This creates blockages and holds you on a karmic treadmill. Release the blockages, renegotiate contracts, reframe soul memories and you change the future. You also activate 'merit karma', the credit balance on your karmic credit card. By placing crystals on and around your body and karmic chakras, the past is released and imbalances rectified. The karmic blueprint, the subtle-energetic body created from past-life experiences, is rejigged, a new pattern is imprinted and soul-learning gifts emerge. You are ready for the next stage of spiritual evolution.

Karma

'Karma is cause and effect operating in everyday life. What is set in motion has consequences. Karma is purposeful, concerned with growth and evolution, rather than punishment. A balancing force, it is all-embracing and has many manifestations. Karma operates at different levels, from the personal to the collective. It shows where balance is needed and may involve reparation, or retribution for past actions, and reward and restitution. Karma does not simply stem from actions and events. It encompasses intention, words, attitudes, thoughts and desires – and ingrained habits.' (*The Book of Why*, Judy Hall)

People tend to view karma as punitive, but it is actually neutral and non-judgemental. What may be termed 'karmic misfortune' is simply the result of past actions coming round again to be balanced out. It is a tool for teaching the consequences of actions – past and present. It is through karma that the soul learns and progresses. Karma simply means that something from the past is manifesting now. It is not a punishment, but an effect. A balancing process that involves action and reaction, response and reparation, it is dynamic and creative. There are deficits and credits on the karmic 'credit card'. Karma may be carried over from previous lives and could also have roots in the present life. Desire, often called craving or wilfulness, creates karma. The human mind has a tendency towards intense attachment to what it wants, or thinks it wants.

Collective karma

Karma arises at a collective level, too, and creates problems for future generations. It arises out of wars, territorial disputes, genocide, religious intolerance and enforced conversion, exile and persecution. No one is responsible for collective karma in the sense of having personally created it, although souls may have been part of its source in conflict, purges, ideologies and mass movements. Lineage-breakers incarnate with the intention of taking on part of this collective karma and clearing it, for the wider whole and for the ancestors.

LEFT Dumortierite
RIGHT Shungite

Exercise

Karma-clearing grid

This grid cleanses and rebalances the karmic chakras.

Suitable karma clearing crystals: Dumortierite, Chrysotile, Blue Kyanite, Shungite, Ancestralite, Flint, Brandenberg Amethyst. *See also* the crystal portraits on pages 68–307.

1 Lie down where you will not be disturbed and place a Smoky Quartz or Flint below your feet.
2 Place a karma-clearing crystal in the hollow at the base of your skull.
3 Place a Brandenberg Amethyst, Trigonic Quartz, Anandalite, Selenite or Blue Kyanite crystal above your head pointing downwards. Allow your hand to intuitively place the crystal in the appropriate place, which may be to one side rather than central.
4 Place a karma-clearing crystal either side of your ears.
5 Lie still and breathe gently, allowing the crystals to gently dissolve the karma, pushing it down to the crystal at your feet for transmutation.
6 The crystal above your head will then input in a new energetic imprint.
7 Gather up the crystals in the reverse order to which they were laid and cleanse thoroughly.

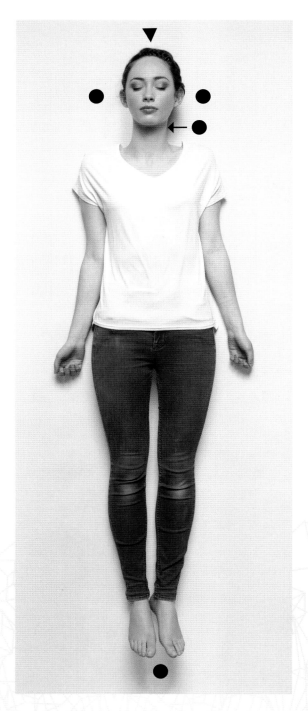

RIGHT A karma-clearing layout. Finger-dowse or pendulum-dowse (*see* page 26) to choose your crystals.

The karmic cycle

Karma demands that an incarnating soul takes responsibility for what is done. What is experienced in the future is the result of present action. Actions have consequences and time has little relevance in the working out of karma. Karma does not become inoperative, but it may go into suspension until conditions are right for it to 'ripen'. The connection between an action and a reaction may be immediately apparent, but this is not always so. Karma may be a delayed reaction. Time is not linear and chronological, it only seems that way from the perspective of Earth. So karma may appear to take a long time to come around, but in the context of eternal time it's the blink of an eye. The smallest of actions or briefest of thoughts produces karma. Every moment is pregnant with consequences. These consequences may not necessarily be 'bad'. Good karma matures in the same way that negative forms do. Karma may occur as a pattern of ingrained actions, attitudes and beliefs that repeat through a cycle of lives; or involve swinging between two opposite extremes until a balance is reached. Break the cycle, find the balance and the karma of grace operates and the soul is freed.

Karmic chakras

Karma is held in two main chakras – the past-life chakra and the causal vortex – and in the karmic blueprint, although other chakras and auric bodies may contain remnants of personal or ancestral karma. An engram can be created in a past life and carried over to the present through the karmic blueprint. An engram is a mental image that records an experience containing pain, unconsciousness and a real or fancied threat to survival. Activating these chakras may bring up memories to be released but could also reconnect to soul gifts previously developed. Crystals entrain the soul back to a more perfect pattern, dissolving karmic imprints and encrustations, freeing up karmic merits.

Past-life chakra

Carried-over dis-ease, unfinished business, attitudes and soul memory are embedded in this chakra (*see* page 23).

Causal vortex

The soul's plan and wider view of past lives are held in this chakra (*see* page 24) together with access to the Akashic Record (*see* page 216).

Healing past-life dis-ease

Karmic dis-ease arising out of soul dis-ease is created from trauma, wounds, injuries, attitudes and patterns or curses carried forward from past to present via the 'karmic blueprint' that creates a new body. Dis-ease may be physical, emotional, mental, spiritual or symbolic. It may offer an opportunity to learn certain attributes: patience, tolerance, compassion, and so on, that the soul feels have been overlooked, or offer someone else an opportunity to grow. It is not a matter of punishment or blame but of balancing out the past and allowing the soul to evolve. Placing appropriate crystals dissolves the cause, if the soul has finished learning through the dis-ease.

Karmic causes of dis-ease

- Soul unrest
- Soul intention
- Need to develop specific qualities
- Closed-mindedness
- Attitudinal karma
- Redemptive karma
- Bigotry or lack of empathy for others
- Unwillingness to hear others
- Direct carryover of affliction
- Organic karma

- Non-development of creative potential
- Curses or ill-wishing
- Conflict from several past-life personas
- Vows, promises, contracts
- Strongly negative past-life self trying to remanifest
- Past-life repression of pain refuses to be ignored any longer

Healing takes place through...

- Reframing the trigger event or cause
- Rejigging the karmic blueprint
- Removing the imprint/engram from the chakras
- Replacing with a positive imprint/engram

If healing does not occur...

- Soul may not have finished evolving through the condition
- Soul may be trying to 'get better' for inappropriate reasons, such as trying to get rid of the condition without learning the lessons behind it
- Soul may be entrenched in 'reparation-restitution' mode, aiming to get back what is felt to be 'owed' or to pay someone back
- Soul may have learned all it needs, and must incarnate again to put learning into practice
- Soul may be offering someone else an opportunity to change or grow

ABOVE LEFT AND LEFT The past-life chakra is behind the ears on the bony ridge. The causal vortex is located over or to the side of the head.

Reading the Akashic Record

The Akashic Record is a cosmic memory bank containing all that has been or that might be in any timeframe and all dimensions. It is rather like a computer that runs numerous simultaneous programmes. It can be read to reveal a soul's past lives, present purpose or potential futures. When you first read the record (*see* right), you may see images that move on quickly before you can fix them in place, but with practice it becomes easier. Sometimes information is dropped into your awareness as words or feelings rather than images. Moments of great emotional trauma and soul dramas make the biggest impression on the record, so these are what tend to be seen first. If you find a scene distressing, remember you are seeing it objectively, not reliving or embodying it. The scene can be reframed into a different outcome if it needs healing – all potential outcomes are available in the Record; you only have to ask for the most beneficial to be triggered.

OPPOSITE *Gazing into a Brandberg Amethyst crystal assists in reading the Akashic Record.*

Exercise

Reading the Record

Suitable crystals: A reading crystal such as Brandberg Amethyst, Chrysotile or Dumortierite not only assists in connecting to the Record but also protects while you access it. Opening the causal vortex chakra (*see* page 24) brings the Record closer.

1 Settle yourself comfortably where you will not be disturbed. Place a Flint or other grounding crystal at your feet.
2 Hold the reading crystal in your hands or place it around your head at the causal vortex chakra. With your eyes closed, look up to the third eye above and between your eyebrows.
3 Breathing rhythmically and easily, withdraw your attention from the outside world and concentrate your attention on the reading crystal. Ask it to open your causal vortex and the Record to you.
4 As the Record opens, the spirit of the reading crystal comes forward to be your guide.
5 If you have any specific questions, put them before your guide and ask to be shown the answers as and when appropriate.
6 When you have completed your Akashic session, disconnect your energies from the scene, thank your crystal guide and be aware of leaving the past behind. Ask the crystal to close your causal vortex chakra. Put the crystal down.
7 Slowly return your awareness to the room. Take a few deep breaths and then slowly open your eyes. Move your fingers and toes and ensure that your grounding cord is in place (*see* pages 262–3).

Brandberg (Brandenberg) Amethyst

The gateway

Source: Brandberg Mountain (Namibia)

Vibration: Exceptionally high

Chakra: All

Physiology: Maintains all organs and systems

Cleansing: All

Gateway to all that is, has been and ever shall be.

MAIN Brandberg point
OPPOSITE LEFT Golden Brandberg
OPPOSITE CENTRE Clear Brandberg
OPPOSITE RIGHT Brandberg Amethyst

Why the name change?

This crystal was introduced to me as 'Brandenberg'. But, having looked at the numerological difference, I've switched to Brandberg here as it equates to 11, a master healing number. The characteristics of number 11 are intuition, illumination, ability to function on a high spiritual plane and immense inner strength. This crystal resonates with those principles and manifests them in your life. 'Brandenberg', an inspirational number 3, expresses unique creativity, bringing spiritual gifts to Earth and anchoring them into practical reality. So, both names are appropriate.

Perfect blueprint

Found only around an ancient sacred massif in Namibia, multidimensional Brandberg Amethyst is a truly magical tool for healing and enlightenment, containing the perfect blueprint for all that is, has been or ever shall be. The crystal does everything required of it, and much more. Although known under the generic title Amethyst, this versatile crystal may be Smoky or Clear Quartz, Hematite Spotted or Citrine. Many Brandbergs contain phantoms, concentrated triangles or wisps of colour. Some encompass 'enhydros', bubbles of water millions of years old. Life-affirming enhydros symbolize the soul incarnated within the body. But no matter what outward form the crystal takes, or which colours are visible, all Brandbergs carry the entire spectrum and perfection of the whole. It is a holographic crystal; every part holds the essence of the whole. Brandbergs tend to be person-centred, getting up close and personal, so find one that matches your inner resonance. You'll identify this by the attraction you feel towards the crystal, as though it has leapt into your hand – or heart – and isn't going to leave. This stone has a compassionate crystal oversoul uniting its scattered parts, a perfect example of unity consciousness. Perhaps more than any other crystal it demonstrates that you are a separate being and part of the whole at one and the same time.

Karmic healing

Brandberg Amethyst takes the soul back to its roots and the pure spiritual essence from which it arose. It imprints that perfection into cellular and subtle bodies so that the physical body, and incarnated soul, clears the past and returns to a state of perfect balance. Amethyst is an extremely forgiving crystal, and transmutational Smoky Quartz a detoxifying one. Combine these with the high-vibrational master resonance of Clear Quartz, and Brandberg works on every level simultaneously. It repatterns limiting beliefs and automatic reactions buried so deep you didn't even know you had them. The crystal facilitates responding in a new and appropriate way to each moment, rather than relying on how it has always been.

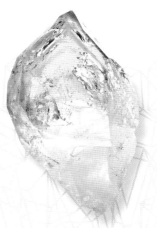

Brandberg removes thoughts or other implants, attachments or inappropriate mental influences from the current or previous lives, releasing their effect. Helpful if you have lost touch with your reason for incarnating, or when stuck in an outdated purpose with past-their-sell-by-date soul contracts and promises that are no longer relevant tying you to specific people or beliefs, the crystal facilitates the release of ties. It pertains only to what is relevant to the highest purpose of your incarnation and quickly clears the way for soul evolution.

Smoky Amethyst Brandberg calls soul-parts home, healing and detoxifying them as necessary before integrating into the overall soul. The crystal forms a

Smoky Brandberg: earth-healing

If land needs karmic or other earth-healing, look no further than a Smoky Brandberg. This is the finest earth-healer there is. It dissolves ancient trauma, loss or invasion, and returns the site to a state of energetic perfection. It reconnects breaks in Earth's etheric energy system. The healing is passed around the world via Earth's chakra and meridian lines.

temporary store for a soul-part that is reluctant to return or for one inadvertently held onto that actually belongs to someone else. The crystal oversoul conveys the soul-part to its rightful home.

Other properties

Brandberg opens the third-eye and soma chakras, giving deep insights into causes of problems and challenges. It connects to the Higher Self, the part of the soul not bound by the physical body that has much greater awareness of the soul's purpose and gifts and the soul-learning inherent in all experiences. Skeletal Brandbergs – and those with windows, external etchings and internal bubbles – take you into multidimensions that surround the physical world. The crystal expands intuition, facilitating being more mindful in the present day.

Brandberg creates emotional clarity. It teaches how to stand in your core, viewing the external world but not overwhelmed by it. It facilitates healing emotional wounds, reimprinting the subtle emotional body with a healthy resonance. Returning all energetic bodies to a state of perfection, the physical body is entrained into a more beneficial level of functioning.

A truly magical tool for healing and enlightenment.

LEFT Smoky Brandberg Earth-healer mentor
OPPOSITE LEFT Smoky Amethyst soul-keeper Brandberg
OPPOSITE RIGHT Clear Brandberg self-healed

Dumortierite

Past-life revealer

Source: Namibia, USA, Brazil, Sri Lanka, Madagascar, Canada, France, Poland, Peru

Vibration: High to extremely high

Chakra: Past life, soma, causal vortex, throat

Physiology: Psychosomatics, cellular memory

Cleansing: All

Dumortierite breaks a cycle of karmic co-dependency.

Characteristics

Dumortierite activates past-life memories, accessing the Akashic Record and the interlife, taking you to examine contracts, promises and agreements operating over aeons of time. It renegotiates these, rescinding ties or vows that no longer serve. Pinpointing patterns that underlie addictions and obsessive contacts, it highlights why you chose to learn through difficulties and challenges in toxic relationships. Thanking people for their role in your karmic learning process, you then let them go. Dumortierite breaks a cycle of karmic co-dependency, facilitating realization that it is not possible to control addictive, needy or self-destructive behaviour on someone else's behalf. You stand placidly by, unconditionally loving but not enabling or being overwhelmed by their traumas and dramas. The other person works it out themselves as you practise boundaried tough love.

MAIN Dumortierite
BELOW Shaped Dumortierite
RIGHT Dumortierite Palmstone
FAR RIGHT Dumortierite in Quartz

Confidence

Dumortierite instils unshakeable self-confidence, facilitating the ability to stand up for yourself in the everyday world. Supporting patience and courage, it activates your self-preservation instinct. Calming over-excitability, promoting detachment and opening positive self-love, Dumortierite creates a constructive attitude to life. For those who deal with crisis and trauma on a daily basis, it creates calm and focuses relief efforts. If you are chaotic and disorganized, Dumortierite helps you take control. ❶

Dumortierite in Quartz

In Quartz matrix, Dumortierite properties are heightened and easily assimilated, replacing toxicity with inner light. Issues are reframed in the interlife. Particularly helpful at the throat, past-life patterns are discussed and resolved with ease, as is facing up to personal or family addictions and extreme wilfulness or obstinacy.

Ocean Jasper

Integration

Reminding you that everything is fluid and cyclical, Ocean Jasper facilitates healing interventions related to Atlantis, particularly rectifying misuse of power. It reveals gifts in experiences, encouraging taking responsibility for your past. The whorls connect to spiritual wisdom and orbs symbolize the interconnectedness of all things, stimulating the desire to serve. Ocean Jasper retrieves lost soul-parts, integrates them and returns them to wholeness. A stone of strength and renewal, it is empathetic and objective, bringing unresolved emotional trauma to the surface, balancing out compulsions and assisting moving out of dis-ease into peaceful harmony.

Picture Jasper

Global awareness

Picture Jasper has a powerful connection to Earth, its energy system and meridians, electromagnetic forces and memories. Grounding you into the physical body, it heals the karmic blueprint. Reading the past by logging into the mineral kingdom's memory bank, the stone reveals knowledge that lies hidden at sacred sites. Linking together all cultures and timeframes, it provides protection during shamanic and soul-retrieval journeys and releases fears. Picture Jasper reminds us that humankind is not on the planet for purely selfish reasons, but that we are here to support one another and care for our planetary home.

Source: Madagascar

Vibration: Medium to high

Chakra: Heart, solar plexus, soma chakra, causal vortex

Physiology: Lungs, lymph and circulatory systems, female reproductive organs, digestive tract, skin, upper torso

Cleansing: All

Source: Brazil

Vibration: Earthy

Chakra: Earth star, base, sacral, solar plexus, third eye, past life, causal vortex

Physiology: Immune system, lungs, kidneys, skin, allergies

Cleansing: All

Pietersite

Walk your truth

Linking everyday consciousness to spiritual awareness, Pietersite reminds you that you are a spiritual being on a human journey. Assisting in processing ancient conflicts and suppressed feelings, it keeps you grounded in your etheric body when reading the Akashic Record, correcting the karmic blueprint. Pietersite dispels the illusion of separateness. It reveals the truth, or otherwise, of other people's words. Pietersite clears dis-ease created by not following your own truth, releasing mental and verbal conditioning imposed by authority figures, and dispelling spiritual illusions. The stone releases from vows and promises made in other lives carried into the present life. ⬤

Freedom Stone

'Don't make me over'

Freedom Stone teaches how to fearlessly stand up for your beliefs and encourages valuing every soul equally, especially the older generation. It shifts domination, racism and over-compromise. The stone lifts oppression and reassesses ideals for which you were prepared to die. If still relevant to your soul purpose, it reframes them into language more suited to your authentic Self. If no longer relevant, the stone releases them with grace. It helps you to never lose sight of why you are here, or to try to make anyone, including yourself, over to fit another person's demands.

Source: Namibia

Vibration: Medium

Chakra: Higher heart, third eye, past life, causal vortex

Physiology: Pituitary gland, endocrine and hormonal systems, metabolism, blood pressure, temperature, lungs, liver, intestine, feet, legs, absorption of nutrients

Cleansing: All

Source: Robben Island (South Africa)

Vibration: Earthy

Chakra: Past life

Physiology: Karmic blueprint

Cleansing: All

Nuummite

Stealth-giver

Protecting against ill-wishing and psychic manipulation, Nuummite clears ancient sorcery. Pulling out negative energy, imprints and implants, it must be approached with right intention or else it rebounds. Nuummite recognizes past-life contacts and highlights debts stemming from misuse of power. Drawing karmic debris out of physical and energetic bodies, it restores power depleted by karmic debts, or other causes, and clears blockages, reprogramming cellular memory. Severing present-life ties stemming from past manipulation or incantations, Nuummite assists lower-world journeys, travelling invisibly to retrieve a lost soul-part.

Source: Greenland, Canada

Vibration: High

Chakra: Past life, soma, causal vortex

Physiology: Tissue regeneration, insulin regulation, eyes, brain, kidneys, nervous system, triple-burner meridian

Cleansing: All

Wind Fossil Agate

Soul-scourer

Scouring karmic encrustations from body and soul, Wind Fossil Agate is excellent for past-life regression work. It highlights lessons yet to be learned, outdated vows, situations and relationships that need reframing. Wind Fossil Agate reveals soul contracts, pacts and promises holding the soul mired or hexed, which must be left behind in order to move forward. It highlights soul gifts and survival skills and teaches how to apply them to the present. This stone assists during challenging situations where strength and endurance are needed to overcome situations over which the soul, seemingly, has no control.

Source: Manufactured

Vibration: Earthy

Chakra: Past life, causal vortex

Physiology: *See* Agate, pages 46–7

Cleansing: All

Sea Foam Flint

Energetic extractor

The fossilized remains of ancient sponges on the sea floor, Sea Foam Flint filters toxicity from the soul and energetic bodies, drawing off karmic debris, removing even the smallest particles that have been left behind when clearing work has appeared to be complete. This Flint is different in action from the normal grounding qualities of the stone. Perfect for earth-alchemy and grounding cosmic light, it opens the Gaia gateway chakra and attunes it to Mother Earth, taking you deep into the soul of the planet and the divine feminine in the secret heart of Gaia.

Mystic Merlinite

Door-opener

Mystic Merlinite opens psychic abilities, moving into expanded consciousness to read the Akashic Record. During karmic clearing, Mystic Merlinite gathers up fragmented soul-parts, purifying them and reintegrating them into the incarnated soul or Higher Self, if it is inappropriate for a soul-part to return to Earth. The stone explores hidden parts of the psyche to better understand previous life situations that had a profound effect on how you live now. Contacting the elementals and devas of the planet, the stone assists karmic clearing for Earth.

Source: UK and elsewhere

Vibration: Earthy

Chakra: Gaia gateway, earth star

Physiology: Etheric bodies

Cleansing: All

Source: Madagascar

Vibration: Earthy

Chakra: Past life, causal vortex

Physiology: *See* Merlinite, page 166

Cleansing: All

Gaia's Blood Flint
(Red/Pink Flint)

Empowering women

Gaia's Blood connects to blood in all forms, but particularly menstrual and menopausal fluid flow. It belongs to a time when blood formed a sacred rite of initiation, connecting with sacred Earth. Pulling energetic remnants of previous abuse and traumas around childbirth and menses out of the body, it clears ancestral patterning from disempowered stereotypical women regarded only as 'mother', looking after everyone else and not being seen for who they really are. It releases being taken for granted or not heard. Gaia's Blood helps women to regain feminine power, especially when combined with blue-grey Milky Way Flint.

Vanadinite

Accepting physicality

Vanadinite assists people who have problems accepting their physicality, particularly when this has past-life causes such as over-indulgence, famine or fasting or flagellation. Grounding the soul into the physical body, it releases previous abuse and misuses of the body. It restores breathing patterns shut down by fear in this or any other life. The stone guards against squandering resources and teaches how to conserve physical energy. It shuts off mind-chatter during meditation, allowing insight and rational thought to combine into an inner voice of guidance. Vanadinite is excellent for creativity on all levels. ❶

Source: UK and elsewhere

Vibration: Earthy

Chakra: Gaia gateway, dantien, navel, base, sacral

Physiology: Female reproductive, lymphatic and hormonal system, puberty, PMS, menopause

Cleansing: All

Source: Morocco, New Mexico and Arizona (USA)

Vibration: Medium

Chakra: Earth star, base, sacral

Physiology: Respiratory system, bladder, energy utilization

Cleansing: Avoid water

Record Keeper Ruby

Akashic Record holder

Record Keeper Rubies contain ancient knowledge and past-life information. Many link to ancient Lemuria, Atlantis and early civilizations in India or the Middle East. Ruby passes energy throughout the entire body, revitalizing and repairing blueprints carried in auric bodies. It assists women who have had problems with child-bearing and menses in other lives and brought those patterns forward, and heals similar problems carried along the matriarchal line. The stone clears past-life blocks on libido, releasing vows of chastity, and calls in a twinflame or soulmate.

Sonora Sunrise
(Cuprite with Chrysocolla)

Empowerment

Sonora Sunrise combines Chrysocolla with Cuprite. Facilitating the exploration of past lives, it rectifies previous lack of integrity. Reframing destructive mental patterns and noxious emotions, it instils security to underpin your present life. Sonora Sunrise helps face with equanimity situations over which you have no control. It attracts a spiritual mentor, or releases from a past-life authority figure who has you under mind control. Its dynamism assists when you are weighed down by the past and lack courage to move forward. This stone sets you free. It instils new life-force into the subtle bodies and restores creative vitality. ⓘ

Source: Madagascar, India

Vibration: Medium

Chakra: Heart, past life, causal vortex

Physiology: *See* Ruby, page 108

Cleansing: All

Source: Mexico

Vibration: Earthy to medium

Chakra: Past life, causal vortex, soma, base, sacral, throat

Physiology: Throat, heart and blood, muscle tissue, skeletal and metabolic systems, bladder and kidney

Cleansing: All

Heulandite

Emotional release

Heulandite reconnects to ancient knowledge from Lemuria, Atlantis and other lives. Accessing multi- and internal-dimensional spaces, it reads the Akashic Record, taking you back into the karmic past to recover from loss or trauma. It shows how knowledge gained can be applied to your present life. Heulandite facilitates changing ingrained habits or behaviours, especially those at a cellular level or within junk DNA, replacing these with openness to new ways and future possibilities. The stone releases ancient jealousy and other negative emotions, alleviating superiority and condescension and judgemental or condemning attitudes.

Atlantasite

Atlantis-connector

Atlantasite accesses past lives in Atlantis, assisting those who misused their spiritual powers at that, or any other, time, making reparation, where appropriate. Reconnecting to ancient wisdom, it facilitates completing projects whose time has now come. Gently encouraging children to modify inappropriate behaviour, it helps break away from results of poor choices or old wounds, healing detrimental patterns and instilling a positive approach. An effective harmonizer of disputes and useful earth-healer, Atlantasite brings peace into the environment and undertakes earth-clearing and energy restructuring where there has been death or destruction.

Source: India, Iceland

Vibration: High

Chakra: Past life, causal vortex, heart

Physiology: Brain and nervous system, endocrine system, heart, cellular memory, joints, lower limbs, blood flow, kidneys, liver

Cleansing: Avoid water

Source: Australia, South Africa

Vibration: High

Chakra: Aligns all

Physiology: Cellular memory, blood, pancreas

Cleansing: All

Chrysotile or Chrysotile in Serpentine

Primeval language

Tumbling Chrysotile reveals ancient writing imprinted onto its surface that contains the knowledge of ages. Rapidly accessing the history of the soul, Chrysotile reads the Akashic Record to discover causes of soul dis-ease or distress. It clears toxic dross, particularly at the emotional level, so that a more beneficial pattern manifests. Helpful where a soul has been a control freak, either with regard to its own life or that of others, the stone gently encourages letting go and moving with the flow of life. This stone contains asbestos; exercise caution and always use tumbled crystals. ❶

Variscite

Encouragement

Facilitating past-life exploration, Variscite enhances visual images while exploring feelings and experiences. Stimulating insights into causes of dis-ease, contracts or patterns that have been carried over, it releases and reframes situations. Variscite facilitates moving out of deep despair into hope. This stone does away with pretence, enabling you to show yourself to the world as you are. Calming nervousness, it instils a quiet heart. Variscite supports sobriety and yet has a lively energy that prevents you from becoming too serious. It induces peaceful sleep and an untroubled mind. ❶

Source: USA, Canada, India, Russia, Australia

Vibration: Medium

Chakra: Throat, past life, alta major, causal vortex

Physiology: Parathyroid, throat, lungs, brainstem, central meridian channels, etheric blueprint, cellular memory

Cleansing: All

Source: USA, Germany, Austria, Czech Republic, Bolivia

Vibration: Medium

Chakra: Past life, causal vortex

Physiology: Energy reserves, nervous system, abdomen, blood circulation, veins, skin, male reproductive organs

Cleansing: Avoid water

Paraiba Tourmaline

Radiant compassion

Paraiba Tourmaline instils infinite compassion for yourself and the planet. Bringing harmony and light into the darkest of situations, it finds the gift at the heart. Encouraging forgiveness at multi- and inner-dimensional levels, it brings unfinished business to a conclusion, providing closure. Paraiba Tourmaline breaks self-defeating programming, replacing it with the present soulplan. Assisting in living according to your goals, the stone identifies where you have strayed from your truth. Paraiba invokes tolerance of others, overcoming judgementalism and fanaticism. It offers support to anyone overwhelmed by responsibility and encourages accountability for your Self. ●

Covellite

Doorway to past

Covellite opens a doorway to wisdom acquired in other lives and releases ingrained beliefs from repressive lifetimes. It assists when you feel vulnerable and are too easily influenced by others, overcoming discontent and instilling satisfaction with life. Covellite facilitates coming to terms with sexuality, releasing past-life celibacy vows and enhancing libido. It harmonizes body, mind and soul and facilitates loving yourself unconditionally while eliminating vanity and arrogance, despondency and anxiety, replacing negative emotions with loving serenity. Covellite transforms dreams into realities and stimulates metaphysical abilities. ●

Source: Brazil, Nigeria (heat-treated)

Vibration: Exceedingly high

Chakra: Three-chambered heart, third eye

Physiology: Metabolism and hormone production. *See* Tourmaline, pages 56–7

Cleansing: Avoid water

Source: Italy, USA, Germany, Sardinia, Wales, Alaska

Vibration: Medium

Chakra: Past life, causal vortex, navel

Physiology: Uterus, digestive organs, ears, eyes, nose, mouth, sinuses, throat, energy management

Cleansing: All

Datolite

'This too shall pass'

Datolite connects to the Akashic Record and downloads knowledge into the third eye. The information slowly but surely reveals the overall soulplan running through your lives. Inducing karmic and ancestral healing, Datolite retrieves data encoded in subtle bodies and junk DNA, connecting to ancestral patterns and events so that you understand why your family is as it is, before healing the past. It activates personal soul far-memory. During violent upheaval or tumultuous change, Datolite provides comfort and inner peace, recognizing and accepting the transience of all things, reminding that everything passes.

Ice Quartz

Karmic solace

Ice Quartz lets go of control mechanisms that, historically, made you feel safe from hurt, but which no longer serve. It opens a new relatedness to yourself and others. An emotional healer that releases anything emotionally entangling from past lives, Ice Quartz facilitates stepping off the karmic treadmill of relationships. Teaching emotional independence and autonomy, it brings about realization that you alone are responsible for creating and maintaining your sense of wellbeing, releasing dependence on any external source, including a loved one, and finding solace in being with your Self.

Source: Mexico, USA, South Africa, Tanzania, Scotland, Russia, Germany, Norway, Canada

Vibration: High

Chakra: Third eye, past life, causal vortex, navel

Physiology: Brain, cellular memory, spleen

Cleansing: All

Source: Himalayas, Pakistan

Vibration: High

Chakra: Higher crown, causal vortex

Physiology: *See* Quartz, pages 38–45

Cleansing: All

Lodalite
(Shaman Quartz)

Shamanic dreams

Gazing into Lodalite Quartz shifts consciousness on to a visionary level, giving insight into past lives and multidimensions. A powerful journeying tool, it provides protection during shadow work and karmic clearing. Facilitating getting in touch with repressed emotions, Lodalite releases fear and promotes understanding of the impermanence of body and ongoing cycles of birth, death and rebirth. The stone radiates love and strength, bringing deep healing from past-life attachments and traumatic events. Removing fear of change, Lodalite shifts rapidly through transformation, harmonizing higher-vibrational energies into the aura, subtle bodies and lightbody.

Phantom Quartz

Releasing the past

Phantom Quartz puts the past into context. Accessing the Akashic Record, it releases repressed memories. Phantom Quartz stimulates karmic clearing for the planet and activates healing abilities. Amethyst Phantom accesses the pre-birth state and present lifeplan. Chlorite Phantom facilitates the removal of energy implants, and planetary healing. Smoky Phantom takes you back to before you left your soul group, linking into the purpose of a group incarnation and identifying members of that group. Where negative energies have intervened in a group's purpose, Smoky Phantom removes these, taking the group back to purity of intention.

Source: Brazil

Vibration: Extremely high

Chakra: Harmonizes with aura

Physiology: *See* Quartz, pages 38–45

Cleansing: All

Source: Worldwide

Vibration: Depends on type

Chakra: All

Physiology: *See* Quartz, pages 38–45

Cleansing: All

Pollucite

Toxic clearer

A powerful detoxifier, Pollucite removes fragments of leftover negativity from the auric bodies, when slowly swept from the top of the head down to the feet (place a transmuting crystal at the feet before commencing). Over the heart, it removes previous heartbreak. Over the third-eye or soma chakra, it clears pernicious thoughts and outdated soul intentions or contracts. Over the past-life or causal vortex chakras, it dissolves ingrained karmic patterning. The crystal facilitates access to angelic realms and those who have passed on, encouraging ancestral healing. It draws together people of all nations to create peace.

Source: Skardu Valley (Pakistan)

Vibration: High

Chakra: Past life, causal vortex, soma, third eye, crown, heart

Physiology: Etheric bodies

Cleansing: Avoid water

Celestial Quartz

Celestial connector

Grey or reddish-coated white Celestial Quartz from Madagascar has a grounded energy that assists people who only have a toehold in the physical body take up residence on Earth, while maintaining a strong connection to the lightbody and retaining full spiritual awareness. Connecting to the Akashic Record, it checks the progress of soul intention. The stone reminds that, when sufficient work is done, the karma of grace sets the soul free from the past. Celestial energies are expressed within the everyday physical world. Extremely effective in grids for earth-healing, it repairs Earth's meridian system.

Source: Madagascar

Vibration: Earthy and high

Chakra: All

Physiology: *See* Quartz, pages 38–45

Cleansing: All

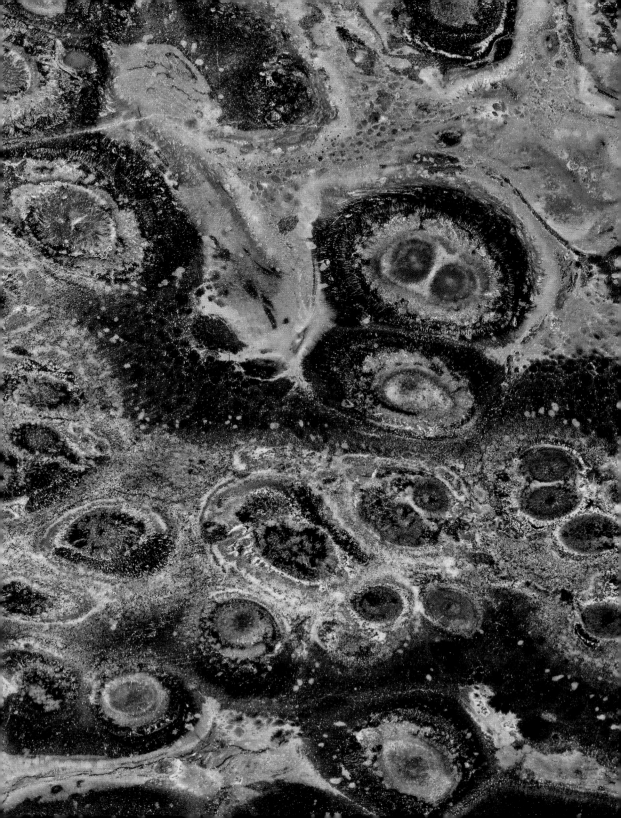

Crystals for ancestral healing

Transgenerational trauma (ancestral trauma that is passed down the family line) is becoming more widely recognized as a cause of dis-ease in second, third and future generations. An ancestral theme can arise from a single, potent act of trauma, oft-repeated abuses or inherited intransigent attitudes, beliefs and events. Transgenerational themes play out through several generations experiencing the same issue or dis-ease. Themes passed down the ancestral line are encoded in junk DNA, and may be expressed through constriction of the psoas or 'soul' muscle and flawed cellular memory.

Transgenerational trauma

Transgenerational contracts and outdated ancestral soul intention are cut off from your conscious mind. but may nevertheless affect your behaviour as they are lodged in your cellular memory and junk DNA.

Toxic family karma

Toxic karma consists of collective karma passed through the family line created from traumatic situations, intransigent attitudes, pernicious emotions and 'banned feelings' – deemed unacceptable or inappropriate to the family's status – limiting belief systems, soul contracts, curses, abuse and the like. It particularly applies to transgenerational trauma carried in genes and to survivor guilt or being rootless, in exile from 'the homeland'.

Junk DNA

Junk DNA is the 98 per cent of DNA for which science couldn't immediately find a use. It didn't 'code', so they called it junk. But 'junk' is giving up its secrets and offering a recycling opportunity for personal trauma and transgenerational memories. It's like a computer memory chip with Random Access Memory (RAM) – something we can access and reprogramme. Junk DNA is passed through the ancestral line, so it's where we tune into a vast field of transgenerational experience. Junk DNA is found in every cell of our bodies, and epigenetics has important implications for healing and transforming the past,

switching off inappropriate, detrimental genetic reactions and switching on positive, beneficial responses. Crystals hold the purest energy pattern, one that is radiated through their vibrations. They bring the body, junk DNA and the ancestral line back into balance.

Breaking 'stuck-memory syndrome' and PTSD response

Past life and 'stuck-family memories' are passed on through junk DNA. Eye Movement Desensitization and Reprocessing (EMDR) desensitizes stuck-memory syndrome, treating past-life memories, phobias, post-traumatic stress disorder (PTSD) or transgenerational trauma. EMDR uses rapid eye movements to shift focus and take you into a calm space. A crystal with distinctive markings assists your eyes to make the movements. Choose a chunky, flat-faced crystal with pronounced bands or spirals, such as Shiva Shell, Banded Agate, Sardonyx or Malachite. This exercise works particularly well if you have the memory in your mind's eye, or you could concentrate on a feeling that a trigger has aroused. Don't try to push the picture or feeling away, let it fade naturally as your eyes move around the crystal. Lying down and placing past-life memory release crystals on the past-life and causal vortex chakras, or emotional release on the heart and solar plexus, further assists.

Exercise

Breaking the response

Suitable crystals: Choose a chunky, flat-faced crystal with pronounced bands or spirals such as Shiva Shell, Banded Agate, Sardonyx or Malachite.

1 When a memory or feeling surfaces, hold the crystal level with your eyes with your arm partially bent so that it fills your field of vision.
2 Look left and focus on the topmost corner at the starting point of a band or spiral. Follow the circle right around to your starting point, or follow a spiral into the centre and out again.
3 Time your breathing to fit in with the movements:
    – Breathe in as you go across to the right.
    – Breathe out as you go down and back to the left.
    – Breathe in again as you move up to your starting point.
    – Repeat the cycle.
4 As you do so, repeat to yourself, 'This is a memory, it is fading. I am healing.'
5 Repeat 10–15 times and repeat whenever the memory or feeling arises again, until it is negated.
6 Keep the stone in your pocket and touch it frequently.

ABOVE The lines on a Malachite assist in breaking PTSD response.

RIGHT Ancestral trauma and toxic family karma are stored in the DNA.

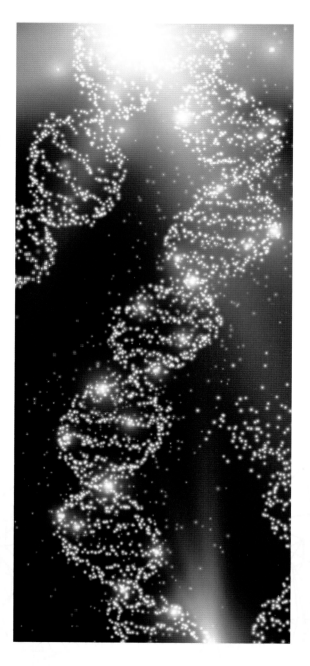

ABOVE Placing a Shiva Shell or other PTSD-releasing crystal on the third eye can assist in breaking the PTSD response.

The soul muscle

The core-stabilizing muscle of the body, the psoas connects your trunk, legs and spine. A healthy psoas grounds you into the planet, acting like an earthing wire. When holding traumatic personal or ancestral memories, the psoas affects your structural balance and keeps the body in permanent 'fight or flight' mode.

Exercise

Relaxing the psoas

Releasing psoas tension can have a dramatic effect on the body.

Suitable crystals: Magnesite, Magnetite, Smoky Quartz, Flint, Hematite. *See also* the crystal portraits on pages 68–307.

1　Place a Smoky Quartz or other grounding crystal at your feet.
2　Place Magnesite or other tension-releasing crystal on the tip of your breastbone.
3　Place two more crystals on either side of your hips in the groin crease.
4　Place your hands over the groin-crease crystals and lie still for ten minutes or so, breathing deeply into your belly and pushing the energy down to your feet. You will feel your body relaxing and lengthening as you do so.
5　When you are ready, remove the crystals, stand up and re-anchor yourself to the planet through your feet.

ABOVE Flint
ABOVE RIGHT Magnetite
RIGHT Magnesite

Healing ancestors

ABOVE An ancestral healing grid laid out on a Tree of Life board.

OPPOSITE Use this ancestral tree illustration for your own ancestral healing layout.

The ancestral line is not only your family tree, but that of all humanity. Placing ancestral healing crystals on the family tree – an actual one if you have one, or else a symbolic version like the tree shown here – sends healing down the family line and forward into future generations. You can seed gifts into the future too. Placing Ancestralite on the roots, an anchoring stone such as Preseli Bluestone or Petrified Wood on the trunk, and light-bearing crystals such as Anandalite or Selenite on the upper branches sends healing and forgiveness right back to the earliest generic ancestors and then out to the future, bringing previous soul learning forward for the benefit of those who have yet to be born.

Ancestral healing grid: Petrified Wood, Ancestralite, Selenite, Cradle of Life, Flint and Eye of the Storm.

Exercise

Healing the ancestral tree

Suitable crystals: Ancestralite, Cradle of Life, Preseli Bluestone, Petrified Wood, Anandalite, Selenite, Eye of the Storm. *See also* the crystal portraits on pages 68–307.

1 Place anchor crystals around the base of the tree.
2 Place a keystone in the centre of the trunk.
3 Place Ancestralite or another suitable stone around the outside of the tree.
4 Picture healing going deep down into the ancestral roots.
5 Place light-bringing crystals in the branches.
6 Picture healing going forward to generations yet to come, seeding the gifts they will need.
7 Leave the grid in place for as long as possible, cleansing the crystals frequently.

Preseli Bluestone

Inner compass

Source: Preseli Mountains (Wales)

Vibration: High

Chakra: Heart, thymus, throat, third eye, soma

Physiology: Karmic and etheric blueprint, sensory organs, DNA

Cleansing: All

This is a visionary stone for all past-life exploration.

Characteristics

Preseli Bluestone is an immensely physical stone, involving the senses and balancing energy. Bluestone moves out of space and time to access multidimensions. With its powerful electromagnetic charge, it creates an unshakeable core solidity to stabilize you through Earth changes and allows waves of energy to pass through your body to ground themselves in the planetary centre. Bluestone warns that whoever violates the planet violates themselves. The stone heals past defilements, however. A strong battery, generating, earthing and grounding spiritual power, it enhances psychic ability and metaphysical gifts. Large pieces may need to be moved out of a bedroom or healing room to avoid over-stimulation. Its directional quality channels Earth's electromagnetic forces and heals the grid where this has been damaged. If power is being drawn from a sacred site for inappropriate purposes, Bluestone breaks the connection and restores the vitality of the site.

Celtic roots

A visionary stone for all past-life exploration, Preseli Bluestone specifically tracks Celtic and ancient British heritage and links to Egyptian knowledge held deep within the stone. On the soma or past-life chakras, it assists soul and power retrieval, reaching way back into the past. The perfect dreaming stone, Bluestone rapidly brings answers, accessing and integrating spiritual information. It has a strong connection with herbs and herbalism, especially those grown on mountains.

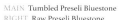

MAIN Tumbled Preseli Bluestone
RIGHT Raw Preseli Bluestone

Ancestralite

'The buck stops here'

Source: Canada

Vibration: Earthy and high

Chakra: Past life, causal vortex, navel

Physiology: DNA, RNA, etheric blueprint, bones, teeth, jaws, structure, inherited diseases

Cleansing: Avoid water

Ensures that toxic karmas and attitudes do not carry into future generations.

Characteristics

A powerful and exceedingly ancient combination, Ancestralite underwent profound metamorphic change, being thrust to the surface by volcanic action, making it suited to ancestral healing. It literally gets down to bedrock, sinking through layers of the past to reach the collective level. Ancestralite clears the generic ancestral line of trauma, dramas, ingrained emotions, attitudes, soul contracts and imperatives passed down the family tree for generations, while preserving soul learning. It assists lineage-breakers, so that toxic karmas and attitudes do not carry into future generations.

Putting down burdens

In situations where a parent needs to stop feeling overly responsible for a child who has now grown to adulthood, Ancestralite assists 'the child' to step into an independent life. It renegotiates and releases soul contracts and vows or promises made in previous lives or the interlife. Placed in a pentagram, Ancestralite connects the past and the Akashic Record to the ever-present now. Used as a grid (*see* pages 242–3), it sends healing far back into the family past and out into future generations. This crystal heals inherited dis-eases transmitted through familial DNA, or dis-eases and ingrained attitudes passed down the family line. It works with generic ancestors to heal racial issues carried in subtle-energy bodies and junk DNA.

MAIN Ancestralite
BELOW Ancestralite

Stibnite

Tentacle-clearer

Stibnite detaches tentacles from clingy relationships, especially after physical separation. Facilitating past-life and ancestral releases, it assists if you find it difficult to say no to a former partner or family member – although, having tie-cut, a situation may arise that tests whether you can stand your ground. Stibnite creates an energetic shield around the physical body, and is excellent for releasing entity possession or negative energy. It helps to see the gold in your centre, re-membering soul gifts. Shamanically, Stibnite carries the energy of wolf, facilitating journeying with this important power ally. Exercise caution: Stibnite is toxic, as it contains lead. Handle it with care and wash your hands thoroughly after using it. ❶

Snakeskin Agate

Shapeshifter

Traditionally conferring invisibility, Snakeskin Agate shapeshifts. The stone sheds your outgrown skin, sloughing off the past to be reborn. It clears ancestral patterning and outdated soul contracts from karmic and ancestral bodies. Helping to travel unseen in the upper and lower worlds, it is a useful accompaniment for soul retrieval. This stone activates kundalini rise and instigates regeneration. It lends the cunning of a serpent when handling devious or difficult situations, especially within the family. Snakeskin Agate roots you into your body and Earth, fully accepting incarnation.

Source: Japan, Romania, USA, China

Vibration: Medium

Chakra: Base, sacral, soma, solar plexus, spleen

Physiology: Cellular memory, oesophagus, stomach

Cleansing: Avoid water

Source: USA, India, Morocco, Czech Republic, Brazil, Africa

Vibration: Earthy

Chakra: Base, sacral, navel

Physiology: *See* Agate, pages 46–7

Cleansing: All

Leopardskin Serpentine

Ancestral roots

Leopardskin Serpentine keeps you earthed while undertaking ancestral or lower-world journeys. Facilitating trance and deep meditation, it opens a direct channel to spiritual guidance. Taking you back to the roots of your family tree, it shapeshifts to reclaim power, especially that misplaced or stolen in previous lives or in other dimensions. It assists anyone disempowered by ancestral beliefs. Offering insights into why you are living the life you are, or chose that particular family, it highlights qualities being brought out. Leopardskin Serpentine responds to holding or environmental placement rather than placement on the body.

Chalcedony Tear

Unfurling the self

The soul shines under the influence of a Chalcedony Tear. Clearing the throat chakra so that absolute truth is spoken, whatever has been held back unsaid is courageously and straightforwardly communicated, particularly at the emotional level. The stone unfurls the 'you that has never been allowed to shine before'. It inspires self-confidence and creates an open and enthusiastic persona. A Chalcedony Tear releases toxic thoughts, transmuting them into joy. It brings mind, body, emotions and spirit into harmony, eases self-doubts and facilitates constructive inward reflection. Chalcedony Tears are beneficial for breast conditions.

Source: UK, Norway, Russia, Zimbabwe, Italy, USA, Switzerland, Canada

Vibration: Earthy

Chakra: Earth star, base, sacral, soma

Physiology: Thyroid, parathyroid, pancreas

Cleansing: All

Source: Morocco

Vibration: High

Chakra: Throat, higher crown

Physiology: Breasts, eyes, gall bladder, bones, spleen, blood and circulatory system

Cleansing: All

Cradle of Life
(Cradle of Humanity)

Holding catalyst

Cradle of Life strips you back to basics and rebuilds your Self. Highlighting how much of other people's energy is held in your energy field, it clears it together with inherited junk DNA, so that you switch on beneficial DNA to move on from family patterns. If you've been uprooted, it helps find a new home within your Self. Creating a holding space where something has been let go, it keeps it open until new patterns kick in. The Cradle has a profound deep link to Gaia and all that is stored in the DNA of Mother Earth.

Chrysanthemum Stone

Time traveller

Chrysanthemum Stone drifts gently through time, taking healing down the ancestral line and forward into future generations. Radiating harmony, it integrates change and shows how past and present work together. Exuding calm confidence, it facilitates being centred in the present moment rather than the past. Chrysanthemum Stone teaches how to remain childlike, not mired in childhood. Encouraging you to be fun-loving and innocent while on a spiritual path, it kickstarts self-development. The stone overcomes bigotry, ignorance, narrow-mindedness, self-righteousness and jealousy. Encouraging showing unconditional love to the world, it brings more love into your family life.

Source: Magaliesburg (South Africa)

Vibration: Earthy and high

Chakra: Heart, throat, third eye, navel

Physiology: Bones, teeth

Cleansing: All

Source: China, Japan, Canada, USA

Vibration: Earthy and high

Chakra: Soma, heart seed, past life

Physiology: Physical maturation, apoptosis, skin, skeleton, eyes, detoxification

Cleansing: All, if tumbled

Isua

Ancient wisdom

One of the most ancient rocks, Isua takes you travelling through time and space and expands into infinite possibilities. Created when land and sea had already separated – something science had not thought possible that early – the stone helps you to do the impossible. It taps into Earth's own Akashic Record. Its message is 'Chill out, don't take life too seriously – it's all happened before and will do again.' This rock is grounding, anchoring the soul into the body and balancing auric bodies. Protective, it removes blockages and shields against negative energy.

Dinosaur Bone

Bones of creation

Dinosaur Bone is excellent for ancestral or karmic healing, taking you far back into the past to understand and heal basic survival issues. Dissipating anxiety and instilling confidence in the future, it sends reassurance down the family line, communicating to future generations that all will be well. Switching off the 'fight or flight' mechanism and adrenal overload passed through junk DNA, it frees the family from transgenerational trauma. As it is basically an infill of the original bone, it takes you back to first causes and dissolves patterns that do not belong in your spiritual DNA.

Source: Greenland

Vibration: Earthy and high

Chakra: All

Physiology: Ancestral blueprint

Cleansing: All

Source: UK, USA, Australia

Vibration: Earthy

Chakra: Navel, past life, causal vortex

Physiology: Bones, teeth, adrenals, temperature, cell growth, hearing

Cleansing: All

Stromatolite

Eternal knowledge

Stromatolite carries eternal knowledge. Acting as a portal to the far past of Earth, it delves deep into closely guarded ancestral secrets. It reads the Akashic Record and looks to the future. Having weathered billions of years of chaos, catastrophe and transformation, it is an excellent support during evolutionary change. It encourages standing in your own power, acting under your soul's direction to fulfil personal and planetary goals. If you have been imprinted with outdated ancestral mental programmes that insist you conform to someone else's agenda, Stromatolite releases these. It facilitates being less emotionally stressed.

Ammolite

Personal empowerment

Ammolite is a stone of personal empowerment showing that perseverance pays off. It stimulates creativity and stamina and promotes wellbeing on all levels. Opening connection to your spiritual gifts, it attracts mentors from the spirit world. On the base chakra it activates your survival instincts, and on the third eye promotes insight. On the soma chakra, it connects to your soulplan for the present incarnation, releasing ingrained pernicious thoughts and emotions that are holding you back. A stone of prosperity, its magnetism brings a project to fruition.

Source: USA, Russia, Madagascar, Australia

Vibration: Earthy and high

Chakra: Earth star, base, sacral, navel

Physiology: Autonomic processes, brain hemispheres, thymus, throat, hands, feet, brain stem, bones, teeth, kidneys, bladder, fluid regulation

Cleansing: All

Source: Rocky Mountains (Canada and USA)

Vibration: High

Chakra: Base, third eye, soma

Physiology: Cell metabolism, cellular memory, pulse, cranium, inner ear, lungs, limbs

Cleansing: Avoid water

Petrified Wood

Ancient records

Petrified Wood keeps you firmly grounded while exploring the multidimensional universe. Helpful when exploring past lives, it connects to the Akashic Record of your soul and the planet. The stone offers support during spiritual growth and the work necessary to evolve. It facilitates the release of all that no longer serves, while retaining what does. If everything is too much to bear, Petrified Wood provides emotional comfort and sustenance. Overcoming chronic fatigue syndrome or ME, it provides support during the ageing process. Petrified Wood is excellent for all earth-healing work.

Montana Agate

Planetary Tree

Mossy Montana Agate contains an ancestral tree for the planet that goes back to the earliest ancestors and their intimate relationship to Mother Earth, so is perfect for ancestral and earth-healing. The stone discerns the truth about the ancestral past, accepting circumstances with grace and healing toxic emotional residue. This grounding stone cleanses the earth star and works up the chakric line, balancing yin and yang and taking controlled kundalini flow with it. Bringing about emotional balance, it integrates subtle bodies with the physical body so that the soul accepts the reality of physicality.

Source: Worldwide

Vibration: High

Chakra: Earth star, base, sacral, solar plexus, higher heart

Physiology: Oxygenation of cells, bones, joints, muscles

Cleansing: All

Source: Montana (USA)

Vibration: Earthy

Chakra: Earth star, base, navel

Physiology: *See Agate, pages 46–7*

Cleansing: All

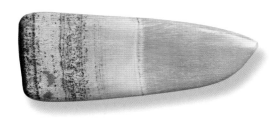

Celestobarite

Janus face

Celestobarite looks to past, present and future and explores multidimensional layers of being. A powerful shamanic shield, Celestobarite cuts through blockages and takes you to the edge and beyond. It conveys you down the ancestral tree to where ancestral soul aspects reside, assisting in reintegrating the family line. This oracle stone shows you both sides of an issue, elucidating what is not clear but leaving you to decide what to believe or put into practice. Its energy reminds you that nothing stays the same, teaching how to laugh at yourself and the absurdities of the human condition.

Celtic (Welsh) Golden Healer

Patriarchal-line healer

Celtic Golden Healer Quartz is deeply nurturing and joy-full, infused with sunshine and good vibes. It is an excellent crystal for clearing the patriarchal line. Place it on the ancestral tree and leave it to do its work. It is a powerful cleanser, both physically and psychosomatically. Releasing all that no longer serves, especially toxic thoughts, it infuses new energies. Healing back to the beginning of time, it takes the healing insights out through the ancestral line into the future so that new generations benefit. It heals the planetary past, anchoring healing light for the future.

Source: England, Poland, Denmark, Australia, USA

Vibration: Earthy

Chakra: All

Physiology: Beyond the physical

Cleansing: Avoid water, unless polished

Source: Wales

Vibration: Exceedingly high

Chakra: All

Physiology: *See* Quartz, pages 38–45

Cleansing: All

Lakelandite

Potent combination

Lakelandite returns to a time before the soul was shaped and fashioned by outside influences, to find your true Self once again. Born at a violent and cataclysmic time, Lakelandite was buried and eventually exposed by glacial action and erosion. Lakelandite deals with transgenerational trauma, bringing order out of chaotic situations and peace to the ancestral line, dissolving limiting belief patterns. It breaks restrictions imposed in the past on using metaphysical sight, and grounds the information received, expressing its potential. This combination integrates higher dimensional information into the planet.

Kambaba Jasper

Stability

Holding a profoundly wise earth energy, Kambaba Jasper goes right to your foundations. Deeply grounding, it harmonizes with the cycles of the natural world, attuning your personal biorhythm to that of the planet and resetting ancestral cycles in your genes. This stone takes you back to your roots and reconnects to the energy of Mother Earth and your purpose in incarnating. Kambaba Jasper resonates with the oldest part of the brain stem and autonomic processes. It removes karmic blockages and programmes and encourages the assimilation of new patterns, enhancing neurotransmitters.

Source: England

Vibration: Earthy and high

Chakra: Aligns all

Physiology: Ancestral blueprint, DNA

Cleansing: All

Source: Madagascar

Vibration: Earthy and high

Chakra: Earth star, base, sacral, heart, past life, causal vortex

Physiology: Digestive system, detoxification, assimilation of vitamins and minerals, bile, gall bladder, cellular structures, cerebellum, autonomic and sympathetic nervous systems

Cleansing: All

Shiva Shell

Seeding future generations

Gently nurturing, Shiva Shell represents the flow of life. Blending spiritual knowledge with inspired visualization, the Shell stimulates the third eye and accesses higher consciousness. Follow the line to journey to an inner or outer source of inspiration – ultimately, the two are one and the same. If you have lost your sense of mission or are missing out on inner joy and spontaneity and need to recreate your Self, the stone assists. Whisper your innermost secret wisdom into the Shell, knowing that it will reach your unborn child and that seeds sown will blossom in future generations.

Celtic Chevron Quartz

Matriarchal-line healer

White Celtic Chevron Quartz is attuned to the moon and matrilineal line. If you have become the scapegoat for the matriarchs, or are clearing emotionally for ancestors or relatives, the crystal releases you. It transmutes everything that needs to be let go. You may feel despairing at the loss of a surrogate role at first, but ultimately you are better for it. Do the necessary grieving and move on. The stone releases fear from the environment and from the ancestral line so that something new emerges. Feel the fear and then let go.

Source: India

Vibration: High

Chakra: Third eye

Physiology: Female reproductive system, testes

Cleansing: All

Source: Wales

Vibration: Extremely high

Chakra: All

Physiology: Brain, nervous system

Cleansing: All

Ancestral Timeline

Family dis-ease healer

An Ancestral Timeline has a flat ledge going down from the apex of a Quartz-family crystal towards the base. It takes you back in time to follow the ancestral tree towards its roots. It frequently has a fault line showing where family pain is located and how far back into the ancestral line it goes. The formation brings the source of family dis-ease to the surface to be healed and sends healing back through the generations to a point before the dis-ease manifested. This transforms the whole family line, radiating its benefits forward into future generations.

Cathedral Quartz

Cosmic computer

A Light Library or computer chip for the planet that holds a record of all that has occurred on Earth, Cathedral Quartz looks like separate pieces, but they are all part of the main crystal, which has multiple terminations with at least one apex point, representing the family tree. Attuned to the Akashic Record and the universal mind, it acts as a receptor and transmitter for group thought. Cathedral Quartz assists the evolution of consciousness by raising thought to a higher vibration, releasing from the ancestral past of humankind and the planet. Programme it to bring about a better world.

Source: Worldwide

Vibration: Depends on matrix

Chakra: Past life, causal vortex

Physiology: *See* Quartz, pages 38–45

Cleansing: All

Source: Brazil

Vibration: Extremely high

Chakra: All

Physiology: *See* Quartz, pages 38–45

Cleansing: All

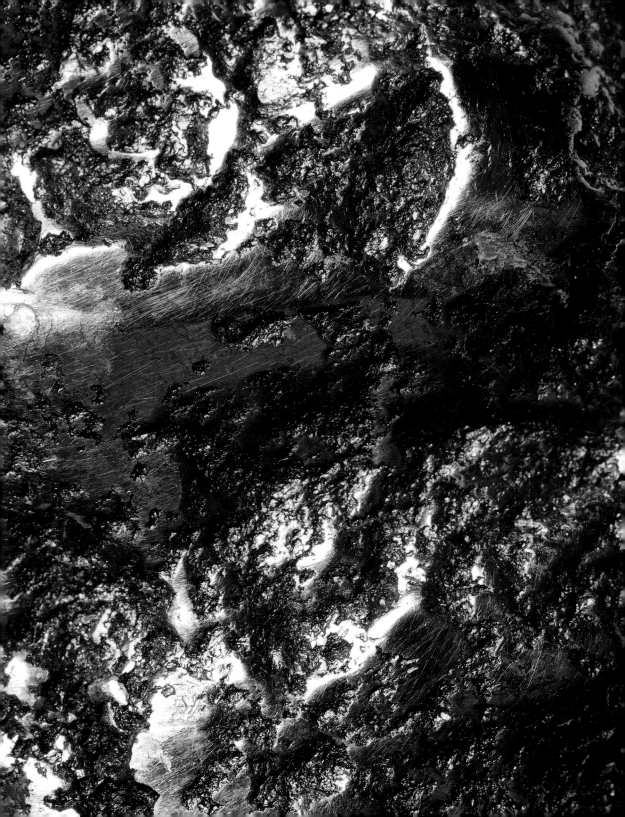

Crystals for grounding and protection

You can only be fully protected if your energies are grounded and you stand firmly anchored on Earth with all your chakras in full working order. Being ungrounded leaves you open to psychic attack, spirit attachment, auto-immune deficiencies and the like. Similarly your space needs to be protected if you are to live safely. Perhaps the single biggest threat to your health and wellbeing is sensitivity to electromagnetic frequencies (EMF), and blocking these can make a huge difference to your overall wellbeing.

EMF protection

In our modern-day world geopathic stress and subtle-energy pathogens surround us virtually everywhere. We are enveloped in constant manmade EMF smog, an intrusive and detectable field given off by power lines, wi-fi and electrical equipment that raises background oscillation frequency beyond what the human body is adapted to deal with. Correct functioning of biological rhythms, cell metabolism, physiological and mental wellbeing depend on communication between the electrical system of brain, body and endocrine system and weak electromagnetic and magnetic fields generated by the planet. Disruption leads to compromised immunity.

ABOVE Placing a mobile phone or tablet on Shungite affords instant protection against EMF pollution.

Symptoms of geopathic and EMF disruption

- Sleep disturbances, chronic fatigue
- Inability to heal
- Sugar or other cravings
- Excessive yawning or choking cough
- Nausea, drowsiness, dizziness
- Cancer, auto-immune and neurological diseases
- Mood dysfunction, depression and apathy
- Formerly clear crystal rapidly looking murky
- Sick-building syndrome
- Electrical apparatus malfunctions
- Feels like walking through treacle
- Better when away from home

Sick-building syndrome

A building with air pollution or inadequate ventilation, excess static electricity, electromagnetic smog, geopathic stress and the like. Symptoms include lack of concentration, headache, chest and skin problems, nausea, excessive fatigue, dizziness.

Crystal solutions

Crystals such as Shungite and Selenite create subtle-energetic grids to protect from the effects of EMFs. They support healthy energy fields, instilling beneficial bio-energy patterns and easing physiological and psychological effects. There are five main approaches:

Shield: Surround the outer edge of the aura or environment with a protective crystal coating. Place crystals next to an EMF source to shield it.

Support: Strengthen bio-energy and align it with the physical body, stimulating your immune system to defend itself.

Transmute: Convert toxic energies into beneficial ones, the crystal acting like a voltage converter.

Ground: Anchor your energies to Earth, strengthening lower chakras and discharging EMFs into the ground.

Negative ions: Negatively charged ions stimulate the body's defensive mononuclear phagocyte system, a network of cells that filter out dead and toxic material. Negative ions repair cellular damage. Crystals such as Amethyst and Tourmaline create negative ions and build a shielding field with them.

BELOW LEFT Shungite
BELOW RIGHT Selenite

Exercise

Grounding cord visualization

Grounding yourself is essential if you are to be comfortable – and energetically safe – in incarnation. The simplest way to do this is with a visualization.

Suitable crystals: Flint, Hematite, Smoky Quartz. *See also* the crystal portraits on pages 68–307.

1 Hold a grounding crystal such as Flint, place your hands either side of your navel.
2 Picture roots spreading out from the crystal to your hips.
3 At your hips the roots turn downwards and pass through your thighs, knees and ankles to the bottom of your feet.
4 Picture the earth star chakra about a foot beneath your feet, opening like petals (Smoky Quartz or Flint at your feet assists).
5 Feel cords growing from the soles of your feet to the earth star where they twist together. The entwined cord passes down to the Gaia gateway and deep into Earth. The cord reaches the big iron crystal ball at the centre of the planet and hooks around it.
6 Feel the energy and protection flow up this cord to keep you energized and safe, as well as anchored.

ABOVE LEFT Sea-tumbled Flint
LEFT Blue Flint

OPPOSITE Flint can instantly help you to ground yourself.

Shungite

Ultimate geopathic stress-blocker

Source: Russia

Vibration: Earthy and high

Chakra: All

Physiology: Cellular metabolism, neurotransmitters, immune, cardio-vascular, digestive and filtration systems, enzyme production, throat, kidney, liver, gall bladder, pancreas

Cleansing: All – cleanse frequently

Shungite clears physical, mental and emotional pollutants.

Characteristics

Profoundly earthing and anti-geopathogenic, Shungite protects your space, aura and physical body against harmful fields such as EMF smog and geopathogens. Its phenomenal shielding power arises from its unique formation. A rare carbon mineral, it is composed of hollow 'bucky balls', fullerenes (carbon in the form of a hollow sphere or tube) that absorb EMF emissions from computers, smart meters, cell phones and the like to eliminate the detrimental effect on sensitive human energy systems.

Biological life-enhancer

Shungite clears physical, mental and emotional pollutants so that fresh patterns imprint. Restoring emotional equilibrium, it transforms stress into a potent energetic recharge. Research has shown that Shungite absorbs that which is hazardous to health, whether it be pesticides, free radicals, bacteria and viruses or microwaves and other vibrational emissions. Shungite transforms water into a biologically active life-enhancing substance, while removing harmful micro-organisms and pollutants (*see* page 31). It boosts physical wellbeing and has a powerful effect on the immune system. A Shungite pyramid placed by the bed counteracts insomnia and headaches and eliminates the physiological effects of stress.

MAIN Shungite sphere
ABOVE RIGHT Elite Shungite
RIGHT Shungite

Flint
Portal-opener

Source: Worldwide

Vibration: Earthy

Chakra: Gaia gateway, earth star, sacral, soul star, base, sacral

Physiology: Jaw, skeleton, joints, reproductive system, cellular and tissue structures, skin

Cleansing: All

Flint provides a deep connection to the heart of Mother Earth.

MAIN **Flint**
LEFT **Ohio Flint**
OPPOSITE LEFT **Orange-brown Flint**
OPPOSITE RIGHT **Blue Flint 'Milky Way'**

Characteristics

Powerfully protective and extremely stable, Flint provides a deep connection to the heart of Mother Earth. Standing at the interface between the material and spiritual worlds, it grounds downloads from higher dimensions into the physical body while protecting the body from harmful vibrations. Flint detoxifies negative energies and filters energies so that only that which is beneficial reaches the body. It cauterizes past-life wounds, clearing the etheric blueprint. With its stabilizing action, it brings structural integrity to all bodies. This nurturing stone takes you into the womb of Mother Earth to reconnect to the wise feminine and priestess power. Perfect for rites of passage that mark the transitions of womanhood, it assists men to connect to their feminine side. A shamanic tool, Flint assists underworld journeying and contacts power-animal allies. It overcomes depression and obsessive disorders. The stone dispels fear and brings comfort and peace of mind. Clearing the aura, Flint cuts through blockages and past-life ties, removing energetic dis-ease and raising your energetic frequency so that nothing negative sticks to your aura.

Different-coloured Flints connect to different chakras and bring varying frequencies to the physical and subtle-energy bodies:

Black or Brown Flint understands the deeper causes of depression and accepts the shadow side of your nature, highlighting the gift within. Earth star chakra.

Orange Flint gives inner strength during difficult times, lifting obsessive tendencies. Base and sacral chakras.

Blue or Grey (Milky Way) Flint lifts you above the mundane into a higher spiritual understanding of dis-ease. Supportive when struggling with causes of problems and blockages, it clears these, facilitating concentrated, focused thought. Past life, brow and base chakras.

Blue-grey Flint rebalances masculine energy, uniting it with the feminine. Base and sacral chakras in men, navel energy centre in women.

Pink Flint is exceptionally vibrant. While pink is the colour of unconditional love and harmony – and pink stones are gentle and kind – Day-Glo pink really wakes you up. It's close to the colour of the causal vortex and soul star chakras.

See also Gaia's Blood Flint, page 228, and Sea Foam Flint, page 227.

Mohawkite

Auric interface

Mohawkite shields, transmutes and stabilizes energies. Releasing the past, it focuses on the present moment. A psychic shield when other methods have been outgrown or lost their effectiveness, creating core strength and stability, the stone wraps itself around the aura and creates an interface between one psyche and another. An effective healer for the ancestral line, Mohawkite releases outdated core beliefs and attitudes that are detrimental to wellbeing, such as self-loathing or judgementalism, replacing them with self-assuredness and inner confidence. The stone grounds vibrational change through the physical body and into the planet. ⚠

Source: USA

Vibration: Earthy

Chakra: Aligns all

Physiology: Vitamin and mineral assimilation, ear, sinus, throat, vocal cords, thyroid.

Cleansing: All

Peanut Wood

Walking lightly on Earth

Peanut Wood assists those who have difficulty in living on the planet, whether physically or energetically, to feel connected and yet remain light of spirit. As with all Petrified Wood, it grounds energy into the physical body, keeping that body anchored to Earth. It helps you to feel at home in the physical realm, which in turn protects your auric field. A stable, calming stone, Peanut Wood supports during trauma and healing or emotional challenges. A useful stone for past-life healing, it facilitates previous-life exploration and going to your soul's roots.

Source: Australia

Vibration: Earthy

Chakra: Earth star, base

Physiology: Ears

Cleansing: All

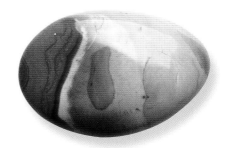

Pearl Spa Dolomite

Pragmatic spirituality

Pearl Spa Dolomite harmonizes the effect of crystal combinations in grids. It makes a useful integration keystone for an environmental grid. This crystal protects by activating the realization that spirituality is a matter of pragmatic interaction with the everyday world, rather than something experienced in another dimension. It brings awareness that you are a spiritual being currently on a human journey, and facilitates feeling more comfortable in incarnation, loving your physical body. Dissolving outdated patterns and negative behaviours, it encourages a spontaneous response to life rather than reacting as you've been taught you ought to do.

Polychrome Jasper

Magical colour web

Polychrome Jasper weaves a magical web of protection around the aura that transmutes and deflects negative energy of any kind, but particularly ill-wishing or jealousy. This exuberant crystal ensures that your physical vitality is always at its peak, a protection in itself. It carries vibrant fire energy which, when channelled with focused intention, motivates and energizes you and your passions into fresh life. It revitalizes creativity and imagination. Polychrome Jasper balances and aligns the chakras and physical, mental and emotional bodies with the etheric realm. It is a stone of courage and determination.

Source: Spain, India, Italy, UK, Switzerland, Namibia

Vibration: Earthy

Chakra: All

Physiology: Musculoskeletal and reproductive systems, nails, skin, metabolism, appetite

Cleansing: Avoid water

Source: Madagascar

Vibration: High

Chakra: All

Physiology: *See* Jasper, pages 48–9

Cleansing: All

Turritella Agate

Earth-connector

Deeply connected to Earth and roots, Turritella Agate links to ancestry and 'homeland', offering strong personal or environmental protection. In past-life recall, it reveals survival issues passed down the family or karmic line. Its fossilized shell fragments hook out the last remnants of trauma. When buried in polluted land or land that carries aggressive memories, Turritella Agate cleanses and revitalizes. Placed on a map or photograph, its healing energies pass to the site. The crystal opens communication between the plant and mineral kingdom, accessing information that is beneficial in healing the planet.

Source: Wyoming (USA)

Vibration: Earthy

Chakra: Earth star, base

Physiology: *See Agate, pages 46–7*

Cleansing: All

Basalt

De-stresser

Strongly magnetic, Basalt grounds 'floaty' people, anchoring the physical body to the planet and the soul to the body. Maintaining the structure of the body, it gives muscular strength and cohesion. Gridding Basalt in areas of environmental instability realigns Earth's meridians and facilitates the free flow of energy – although living on Basalt rock may impart melancholy to sensitive people. Basalt has undergone metamorphosis, so assists transformation and provides a solid support during life challenges. It helps you be more resilient under pressure and achieve a positive perspective on your situation.

Source: Worldwide

Vibration: Earthy

Chakra: Earth star, base

Physiology: Muscles, intestines

Cleansing: All

Master Shamanite

Profound metaphysics

Master Shamanite is deeply cleansing and profoundly metaphysical. It strengthens personal will, purifying and protecting the energy bodies, infusing power. It assists remaining centred and focused, no matter what is occurring. The stone connects to ancestral wisdom and heals ancestral pain. Facilitating multidimensional access while remaining grounded, it assists journeying and soul retrieval, teaching that death is not The End. The stone connects to power animals in the lower worlds, and spirit guides and mentors in other dimensions. It assists with entity detachment, especially that carried through the family line.

Banded Agate

Tie-releaser

Banded Agate is a tie-releaser for the third eye. It quickly cuts mental cords to a guru, partner or parent who capitalizes on a previous connection to retain manipulative control in the present, replenishing energy lost in such situations. Where someone is being 'prayed for', whether by a priest or cult-leader, to bring that person 'back to the fold' – under control once again – Banded Agate returns the coercing energy to its source, and frees the person to live life as they wish. A useful environmental healer, when gridded around a house it prevents out-of-body visitations from another soul.

Source: USA

Vibration: High

Chakra: Aligns all

Physiology: All

Cleansing: All

Source: Botswana, USA, Morocco, Czech Republic, Brazil, South Africa

Vibration: Earthy

Chakra: Base, earth star, spleen, third eye

Physiology: *See* Agate, pages 46–7

Cleansing: All

Granite

Stabilizing

Emitting measurable paramagnetic frequencies and high in Qi, Granite passes lifeforce into the body so that an energy field is stabilized and energized, although its harshness may exacerbate depression. Granite realigns subtle bodies with the physical, activating electrical activity in cells and stimulating the immune response. The rock neutralizes the ill-effects of noxious earth-energy lines and re-energizes Earth's magnetic grid. It is an excellent gridding stone to create safe, sacred space in which to practise magical and transformational rituals. The stone energetically regulates apoptosis, the essential biological process of cell birth, death and rebirth.

Black Tourmaline

Ultimate protector

Black Tourmaline forms a powerful shield against psychic attack, spells, ill-wishing and toxic energy, absorbing the impact, including EMFs and geopathic smog. It cleanses, purifies and transforms noxious energy into a lighter vibration. Taking you deep into your inner shelf and your shadow, Black Tourmaline facilitates understanding yourself and others, promoting self-confidence and diminishing fear. The crystal clears negative thoughts and ingrained emotional patterning and promotes a positive attitude to life. It balances male–female energy within the body and has a strong connection to devic energies in the planet. ●

Source: Worldwide

Vibration: Earthy

Chakra: Earth star, base

Physiology: Bones, hair, face, head, apoptosis, auto-immune system

Cleansing: All

Source: Brazil, Sri Lanka, Tanzania, Nigeria, Kenya, Madagascar, Mozambique, Namibia, Afghanistan, Pakistan, Malawi

Vibration: Earthy and high

Chakra: Earth star, base, higher heart

Physiology: Neural pathways. *See* Tourmaline, pages 56–7

Cleansing: All

Schalenblende

Solutions

Keeping you grounded and functioning optimally on Earth, Schalenblende energetically regenerates the physical body. Use it when you feel you have no resources left with which to cope with life's challenges. Providing a shield during journeying and out-of-body working, Schalenblende assists the soul to return. Synthesizing intellect and intuition, it enhances communication, facilitating solution-finding between those who are not of like mind or between different species. If you lie awake at night worrying, place Schalenblende under your pillow to bring a good night's sleep. The situation looks different in the morning.

Tantalite

Pollution-protector

Tantalite soaks up negative energy and protects against psychic vampirism and environmental pollution. Gridding this stone stabilizes the environment, deflecting radiation and other adverse energies. It overcomes chemical pollution, energetically removing disharmony at a cellular and etheric level. Clearing hooks, attachments, implants, mental imperatives and core beliefs from the physical and subtle-energy bodies, it overcomes obsession, cravings and addiction. Excellent for decision-making, Tantalite holds back until the full picture is obtained. It suspends judgements based on past events and revitalizes a sense of purpose and direction, connecting to the guidance of higher beings. ❶

Source: Germany

Vibration: Earthy and high

Chakra: Soma

Physiology: Immune and endocrine systems, pancreas, prostrate gland, brain, prostate, testicles, ovaries, retina, sense organs

Cleansing: All

Source: Australia, Afghanistan, Namibia, USA, Nigeria, Canada, Europe, Brazil, Madagascar

Vibration: Earthy

Chakra: All

Physiology: Bone development, assimilation of minerals, metabolic function, tissue and cellular repair, joints, heart

Cleansing: Avoid water

Tiger Iron

Refuge

Grounding and protecting, Tiger Iron creates a place of refuge when danger threatens. Assisting people who are deeply exhausted, especially those suffering from emotional or mental burn-out or family stress, Tiger Iron infuses vitality and supports while passing through change or persevering in the face of overwhelming odds. The stone promotes change by opening a quiet space to contemplate what is needed, supplying the energy necessary for action. Tiger Iron's solutions are pragmatic and simple. This is a creative and artistic stone that brings out inherent talents.

Boji Stone

Balanced polarity

Boji Stones gently but firmly return you to Earth and into your body, grounding you into the present moment, especially after multidimensional work. In pairs, they assist people with only a toehold on incarnation. They have a strongly protective function. Realigning the chakras and repairing holes in the auric body, they overcome blockages and assist in shadow work. Balancing and energizing, a pair rebalances male–female energy structures within the body and aligns chakras and subtle bodies, clearing blocked emotions and hurtful memories. Blue Bojis guard the body during out-of-body experiences until the soul returns. ⓘ

Source: England, Mexico, Australia, USA

Vibration: Earthy

Chakra: All

Physiology: Red-white blood count, detoxification, hips, lower limbs, feet, muscles, assimilation of vitamin B

Cleansing: All

Source: USA

Vibration: High

Chakra: All

Physiology: Tissue regeneration, energy management

Cleansing: Avoid water

Bronzite

Courtesy

Sold as effective against curses and as a magical protector, Bronzite turns back negative thoughts and psychic attack. However, it bounces ill-wishing, curses or spells back to the source considerably magnified, perpetuating the problem. Where Bronzite comes into its own is that it facilitates simply 'being', entering a dynamic state of non-action and non-doing, bringing total serenity. Bronzite strengthens non-judgemental discernment, pinpoints your most important choices and promotes decisive action. Helpful when feeling powerless in discordant situations or in the grip of events beyond your control, Bronzite increases self-assertion, restoring composure and a cool head. Combine with Black Tourmaline (*see* page 272).

Mahogany Obsidian

Closure

Mahogany Obsidian removes energy blockages and cuts cords with psychic vampires that sap your energy. Indispensable for shadow and soul-retrieval work, it shows where you have been in denial and brings closure to the vicious circle that it creates, breaking out of negative habits and unhealthy or outgrown life patterns. Resonating with Earth, Mahogany Obsidian grounds and protects, giving strength in times of need. This stabilizing stone strengthens a weak aura and restores correct spin to the sacral and solar plexus chakras so that you are naturally protected. It vitalizes purpose and stimulates growth at all levels.

Source: Germany, Finland, India, Sri Lanka, USA

Vibration: Earthy

Chakra: Base, sacral, earth star

Physiology: Yang energy, assimilation of iron, nervous system, alkaline balance

Cleansing: All

Source: Mexico

Vibration: Earthy

Chakra: Spleen, base, earth star

Physiology: Circulation

Cleansing: All

Chiastolite

Gateway to mysteries

Chiastolite transmutes dissension and conflict into harmony. It dispels negative thoughts and feelings, releases outworn patterns and conditioning and assists problem-solving and change. Chiastolite facilitates journeys out of the body. Linked to death and rebirth, it helps those making transition beyond death, protecting the soul on its journey. Dissolving illusions and calming fears, it enables reality to be faced and is helpful if you fear you are going mad. Chiastolite assists problem-solving by strengthening analytic capabilities. It removes feelings of guilt and stabilizes emotions. Chiastolite maintains spirituality during illness or trauma, invoking protective forces.

Healer's Gold

Healer's ally

Healer's Gold is excellent for all who work therapeutically. It provides an interface between your personal energy field and the outside world, so that impartial observation and healing of someone else's field are made without them impinging personally. This powerful stone combines Pyrite and Magnetite and restores energy depleted during healing – reminding that universal energy should be channelled rather than using one's own. Healer's Gold heals the aura and provides a protective shield against electronic devices. The stone draws high-frequency energy into the body and grounds it in the earth-plane. ●

Source: Chile, Russia, Spain

Vibration: Earthy

Chakra: Earth star, base, sacral

Physiology: Blood, acid–alkaline balance, lactation, chromosomes, immune and nervous systems

Cleansing: All

Source: Arizona and New Mexico (USA)

Vibration: Earthy and high

Chakra: Solar plexus

Physiology: Oxygenation

Cleansing: All

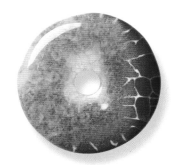

Hematite

Grounded contact

A powerful grounding and protecting stone, Hematite imparts confidence and helps you to feel stable and secure. It focuses on basic survival needs, while remaining untroubled about the future. Assisting concentration and memory, it facilitates coming to terms with 'mistakes', recognizing them as learning experiences for the soul. Hematite mitigates any form of over-indulgence, especially over-eating. The stone harmonizes body, mind and spirit, anchoring you if you only have one foot in incarnation. It establishes a connection to the core of the planet, while allowing you freedom to roam the cosmos and always know the way home.

Fire Agate

Fortitude

Building a protective shield around the body, Fire Agate returns ill-wishing back to its source so that the sender understands the harm it is doing. With its deep connection to Earth, Fire Agate is calming, bringing inner security and safety. Its strong grounding powers support during difficult times. The stone encourages introspection, effortlessly bringing up inner problems for resolution. It eliminates cravings and destructive desires, and overcomes addictions. Fire Agate facilitates relaxation so that the body 'mellows out', reducing stress and enhancing meditation.

Source: Worldwide

Vibration: Earthy and high

Chakra: Earth star, base, past life and crown

Physiology: Blood, heart and circulation, kidneys, blood cells, iron assimilation

Cleansing: All

Source: USA, Czech Republic, India, Iceland, Morocco, Brazil

Vibration: Earthy to high

Chakra: Base, sacral, dantien

Physiology: Triple-burner meridian. *See* Agate, pages 46–7

Cleansing: All

Rosophia

Dragon-shaper

Rosophia carries strong bioscalar wave energy and effects multidimensional healing. Its profound earth connection links to Sophia, divine feminine wisdom. Rosophia facilitates discerning spiritual truth from illusion. Although gentle, Rosophia has a powerful intensity. It strengthens and raises the energies of the lower chakras so that you feel more comfortable in incarnation and adapt to energetic changes, maintaining constant equilibrium but setting mind and spirit free to explore infinite possibilities. Rosophia adjusts the dragon energy of the planet to accommodate raised frequencies. Reconnecting Earth's grid, it de-energizes stuck patterns and revitalizes Earth's subtle etheric body.

Source: California and Colorado (USA)

Vibration: Extremely high

Chakra: Gaia gateway, earth star, base, sacral, three-chambered heart

Physiology: Heart and circulatory system, kidneys, lower intestine, bowel, bladder, muscles, tendons, cellular-organization, auto-immune system, eyes

Cleansing: All

Amber

Aura-sealant

A powerful protector against EMF smog and negative energies, Amber cleanses and seals the aura and chakras. A natural antibiotic, Amber promotes tissue revitalization. It imbues the energy bodies with vitality and encourages the physical body to rebalance and heal itself. The crystal promotes trust and instils peacefulness. It stimulates the intellect, motivating you to move forward, bringing stability to life. An antidepressant, it strengthens your sense of self-worth. Amber resonates with the throat chakra and assists the assimilation of air. The crystal absorbs pain and alleviates joint problems.

Source: Worldwide

Vibration: Earthy and high

Chakra: Throat, sacral, higher heart, throat

Physiology: Tissues, immune system, throat, lungs, joints

Cleansing: All

Golden Herkimer Diamond

Regeneration

Golden Herkimer Diamond is a brilliant cleanser and regenerator. A powerful healer for the solar plexus and karmic emotional disturbances, it restores vitality to energy bodies and chakras. Attuning higher-dimensional chakras to receive downloads of accelerated vibrational energy and ground it into the planet, Golden Herkimer offers deep transmutation. Developing spiritual gifts, it clears implants and removes restrictions placed on spiritual sight in this or any other life. This stone eliminates gender confusion or ambivalence in those who have changed sex from one incarnation to another or during the present life. Use it for deep environmental transformation.

Amazonite

EMF barrier

Amazonite opens intuition and grounds it in everyday reality. Protecting against electromagnetic fields, it blocks geopathic stress. Grid it around a room or source of EMF smog. Harmonizing aspects of the personality, Amazonite assists in seeing both sides of a problem and taking different points of view into consideration. It soothes emotional trauma, alleviating worry and fear, and supports friendship. Amazonite provides powerful protection when travelling through multidimensions in an expanded state of consciousness. It disentangles karmic ties, realigns the physical body with the etheric and balances masculine and feminine energies. ◑

Source: USA, Himalayas

Vibration: Extremely high

Chakra: Stellar gateway, soul star, soma, third eye, causal vortex, alta major, solar plexus, sacral

Physiology: All. *See* Quartz, pages 38–45

Cleansing: All

Source: Russia, Myanmar (Burma), India, Ethiopia, Madagascar, Brazil, USA

Vibration: Medium

Chakra: Heart, spleen

Physiology: Metabolism, heart, muscles, teeth, bones, immune and nervous systems

Cleansing: All

Serpentine

Serpent wisdom

An earthing stone that deepens meditation, Serpentine opens metaphysical abilities and controls the rise of kundalini up the spine. It removes blockages from chakras and energy bodies, aligning them and providing protection. The Romans used this stone as protection against sorcery and the dark arts. It assists retrieval of ancient wisdom, and regains memory of past lives. Correcting mental and emotional imbalances, Serpentine helps you to feel more in control of your life. Serpentine is cleansing for the body and blood. It facilitates the conscious direction of healing energy towards problem areas. ❶

Budd Stone
(African Jade)

Skilful negotiator

Budd Stone grounds 'airheads' by opening the base chakra and anchoring it to the core of the planet. It facilitates the skilful negotiation of pitfalls to reach a successful conclusion to a venture, and supports in dealing with the everyday world. Helpful in the commercial sphere, it accesses hidden agendas. Budd Stone opens the inner ear, attuning to spirit voices, your Higher Self and intuition. Budd Stone interprets the noises your body makes when picking up subtle signals. Bringing order out of chaos, it clears environmental negativity. Sweeping the stone around the aura clears subtle impediments to spiritual growth.

Source: UK, Norway, Russia, Zimbabwe, Italy, USA

Vibration: Earthy

Chakra: Base, crown, third eye, heart

Physiology: Calcium and magnesium absorption, pancreas, blood

Cleansing: All

Source: South Africa

Vibration: Earthy

Chakra: Earth star, Gaia gateway, base, alta major

Physiology: Feet, ears, circulation, fluid balance

Cleansing: All

Green Aventurine

Spleen protector

Green Aventurine protects the spleen chakra. Circling it under the left armpit removes hooks from past relationships and detaches energy vampires who drain your energy. The stone prevents reattachment. It protects and heals the heart. Ameliorating fear, it examines motives and outdated behaviour patterns, dissolving negative emotions and thoughts. Green Aventurine looks forward with joyous expectation and provides support if you are going outside your comfort zone. It increases confidence and brings out leadership qualities, strengthening integrity and compassion. The stone has strong links with the devic kingdom, increasing fertility. It enhances your own creativity.

Source: China, India, Tibet, Nepal, Tanzania, Russia, Italy, Brazil

Vibration: Earthy

Chakra: Base, sacral, heart, spleen

Physiology: Spleen, eyes, kidneys, adrenals, lungs, sinuses, heart, muscular system, blood pressure

Cleansing: All

Prairie Tanzanite

Lullaby

Deeply relaxing, Prairie Tanzanite 'unplugs from the matrix', cleansing past-life chakras and rewiring the karmic blueprint. It heals the ancestral line and emotional body, releasing deeply seated trauma and grief, gently clearing the heart. Relieving symptoms and healing the root causes of PTSD, the stone identifies unexpected gifts in trauma. It creates a grounded spirituality that incorporates a higher state of consciousness. Prairie Tanzanite is profoundly calming and centring during periods of extreme frustration. It supports children, calming ADHD and overcoming insomnia. The stone has a powerful connection to nature spirits and cosmic devas.

Source: USA

Vibration: Earthy and extremely high

Chakra: Heart, heart seed, higher heart, solar plexus, crown, soma, causal vortex, past life

Physiology: Blood pressure, teeth, bones, muscles

Cleansing: All

Bismuth

Complex boundaries

Bismuth settles in new vibrations, and helps the body adjust to higher frequencies, assisting in moving easily between the physical plane and spiritual realms. Calming disorder and directing changes into the right direction, Bismuth strengthens the connection to universal energies, drawing these down into the base and sacral chakras to create a clearer, more cohesive energetic field. The stone changes complex thought patterns that have become obsolete so that a more constructive pattern is imprinted. Laboratory-grown Bismuth ensures group cohesiveness. It assists people who are isolated or who have become institutionalized to find a caring, accepting community.

Source: Russia, Germany, laboratory-grown

Vibration: Earthy and high

Chakra: Crown, base, soul star, stellar gateway, earth star, Gaia gateway

Physiology: Stomach, intestines, muscles, cellular structures

Cleansing: Avoid water

Lepidolite

Stress reduction

Lepidolite is an efficient protection against EMFs as it generates negative ions. A stress-reducer that halts obsessive thoughts, its lithium content stabilizes mood swings and bi-polar disorders. It is excellent for overcoming emotional or mental dependency, releasing from addictions, obsessions or self-harming. Lepidolite encourages independence and achieving goals. Facilitating spiritual journeying, it accesses the Akashic Record, tunes into past lives creating blockages in your life now, and takes you forward into the future to assess the results of current actions. It locates the site of dis-ease, strengthens the immune system, relieves allergies and relieves exhaustion. ❶

Source: Brazil, Russia, USA, Canada, Madagascar

Vibration: Earthy and high

Chakra: Heart, throat, third eye, crown

Physiology: Immune system, DNA, nerves and muscles, female reproductive system

Cleansing: Avoid water

Purpurite

Curse-protector

Purpurite protects against curses, especially on land or property that has been hexed. Affording psychic protection, it stimulates evolution, grounding the resultant shifts into everyday reality. It imparts clarity and confidence to thought and communication, and prevents interference with the transmission of views. The stone breaks outdated habits or attitudes that keep you mired in the past and lifts despair, opening receptivity to guidance and new ideas. Purpurite energizes the physical and mental bodies, overcoming tiredness and despondency at any level. If adverse environmental or community interference or past-life conflict arises, it cuts links to the group.

Sage Amethyst Agate

Spiritual awakener

Sage Amethyst Agate provides protection from negative influences in the environment, opening the higher chakras to receive guidance. Helpful to those whose auras are sensitive, it works slowly at a pace that does not overwhelm. The stone repairs holes and tears in the energy field that could leave you open to entity attachment. Helpful when overcoming addictions and obsessions, it clears negative emotions and anger that could turn inwards and become self-destructive. Releasing resentment and letting go of judgemental attitudes, it encourages you to be more gentle and loving towards your Self and to others.

Source: Namibia, Western Australia, USA, France

Vibration: Earthy and high

Chakra: Base, higher crown

Physiology: Energy management, cellular memory, cardio-thoracic system

Cleansing: All

Source: USA

Vibration: Earthy and high

Chakra: All, especially higher

Physiology: *See Agate, pages 46–7*

Cleansing: All

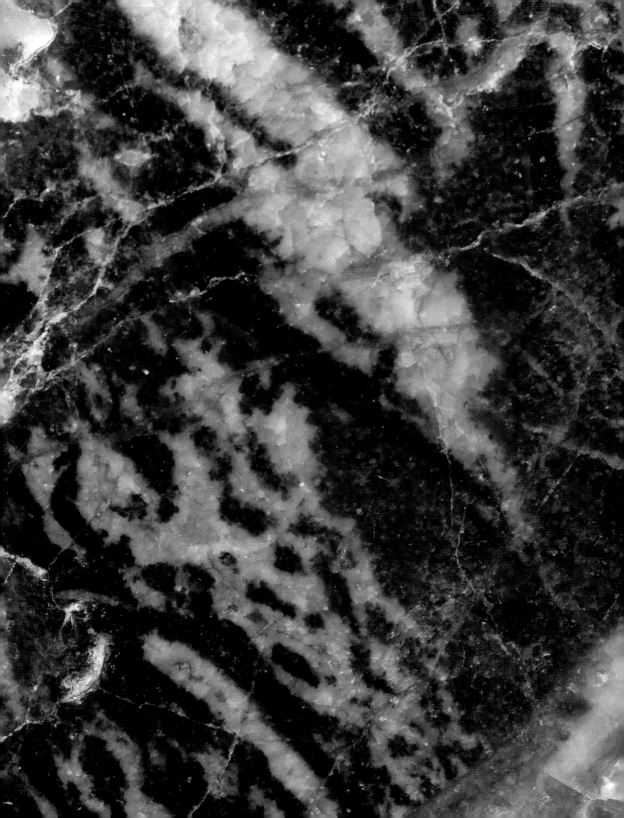

Crystals for the home and environment

Crystals enhance your home and environment in many ways. They bring peace and stability, or abundance and joy. Crystal grids draw prosperity into your home. They facilitate earth-healing and enhanced fertility for the land around you, or heal ancient trauma trapped within it. Crystals create safe space, blocking external influences. Stones such as Shungite, Smoky Quartz and Black Tourmaline placed in the corners of a room or around a house block detrimental energies, including EMFs. Placing a large Quartz or Selenite in the centre of the space fills it with healing light, and Rose Quartz with unconditional love.

Crystals in your home

The ancient Chinese art of Feng Shui helps you to place crystals to best advantage within your home. 'Bagua' is the Feng Shui energy map of your space. Each area of the house, or a single room, governs a specific area of life. To attract assistance to a particular area, place appropriate crystals either directly in that area or on the bagua plan itself (*see* opposite) so that the energetic effect transfers. The titles of each area have a wider meaning. 'Abundance', for example, affects your ability to receive, without which you cannot enjoy abundance. 'Family' affects your ability to initiate, and 'children' your ability to complete projects. The 'career' area just inside the front door also covers social relationships. The 'love' corner represents not only partnerships but also the feminine and your mother, while 'helpful people' encompasses the masculine and your father.

Wealth corner

Keep a Citrine in your purse or the wealth corner of your home to attract prosperity on all levels. The wealth corner is the farthest-left corner from the front door – the perfect place to position abundance grids.

Suggested bagua crystals

Area of the plan	Suggested crystal
Abundance	Goldstone
Fame	Sunstone
Love	Rose Quartz
Family	Spirit Quartz
Health	Que Sera
Children	Carnelian
Knowledge	Blue Lace Agate
Career	Citrine
Helpful people	Imperial Topaz

OPPOSITE Lay appropriate crystals on the bagua plan to enhance different areas of your life.

Abundance
Prosperity
Wealth
Power

Fame
Reputation
Vision

Love
Partnership
Relationship
Marriage

Family
Ancestors, Community
Associates, Employees

Health
Heart of Chi
Balance
Harmony

Children
Creativity
Success
Achievement

Knowledge
Self-improvement

Career
Mission
Courage

Helpful people
Travel
Target market

Front door

Crystal abundance

Crystal spirals draw prosperity and abundance into your life or radiate it out into the environment from a central keystone, depending on which the way the crystals point. Placing the grid on an appropriate crystal baseplate anchors it into everyday reality, or you could use anchoring stones around the grid.

Exercise

Abundance-spiral layout

Create an abundance spiral and place it in the abundance corner of your home, or in the room associated with wealth according to the bagua plan (*see page 287*).

Suitable crystals: You will need sufficient crystals for the spiral, a keystone for the centre and appropriate grounding crystals or a baseplate. These are best dowsed for, as they will vary according to the site.

1 Hold the cleansed crystals in your hands and ask that they bring abundance to you.
2 Lay the keystone at the centre.
3 Place crystals spiralling out from the keystone.
4 Leave in place, cleansing the crystals from time to time.

LEFT Heat-amended, bright orange-yellow Citrines attract abundance.

OPPOSITE Citrine and Herkimer Diamonds spiralling out from a Goldstone keystone anchored on Petrified Wood.

Earth chakras

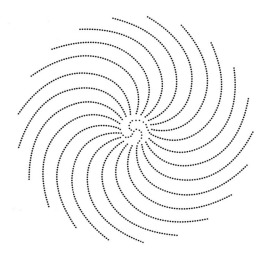

Planet Earth is subject to enormous geopathic and electromagnetic stresses that affect its energetic grid system. Placing crystals into the Earth's chakras in the environment, or onto a map, brings balance and sends healing and stability to the planet, particularly when there is turmoil due to political upheaval, earthquakes, volcanic eruptions or other earth-shaking activity.

Seven major earth chakras

Base: Mount Shasta, California
Sacral: Lake Titicaca, South America
Solar plexus: Uluru, Australia
Heart: Glastonbury, England
Throat: Great Pyramid, Egypt
Third Eye: Kuh-e Malek Siah, Iran
Crown: Mount Kailash, Tibet

Exercise
Stability grid

Suitable crystals: Seven earth-chakra crystals (use site-specific crystals that have come from the site itself or nearby, dowse for appropriate crystals, or use crystals of complementary colours – *see* pages 62–3). Anchor stones such as Flint, Hematite and Smoky Quartz.

1 Hold the cleansed crystals and state your intention.
2 Lay an appropriate crystal on each chakra.
3 Lay anchoring crystals as appropriate or as a straight-line grid on the ground.
4 Thoroughly cleanse the grid.
5 Leave in place for as long as appropriate.

Exercise

Environmental healing on the ground

A multi-armed spiral layout sends healing into the environment. It can be laid with as many arms as appropriate. Three or four may be all that are required, but it is not uncommon to add further arms as earth-healing progresses. It can be left in place in the environment, so choose somewhere it will not be disturbed – neatly cut lawns are best avoided. This layout is particularly potent when laid as Earth bursts into new life in the spring or at the time of a new moon.

Suitable crystals: Lay the grid with alternate arms of cleansing stones such as Flint pointing into the centre, and healing crystals such as Quartz pointing outwards. A central Elestial Smoky Quartz or Flint keystone transmutes toxic energies.

1 Hold your hands over the stones and state your intention.
2 Place the central keystone, restating your intention.
3 Lay a cleansing-crystal arm with the crystals pointing to the centre.
4 Lay an earth-healing crystal arm with the crystals pointing outwards.
5 Continue laying arms until the appropriate number of arms has been arrived at.
6 Use the power of your mind to activate the grid, restating your intention.
7 Remember to cleanse the grid frequently.

TOP Rhodozite
ABOVE Rainforest Jasper
RIGHT Smoky Quartz

Exercise

Environmental healing on a photograph

An inverted pentagram layout draws energy into a large or small area to heal, nourish and sustain it, to bring abundance or for specific purposes such as protection, ameliorating drought or rebalancing excess rainfall. It is particularly useful if there has been toxic spillage or poisoned water sources. Place over a photograph and leave the layout where it will not be disturbed until no longer required. A similar healing grid could be laid on a map.

Suitable crystals: Five earth-healing crystals such as Aragonite, Black Tourmaline, Shungite, Smoky Quartz, Kambaba Jasper, Rainforest Jasper, Rhodozite or Smoky Brandberg Amethyst, one keystone and anchor stones such as Smoky Quartz, if appropriate.

1 Hold the crystals in your hand and state your intention.
2 Lay the top-left corner crystal first and follow the lines to complete the pentagram.
3 Activate the grid by tracing the lines with a crystal wand or the power of your mind.
4 Place the keystone in the centre.
5 Check by dowsing whether anchor stones are required.
6 To dismantle the grid, pick up the stones in the opposite order to which they were laid. Thank the stones for their work. Cleanse them thoroughly and place in sunlight to recharge, then store until required again.

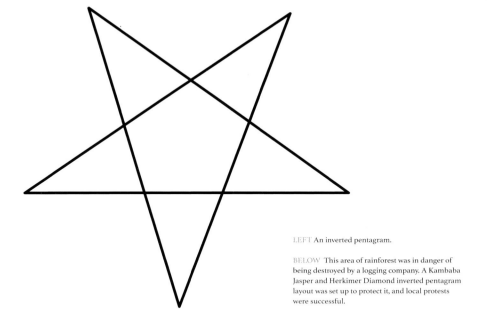

LEFT An inverted pentagram.

BELOW This area of rainforest was in danger of being destroyed by a logging company. A Kambaba Jasper and Herkimer Diamond inverted pentagram layout was set up to protect it, and local protests were successful.

Citrine

Abundance

Source: Congo, Brazil, USA, UK, Russia, Uruguay, France, Madagascar

Vibration: Extremely high

Chakra: Sacral and crown

Physiology: Digestion, kidneys, blood, thymus, thyroid, hormonal and immune systems

Cleansing: All

Encourages generosity of spirit and accumulation of wealth.

Characteristics

Prized for its prosperity-enhancing properties, Citrine encourages generosity of spirit and accumulation of wealth. It reminds you that abundance is a state of mind that encompasses friendship and joy as well as money. Encouraging gratitude for the small gifts in life, Citrine motivates you to freely share your abundance and expand your heart. The bright energy of Citrine counts your blessings and raises your self-confidence. Excellent for counteracting depression, this crystal instils optimism and a positive attitude. It overcomes apathy and hopelessness, and raises self-esteem. A stone of creativity, Citrine capitalizes on your skills and talents. Stimulating your mind, it facilitates seeing new possibilities and actualizing them. Despite Citrine being largely self-cleansing, it benefits from regular clearing. Natural Citrine is much paler than the bright, heat-treated Amethyst often sold as 'Citrine', but is effective in grids and healing.

Forms

All forms bring energy into your physical environment or your body. Point Citrine towards your body to infuse it with joyous vitality. Perfect for the wealth corner, a cave-like Citrine geode collects and conserves abundance. A many-pointed cluster generates wealth and a single point attracts or radiates abundance. A Citrine sphere radiates energy and prosperity out into the environment, and a bright, joyful tumbled version is just right for your purse or for placing on your body.

MAIN Heat-treated Citrine plate
FAR LEFT Natural Citrine
LEFT Heat-amended citrine
ABOVE Kundalini Quartz

Aragonite

Earth-healer

Source: Namibia, England, Spain, Mexico, Peru, China

Vibration: Earthy and high

Chakra: All, according to type

Physiology: Extremities, bones, calcium absorption, discs, muscle, immune system

Cleansing: Avoid water

A reliable earth-healer and anchor stone.

MAIN 'Sputnik' Brown Aragonite
OPPOSITE LEFT Blue Aragonite
OPPOSITE CENTRE Lilac Aragonite
OPPOSITE RIGHT White Aragonite

Characteristics

Aragonite makes you feel comfortable within your own body and your environment. It combats dis-ease, especially nervous twitching and spasms that come out of inner unrest. Attuned to Gaia, Aragonite encourages conservation and recycling and deepens your connection to Earth. A reliable earth-healer and anchor stone, it transforms geopathic stress and clears blocked ley lines, even at a distance. Placed on a map, Aragonite heals trauma or blocked planetary meridian lines. With its ability to centre and ground physical energies, it ameliorates stress. Combating over-sensitivity, Aragonite teaches patience and acceptance and stabilizes spiritual development that is wildly out of control. The stone gently takes you back into childhood or beyond to explore the past. Excellent for people who push themselves too hard, it facilitates delegation and instils vitality. Its practical energy encourages discipline and reliability and develops a pragmatic approach to life. ❶

Colour spectrum

Each colour of Aragonite resonates with a specific element.

Brown Aragonite: Attuned to earth and the lower shamanic world, Brown Aragonite resonates with the earth star and base chakras. The 'sputnik' form (*see* opposite) is an excellent earth anchor when buried at each corner of a property or laid into a stabilizing grid.

White Aragonite: Connected to ether or spirit and interstellar dimensions, White Aragonite's energies are those of love, compassion and forgiveness. It resonates with the higher crown chakras.

Lilac (Lavender/Purple) Aragonite: Attuned to the air element and the upper shamanic world, Lilac Aragonite resonates with the chakras around the head. It helps you to feel comfortable in your own skin.

Pink or Red Aragonite: Resonating with the fire element and the shamanic middle world, Red Aragonite opens the heart to universal love. Pink Aragonite resonates with chakras in the upper torso, and Red Aragonite also stimulates the base and sacral.

Blue Aragonite: Resonating with the water element and interstellar regions, Blue Aragonite clarifies the chakras in the upper half of the body. This colour gently releases stuck emotions and assists with inner-child work and manifesting your own soulplan.

Rhodozite

Wish-granter

Rhodozite packs a powerful punch. Grid it around a site, on a map or on the ground for earth-healing. The crystal switches off mind-chatter, taking you into stillness. It facilitates out-of-body experiences. Removing blockages, Rhodozite powers all chakras, adding vitality to the body and stimulating Qi. It links to previous lives to ascertain effects on the present. Place Rhodozite around a person making a transition so that karmic and etheric blueprints are cleansed and no dis-ease is carried forward. Be careful what you wish for, as this crystal grants your heart's desire!

Tree Agate
(Dendritic)

Plenitude

Tree Agate brings abundance to all areas of life, including business and agriculture. This crystal has a strong connection with the plant kingdom and deepens your connection to Earth. It enhances crop yields and maintains the health of house plants. Repelling insects and other pests, it creates a peaceful environment, inner and outer. Tree Agate encourages remaining centred in times of strife or confusion, bringing stability. It gives you perseverance and the ability to see difficulties as a challenge. Tree Agate urges you to remain connected to your roots as you grow.

Source: USA, Madagascar, Spain

Vibration: Earthy and high

Chakra: Earth star, Gaia gateway, base

Physiology: Tissues, pH balance, brain function, eyes

Cleansing: Avoid water

Source: USA, Czech Republic, India, Iceland, Morocco, Brazil

Vibration: Earthy

Chakra: Earth star, base

Physiology: Nervous system. *See Agate, pages 46–7*

Cleansing: All

Sardonyx

Strength and protection

Grid Sardonyx around your house or around areas of criminal activity or unrest, as it protects and harmonizes the outer environment. However, it reminds you that your own conduct has to be impeccable. This grounding stone supplements willpower and strengthens character, promoting integrity and virtuous conduct. It increases stamina, imparting vigour and self-control. Sardonyx alleviates depression and overcomes hesitancy. It improves perception and assists processing information. On the spiritual level, Sardonyx invokes the search for meaningful existence. It attracts friends and good fortune, and brings lasting happiness and stability to marriage and partnerships.

Aegerine

Strength

Aegerine protects those who are sensitive to low-frequency radiation including wi-fi, computers, mobile phone towers and other types of EMF radiation. It protects against psychic attack and removes attached entities or thought forms from the aura or a location. The stone releases deeply held negative patterning, facilitating emotional healing. Beneficial for overcoming addictions, it reverses feelings of worthlessness or self-pity, instilling the ability to persevere and overcome. Stress-releasing Aegerine assists when you are feeling depressed or filled with negative emotions such as anxiety, replacing these with positive energy.

Source: Brazil, Uruguay, India, Madagascar

Vibration: Earthy

Chakra: Earth star, base, sacral

Physiology: Lungs, bones, sensory organs, fluid balance, cell metabolism, immune system, assimilation of nutrients

Cleansing: All

Source: South Africa, Russia, Canada, USA, Greenland

Vibration: Earthy and high

Chakra: Higher heart

Physiology: Cellular memory, immune, metabolic and nervous systems, muscles, liver, spleen, gall bladder, detoxification

Cleansing: Avoid water

Gobi Desert Agate

'Stripped to the bone'

Gobi Desert Agate results from aeons of scouring by sand particles. This cleansing stone sucks out the last remnants of negative energy from anywhere there has been trauma or grief. It can deal with the physical and psychological effects of past- or current-life torture, including being placed on the rack or having bones broken. This Agate assists anyone who feels they are currently on a psychological rack or undergoing emotional torture. It clears anxiety and calms the whole energy system. Restructuring the past, it heals timelines, handing back control and creating a support structure that harmonizes with the current lifeplan.

Sedona Stone

Vortex energy

Sedona Stone holds the concentrated energy of powerful multidimensional vortexes. Holding Sedona Stone plugs you into an inexhaustible source of power. It immediately transports you into Earth's meridian grid, and the vortex energy whirls you deep within yourself to explore inner dimensions and out to the furthest reaches of the cosmos. Powering ceremonies and shamanic journeying, this stone enhances metaphysical abilities, especially if placed over the soma chakra. Sedona Stone is an immensely powerful healer, with rejuvenating and revitalizing properties. It re-energizes all cells of the body, including blood and lymph.

Source: Mongolia

Vibration: Earthy and high

Chakra: Earth star, past life, causal vortex

Physiology: Blood pressure. *See* Agate, pages 46–7

Cleansing: All

Source: USA

Vibration: High

Chakra: Soma, Gaia gateway, base, sacral

Physiology: Blood, lymphatic system, energy management

Cleansing: All

Elestial Smoky Quartz

Ultimate detoxifier

This crystal creates a safe personal or workspace, pulling noxious energy out of the environment, replacing it with vibrant light, and protecting against geopathic stress or psychic invasion. An outstanding purifier and detoxifier, this exceptional earth-healer transmits energies along Earth's meridians to revitalize power points of the planet. To instantly create a safe space, hold Smoky Elestial over your dantien or earth star. Smoky Elestial draws past-life trauma or dis-ease out of the present-life physical body, heals the etheric blueprint and subtle-energy bodies and assists the soul to reclaim power. It heals the ancestral line.

Source: Worldwide

Vibration: Earthy and high

Chakra: Gaia gateway, earth star, dantien

Physiology: *See* Quartz, pages 38–45

Cleansing: All

Cinnabar

Shopkeeper's friend

The wonderful vermilion of Cinnabar led to it being known as 'dragon's blood'. A stone of abundance, it increases takings and holding onto wealth, assisting a seller as it increases persuasiveness. Teaching assertiveness without pushiness, it facilitates prospering in endeavours. Cinnabar is helpful when you want to enhance your persona or change your image, as it invests the personality with dignity and power. This stone makes the outward demeanour aesthetically pleasing and elegant. It imparts fluency to mind and speech. Releasing energy blockages and aligning energy centres, Cinnabar asserts that everything is perfect exactly as it is. 🛈

Source: China, USA

Vibration: Earthy

Chakra: Earth star, base, sacral

Physiology: Blood, female reproductive organs, weight control

Cleansing: Avoid water

Halite

Purification

Halite draws out impurities lodged in your soul or etheric body, creating inner balance. It clears environmental toxins and guards against negative energies, entity attachment or psychic attack, especially when under the influence of drink, drugs or when generally disorientated and ungrounded. Dispelling oppression, Pink Halite detaches entities and spirit possession, sealing the aura against reattachment. Useful if you become the object of someone else's lust or needy feelings, Halite dissolves outdated patterns, negative thoughts and ingrained feelings such as anger. Ameliorating anxiety and bringing contentment, Halite transmutes feelings of abandonment or rejection, promoting emotional wellbeing and increasing goodwill.

Source: USA, France, Germany, Morocco

Vibration: Earthy to high

Chakra: Cleanses all

Physiology: Detoxification, metabolism, cellular memory, intestines, respiratory system, skin, meridians

Cleansing: Avoid water

Pink Zebra Stone

Contentment

Pink Zebra Stone has a grounding and nurturing energy that offers protection from physical and spiritual harm through strengthening the aura. Helping to see beyond illusion and getting to grips with problems, it penetrates beneath the masks people wear, to perceive the underlying reality, assisting personal, social and work relationships. Facilitating seeing both sides of a situation, it encourages being true to your Self. Zebra Stone creates balance, integrating the grounding energy of Mother Earth and the spiritual vibrations of the cosmos. Helpful in overcoming depression or anxiety, it vanquishes apathy and kickstarts ideas into action.

Source: Australia

Vibration: Earthy

Chakra: Base, heart

Physiology: *See* Jasper, pages 48–9

Cleansing: Avoid water

Unakite

Recuperation

Unakite reveals the root cause of dis-ease and blockages, whether arising in the distant or near past, bringing them to the surface for transformation and release. In past-life healing it goes to the source of a problem and reframes it, balancing emotions with spirituality. This stone provides grounding when needed, especially after meditation or psychic work. Gridded in the environment, Unakite radiates a gentle calming energy that negates the effect of EMF pollution and other disturbances. It overcomes insomnia and assists healthy pregnancies. The stone facilitates recuperation after serious illness, returning etheric bodies to the optimum.

Picrolite

Ancient earth-connector

Highly prized in prehistoric times, Picrolite is green Serpentine. Many early statues of the Earth Mother goddess were created from this material, demonstrating how ancient the connection of this earth-healer is to Earth. This powerfully protective stone clears and balances the chakra system and aura, and assists kundalini to rise in a controlled manner. It promotes stamina and insists that you be a thriver, not simply a survivor. It is traditionally gridded to draw rain to areas of drought. Encouraging recognition of positive qualities in a partner, Picrolite transforms a rocky relationship. ●

Source: USA, South Africa, Switzerland

Vibration: Earthy

Chakra: Third eye, earth star, heart, higher heart

Physiology: Reproductive system, pregnancy, skin, hair, recuperation

Cleansing: All

Source: Dominican Republic, Australia, Canada, Czech Republic, Slovakia, Japan

Vibration: Earthy

Chakra: Gaia gateway, earth star, base, heart

Physiology: Heart, adrenals, endocrine system, assimilation of protein

Cleansing: Avoid water

Rainforest Jasper

Being

With a strong connection to Nature and the planet, Rainforest Jasper takes you back to your roots to reanchor yourself and reassess your situation objectively. Encouraging mindfulness, it urges you to accept yourself as you are, without needing to change. However, this 'stone of being' facilitates moving effortlessly back into emotional balance, instilling deep self-respect for yourself and for others. A natural healer, Rainforest Jasper reactivates herbal healing knowledge from the far past, passed through the female line. This stone accesses ancestral matriarchs to reconnect to the beneficial family myths by which they lived.

Chlorite Quartz

Master cleanser

Chlorite Quartz has strong associations with Mother Earth and facilitates healing journeys through nature. The supportive stone assists with self-realization and cleanses the past. It rapidly absorbs negative energy and toxins and clears a build-up of negative energy anywhere in the body or environment. A large Chlorite Quartz placed point down in a lavatory cistern energetically cleanses the whole house. This stone assists the removal of energy implants or thought forms, accessing their source in this or any other lifetime and sealing the aura after removal. Chlorite Quartz ameliorates panic attacks and stabilizes bi-polar disorder.

Source: South America

Vibration: Earthy

Chakra: Earth, base, spleen

Physiology: Cellular memory, fluid imbalance, immune system

Cleansing: All

Source: Worldwide

Vibration: Earthy to high

Chakra: Spleen, third eye

Physiology: Cleansing and elimination systems, nerves, brain

Cleansing: All

Epidote in Prehnite

Crystal of awareness

Healing the healer, Epidote in Prehnite provides a protective shield and a safe space in which to work therapeutically or metaphysically. It heightens the senses and telepathic understanding. Assisting children and adults who are sensitive to spirit but fear contact, it acts as a guardian being. Epidote in Prehnite calms angry emotions and overcomes habitual negativity, cleansing the emotional energy body. It strengthens Qi and increases energy while simultaneously calming the emotions. Prehnite eases worries and restlessness. This stone is helpful for understanding mathematics and programming. ⓘ

Kiwi Jasper
(Sesame Jasper)

Tranquillity

Kiwi Jasper is deeply nurturing. A balancing stone, it aligns physical, emotional and mental bodies with the etheric realm. It facilitates dream recall and shamanic journeys. This stone sustains and supports the soul during times of stress, inducing tranquillity and emotional strength. It is helpful for healers, counsellors and therapists, assisting those who work on behalf of or care for others, and anyone overcoming addictive or compulsive behaviour. The stone supports anyone working to create fairness and justice for all. Kiwi Jasper stabilizes land that has been under stress, so it is an effective earth-healer.

Source: Mali, South Africa

Vibration: Earthy to high

Chakra: Heart

Physiology: Sensory processing, detoxification, kidneys, immune system, digestion

Cleansing: All, when tumbled

Source: New Zealand

Vibration: High

Chakra: Earth star, Gaia gateway. Aligns all

Physiology: Mineral assimilation

Cleansing: All

Candle Quartz

Family unity

Candle Quartz brings the whole family or a group together as one and draws a guardian angel closer. Highlighting soul purpose, it focuses a lifepath towards service. A large Candle Quartz attracts abundance, radiating love. Candle Quartz puts ancient knowledge into practice and draws power allies closer. Restoring trust and innocence, it heals a damaged inner child. Candle Quartz heals the ancestral line and karmic inheritance, dissipating feelings of oppression and despair. This stone develops emotional independence and inter-dependence, showing when it is beneficial to rely on and share with a partner and when to stand alone.

Fire and Ice

Light-worker

Fire and Ice carries inspirational cosmic fire. Uniting polarities, it integrates the full spectrum of consciousness into everyday reality. Cleansing and aligning the chakras, it activates kundalini rise in the etheric bodies. In past-life healing, it resolves the misuse of power. A stone of new beginnings and profound growth, it reveals the soul's purpose. Facilitating awareness of different timelines, it opens connectedness to multiple realities and dimensions. A battery for Earth's grid, when its energy is taken to the heart of Mother Earth it fertilizes the planet, providing a power source for earthly transformation.

Source: Madagascar, Brazil

Vibration: High

Chakra: Heart, navel

Physiology: Heart, carbohydrate and nutrient absorption, insulin regulation

Cleansing: All

Source: Brazil, thermally shocked

Vibration: Extremely high

Chakra: Soma, soul star, stellar gateway, third eye

Physiology: Pineal and pituitary glands, endocrine system, reproductive and urinary tracts, subtle-energy bodies

Cleansing: All

Manifestation Quartz

Great manifestor

Manifestation Quartz has a smaller crystal enfolded within the main crystal. A manifestor of abundance and good fortune, it attracts all that you need to support you, bringing you your heart's desire. The crystal resolves underlying doubts and brings into awareness emotional blockages, preventing manifestation, releasing all that is no longer required in order to make room for the new to emerge. Activating creative endeavours and helpful during a brainstorming session in the early stage of a new project, it births new and exciting ideas while structuring them into physical reality.

Spirit Quartz

Crystallized spirit

This uplifting stone radiates high-vibration energy in all directions while tightly focusing multidimensional healing, reprogramming cellular memory. It facilitates out-of-body journeying, activating the lightbody and facilitating metaphysical work, especially reframing the ancestral past. Rejigging the etheric blueprint, it pinpoints significant karmic connections and gifts or karmic justice in traumatic situations, promoting self-forgiveness. Spirit Quartz balances male and female, yin and yang. It facilitates transition between different brainwave states, stimulating heightened awareness. At death, it guides the soul through the afterlife to the highest possible vibration and into the hands of those waiting to welcome it home.

Source: Worldwide

Vibration: High

Chakra: Base, sacral

Physiology: *See* Quartz, pages 38–45

Cleansing: All

Source: South Africa

Vibration: Extremely high

Chakra: Aligns all

Physiology: *See* Quartz, pages 38–45

Cleansing: All

Glossary

Aura: Subtle-energy bodies surrounding the physical body.

Biomagnetic energy: Subtle, organized electromagnetic energy field existing in and around all living things.

Cathartic: An emotional or energetic release.

Cellular memory: Earlier, past-life or ancestral attitudes, trauma and patterns deeply ingrained in cells or DNA.

Chakra: Energy linkage point between the physical and subtle bodies and environment.

Core beliefs: Deeply held, often unconscious, limiting beliefs passed through the ancestral line or soul lineage. Core beliefs may be outdated or untrue and create internal conflicts through unresolved multiple agendas.

Dantien: Small, spirally rotating, power-generating sphere on top of the sacral chakra.

Dis-ease: State that results from physical imbalances, blocked feelings, suppressed emotions and negative thinking, from this or any other lifetime or the ancestral line, and which, if not reversed, leads to illness.

Earth-healing: Rectifying distortions of Earth's energy field or meridian grid caused by pollution, electromagnetic interference and destruction of its resources.

Electromagnetic smog/EMFs: Detectable electromagnetic fields given off by power lines and electrical equipment that have an adverse effect on sensitive people.

Essence: Energetic vibrations of a crystal transferred by immersing crystals in spring water and placing in sunlight.

Etheric blueprint: The subtle-energetic grid from which the physical body develops and is maintained.

Expanded awareness/consciousness: Wide spectrum of consciousness that encompasses grounded frequencies of Earth and higher multidimensional frequencies. It facilitates accessing every level of reality and all timeframes simultaneously.

Geopathic stress and geopathogens: Earth and physiological stress created by energy disturbance from underground water, power lines and ley lines, quarrying and other subterranean events.

Grids/gridding: Placing crystals around a building, person or environment for energy enhancement or protection.

Grounding: Creating a strong connection between one's soul, core being, physical body and Earth.

Healing challenge: Situation when symptoms may be exacerbated before a condition heals.

High vibration: High-vibration crystals resonate at a lighter, finer, higher frequency, reaching multidimensional consciousness.

Higher Self: The part of the soul not fully incarnated, occupying a higher dimension and therefore able to see further and with greater insight than the incarnated Self.

Incarnation: Being in a physical body and living on the Earth.

Inclusion: Speck or plate of another mineral within a crystal.

Inner levels: Intuition, psychic awareness, archetypes, emotions, feelings, subconscious mind, subtle energies.

Inner terrorist: Part of ourselves that whispers fear and terror into our heart, sabotaging plans and hopes.

Interface: Where two energy fields meet.

Interlife/Between-life: State before physical incarnation takes place, where soul- and lifeplans and agreements or contracts are made.

Journeying: The soul leaves the physical body and travels to distant locations.

Kundalini: A Sanskrit word meaning 'coiled like a snake'. A subtle but extremely dynamic psycho-spiritual energy that can irradiate the cells of the physical and etheric bodies with a new resonance. It awakens the lightbody and the ability to assimilate higher-dimensional frequencies.

Lightbody: Subtle-energy body vibrating at an extremely high frequency.

Matrix: Rock in which a crystal forms.

Mental influence: The effect that other people's thoughts and strong opinions have on the mind.

Meridian: Subtle-energy channel running close to surface of the skin, or the planet, containing acupuncture points and vortexes.

Negative emotional programming: 'Oughts', 'shoulds' and toxic emotions instilled, in childhood or other lives, that remain in the subconscious mind to influence present behaviour.

Physiology: Biochemical, chemical and electrical processes within cells and the organs comprising the physical body.

Psychic attack/ill wishing: Malevolent thoughts or feelings towards another person, consciously or unconsciously directed.

Psychic vampirism: Feeding on the energy of others.

Psychosomatic: The detrimental effect of toxic thoughts or emotions on the physical body.

Qi: Lifeforce energizing the physical and subtle bodies.

Rainbow flash: An iridescent coating on the outside of the crystal, or an internal rainbow that appears when it is turned through light.

Soul: Vehicle for carrying eternal spirit.

Soulplan/lifeplan: Soul's intention and learning-plan for present life.

Soul retrieval: Trauma, shock or abuse, or extreme joy, causes a fragment of soul energy to remain stuck, or at a past-life death. Soul retrieval reintegrates this.

Subtle-energy bodies: Biomagnetic auric layers.

Thought forms: Energetic forms created by strong positive or negative thoughts existing on the etheric level.

Transmutation/transmutative: Converting dense, toxic or otherwise detrimental energies into a beneficial, higher-frequency vibration to enhance wellbeing.

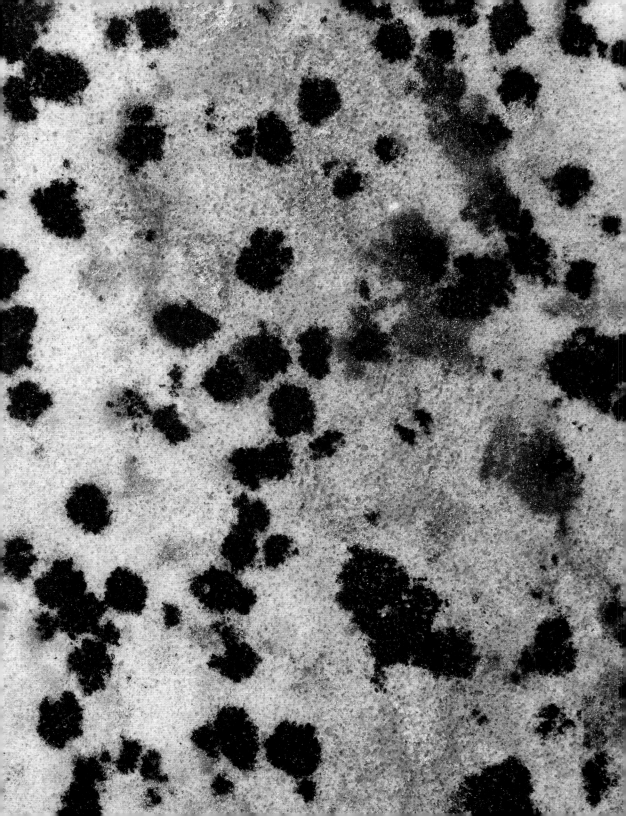

Resources and further reading

Books by Judy Hall

The Ultimate Guide to Crystal Grids: Transform Your Life Using the Power of Crystals and Layouts
(Fair Winds Press, USA, 2017)

Judy Hall's Crystal Zodiac
(Godsfield Press, London, UK, 2017)

Crystal Prescriptions vols 1–6
(O Books, Alresford, UK, 2005–17)

Crystal Mindfulness: Still Your Mind, Calm Your Thoughts and Focus Your Awareness with the Help of Crystals
(Watkins Publishing, London, UK, 2016)

The Crystal Wisdom Healing Oracle
(Watkins Publishing, London, UK, 2016)

The Little Book of Crystals: Crystals to Attract Love, Wellbeing and Spiritual Harmony into your Life
(Godsfield Press, London, UK, 2016)

Judy Hall's Complete Crystal Workshop
(Godsfield Press, London, UK, 2016)

The Encyclopedia of Crystals, New Edition
(Bounty Books, London, UK, 2015)

Earth Blessings: Using Crystals for Personal Energy Clearing, Earth Healing and Environmental Enhancement
(Watkins Publishing, London, UK, 2014)

The Crystal Bible, vols 1–3
(Godsfield Press, London, UK; Walking Stick Press, USA, 2003–13)

Life-changing Crystals: Using Crystals to Manifest Abundance, Wellbeing and Happiness
(Godsfield Press, London, UK, 2013)

101 Power Crystals: The Ultimate Guide to Magical Crystals, Gems, and Stones for Healing and Transformation
(Fair Winds Press, USA. Quarto, London, UK, 2011)

Crystals and Sacred Sites: Use Crystals to Access the Power of Sacred Landscapes for Personal and Planetary Transformation
(Fair Winds Press, USA, 2012)

Good Vibrations: Psychic Protection, Energy Enhancement, Space Clearing
(Flying Horse Books, Bournemouth, UK, 2008)

Purpose-made crystal cleansing essences are available from www.petaltone.co.uk or www.petaltone.usa and www.thecrystalbalance.net

Index

Acknowledgements

Judy Hall would like to acknowledge with thanks the assistance of all those who have explored the properties of new crystals, and the crystal sellers who drew her attention to those crystals.

OVERLEAF Triplite in matrix, orange and red.

Picture credits

Dreamstime.com Incomible (used throughout). **Getty Images** Cyndi Monaghan 189. **Octopus Publishing Group** 26l, 102, 103br, 155; Naomi Edmondson 19, 32–3, 35, 126, 190, 290, 293t; Janeanne Gilchrist 30; Abi Read 43, 44–5; Lyanne Wylde 27. **iStockphoto** Azurhino 62–3; Kotoffei 239r. **Shutterstock** Lindwa 243.